Beyond Essence

Ernst Troeltsch as Historian and Theorist of Christianity

HARVARD THEOLOGICAL STUDIES
58

CAMBRIDGE, MASSACHUSETTS

Beyond Essence

Ernst Troeltsch as Historian and Theorist of Christianity

Lori Pearson

DISTRIBUTED BY

HARVARD UNIVERSITY PRESS

FOR

HARVARD THEOLOGICAL STUDIES

HARVARD DIVINITY SCHOOL

Beyond Essence:
Ernst Troeltsch as Historian and Theorist of Christianity

Harvard Theological Studies 58

Series Editors:
François Bovon
Francis Schüssler Fiorenza
Peter B. Machinist

Pearson, Lori
  Beyond essence : Ernst Troeltsch as historian and theorist of Christianity / Lori Pearson
    p. cm. -- (Harvard theological studies ; 58)
Includes bibliographical references and index.
  ISBN 0-674-01919-9
1. Troeltsch, Ernst, 1865-1923. I. Title.
  BX4827.T7P43 2007
  230'.046--dc22
                                          2007027516

To Celia and Soren

with love

Contents

Chapter Five
FROM ESSENCE TO SYNTHESIS

Acknowledgments

Many people have supported me throughout the process of writing this study, which is a revision of my dissertation. My greatest thanks go to my dissertation adviser, Sarah Coakley, who was a constant source of wisdom, insight, enthusiasm, and encouragement during my graduate school years, and whose guidance was crucial for the success of this project. I am deeply grateful for the countless ways she has continued to invest in my scholarly development. I could not have asked for a better mentor. I was also fortunate to have had the opportunity to work with John Powell Clayton (1943–2003), who was a generous mentor and teacher. My trips to his Boston University office for lively conversations about my dissertation are cherished memories from graduate school. He is greatly missed. Francis Schüssler Fiorenza was my teacher throughout my years at Harvard Divinity School. I have benefited greatly from his encyclopedic knowledge of nineteenth-century Christian thought and from his continued interest in my work. It was also a privilege to have Gordon Kaufman on my committee. I am grateful for his willingness to serve as an engaging dialogue partner on issues related to historicism and theological method. To them all I express my sincere gratitude and admiration.

Three others made particularly important contributions to this study. Friedrich Wilhelm Graf of the University of Munich offered crucial guidance and access to resources during my stay at the Ernst-Troeltsch-Forschungsstelle, then at the University of Augsburg (now in Munich). His scholarly contributions have influenced my work profoundly. I owe a great debt of gratitude to Walter E. Wyman, Jr. of Whitman College, who generously read and offered detailed comments on the penultimate draft of my dissertation. I thank him for mentoring me in my work in nineteenth-century theology. Wendell Dietrich of Brown University has been a consistent contributor to my intellectual development. He offered enthusiastic support and guidance on various segments of this study.

I have also benefited from various forms of institutional support. I thank the Deutscher Akademischer Austauschdienst (DAAD) for funding my research in Augsburg. During that time, Karl Heinz Fix and Markus Schroeder provided valuable guidance and hospitality. I also thank my colleagues at

Luther College for the support they gave me during the years I taught there. My colleagues in the Religion Department at Carleton College have been unfailing in their enthusiasm for my research, and there is no end to my thanks for them. I also thank Dean Scott Biermann, Associate Dean Elizabeth Ciner, and the Roth and Smith Fellowships at Carleton College for support of this project. Many Carleton colleagues have provided valuable feedback on segments of this study: Shahzad Bashir, Andrew Fisher, Jessica Leiman, Michael McNally, Susannah Ottaway, Parna Sengupta, and Serena Zabin. Richard Crouter offered help on the manuscript at a critical time, and has been a cherished and generous mentor and colleague. Many members of the Nineteenth-Century Theology Group of the American Academy of Religion also made helpful responses to my work.

I am deeply grateful for the insight, skill, and professionalism of my proof-reader, Beth H. Morel. For the design of the cover, I thank Danny Mintz. I thank the staff of Harvard Theological Studies for their contributions to this project, especially managing editor Dr. Margaret Studier for her encouragement and support, as well as copy-editor Randall Short, proofreader Eve Feinstein, and typesetters Anne Browder, Rebecca Hancock, and Richard Thompson.

During my years at Harvard Divinity School I benefited from the guidance and collegiality of many teachers, including Richard R. Niebuhr, David Lamberth, Krister Stendahl, and Ronald Thiemann. Colleagues who are also dear friends played a central role in the completion of this study. Melanie Johnson-DeBaufre journeyed with me through graduate school and as a fellow faculty member and loyal friend at Luther College. She put aside her own work to read an early draft of the manuscript; her many suggestions greatly enhanced the final product. Laura Muench-Nasrallah and Susan Abraham provided comic relief, intellectual companionship, and valuable feedback while I was completing the dissertation. Other friends who supported or responded to my work include Maren Batalden, Elizabeth Bettenhausen, Ernest Boyer, Aimee Burant, Valerie Cooper, Jeannine Hill Fletcher, Greg Schmidt Goering, AnneMarie Luijendijk, Ivan Petrella, Rowanne Sayer, Jalane Schmidt, Christine Weigel, Katherine Whitsitt, and Novian Whitsitt.

My most important thanks go to the members of my family for patiently waiting while I worked endlessly on this project. First and foremost I thank my parents for their encouragement, support, and love. I am grateful to my mother, Lois Pearson, for her confidence in me and for her enthusiasm about my work, and for the various forms of practical support she provided throughout the process. Memories of my father Robert Pearson's sense of humor, compassionate heart, and theological depth continue to sustain me. He modeled for me the value and complexity of religious tradition, which is the topic that drives this study. I also thank Mark, Kim, and Finn Pearson as well as the entire Murphy family. By far my deepest gratitude goes to my sweet and generous husband, Brian Murphy, for his unfailing care, patience, friendship, and love. Without his help and unwavering support, this study would still not be finished. Our children were born between the appearance of the dissertation and the completion of this book. Celia's playfulness, thoughtfulness, and love of relationship fill me with happiness and hope, and little Soren is a bundle of pure joy with a sweet disposition and an energetic spirit. This book is dedicated to them.

Abbreviations and Short Titles

BP   *Die Bedeutung des Protestantismus für die Entstehung der modernen Welt*, in *KGA* 8, 199–316.

"Essence"   Ernst Troeltsch, "What Does 'Essence of Christianity' Mean?" In *Ernst Troeltsch: Writings on Theology and Religion.* Edited and translated by Robert Morgan and Michael Pye. Louisville, Ky.: Westminster/John Knox Press, 1990, 124–79. This is an English translation of "WCh"[2] (see below).

ET   English translation

GS   *Gesammelte Schriften*

GS 1   Ernst Troeltsch, *Die Soziallehren der christlichen Kirchen und Gruppen.* Vol. 1 of *Gesammelte Schriften.* Tübingen: J. C. B. Mohr, 1912.

GS 2   Ernst Troeltsch, *Zur religiösen Lage, Religionsphilosophie und Ethik.* Vol. 2 of *Gesammelte Schriften.* Tübingen: J. C. B. Mohr, 1913.

GS 3   Ernst Troeltsch, *Der Historismus und seine Probleme. Erstes Buch. Das logische Problem der Geschichtsphilosophie.* Vol. 3 of *Gesammelte Schriften.* Tübingen: J. C. B. Mohr, 1922.

GS 4   Ernst Troeltsch, *Aufsätze zur Geistesgeschichte und Religionssoziologie.* Edited by Hans Baron. Vol. 4 of *Gesammelte Schriften.* Tübingen: J. C. B. Mohr, 1925.

KGA   *Kritische Gesamtausgabe*

KGA 7   Ernst Troeltsch, *Protestantisches Christentum und Kirche
              in der Neuzeit (1906/1909/1922)*. Edited by Volker Drehsen
              in collaboration with Christian Albrecht. Vol. 7 of *Ernst
              Troeltsch Kritische Gesamtausgabe*. Berlin: Walter de
              Gruyter, 2004.

KGA 8   Ernst Troeltsch, *Schriften zur Bedeutung des Protestantismus
              für die moderne Welt (1906–1913)*. Edited by Trutz Rendtorff
              in collaboration with Stefan Pautler. Vol. 8 of *Ernst Troeltsch
              Kritische Gesamtausgabe*. Berlin: Walter de Gruyter, 2001.

KGA 17   Ernst Troeltsch, *Fünf Vorträge zu Religion und Geschichts-
              philosophie für England und Schottland. Der Historismus und
              seine Überwindung (1924)/Christian Thought: Its History
              and Application (1923)*. Edited by Gangolf Hübinger in
              collaboration with Andreas Terwey. Vol. 17 of *Ernst Troeltsch
              Kritische Gesamtausgabe*. Berlin: Walter de Gruyter, 2006.

PP   Ernst Troeltsch, *Protestantism and Progress: The Significance
              of Protestantism for the Rise of the Modern World*. Foreword
              by Brian Gerrish. Philadelphia: Fortress Press, 1986. (This
              edition follows the original 1912 English translation: *Protes-
              tantism and Progress: A Historical Study of the Relation of
              Protestantism to the Modern World*. Translated by W. Mont-
              gomery. New York: G. P. Putnam's Sons, 1912.)

Religion in Ernst Troeltsch, *Religion in History*. Essays translated by
History   James Luther Adams and Walter F. Bense. Minneapolis,
              Minn.: Fortress Press, 1991.

ST   Ernst Troeltsch, *The Social Teaching of the Christian
              Churches*. Translated by Olive Wyon. London: George Allen
              & Unwin, 1931. Repr., Louisville, Ky.: Westminster/John
              Knox Press, 1992. This is an English translation of *GS* 1.

"¹WCh"   "Was heißt 'Wesen des Christentums'?" *Die Christliche Welt* 17 (1903) 443–46, 483–88, 532–36, 578–84, 650–54, 678–83.

"²WCh"   "Was heißt 'Wesen des Christentums'?" Revised edition (1913). In *GS* 2, 386–451.

Writings   *Ernst Troeltsch: Writings on Theology and Religion.* Edited and translated by Robert Morgan and Michael Pye. London: Gerald Duckworth & Co., 1977. Repr., Louisville, Ky.: Westminster/John Knox Press, 1990.

ZNThG/   *Zeitschrift für Neuere Theologiegeschichte/Journal for the*
JHMTh   *History of Modern Theology*

A Note on Translations

Quotations from Troeltsch's writings generally follow (with occasional revision, as noted in the footnotes) the standard English translations when available; in these cases, footnotes make reference to both the German and the English texts. All translations of Troeltsch's untranslated essays and works are my own. Translations of German-language secondary sources are also my own.

Introduction

So long as Christianity is a living religion, people will be constantly quarreling with one another concerning what it is and what it ought to be; and they will constantly seek through new syntheses to meet present conditions and to adapt it to future exigencies.[1]

One century ago Ernst Troeltsch put forward a new vision of Christianity that conceived of the religion as neither stable nor self-evident. Rather, Troeltsch claimed, the identity of Christianity as a living religion is continuously rearticulated as communities engage in lively debates that speak to concerns about the present and future. As Troeltsch once said in an essay that will be central to this book, "To define the essence [of Christianity] is to shape it afresh."[2]

Today Christian identity is crafted and contested explicitly and implicitly in countless scholarly projects: theologians and philosophers in conversation with cultural anthropologists problematize the boundaries and contours of religious traditions; scholars of late antiquity put forth competing reconstructions of earliest Christianity; and historians of lived religion

---

[1] Ernst Troeltsch, "The Dogmatics of the 'Religionsgeschichtliche Schule,'" *American Journal of Theology* 17 (1913) 20–21. See also 2d rev. ed., "Die Dogmatik der 'religionsgeschichtlichen Schule,'" in *GS* 2:519; ET, "The Dogmatics of the History-of-Religions School," in *Religion in History*, 103. This essay was first published in English in the *American Journal of Theology*, and was then revised and published (in German) in *GS* 2. The ET appearing in *Religion in History* incorporates text from both editions. The quotation excerpted above appears in all three versions. Hereafter citations of this essay offer first the relevant pages from the ET in *Religion in History* (abbreviated "The Dogmatics") followed by the pages from the German edition (abbreviated "Die Dogmatik") from *GS* 2. I cite the first edition (from the *American Journal of Theology*) only when it contains material omitted from the 2d rev. ed.

[2] "Essence," 162; "²WCh," 431; "¹WCh," 654. For an explanation of the different editions of this essay, see note 32 below; see also the list of abbreviations and short titles at the front of this book.

propose new models for understanding and locating religious movements and practices in American Christianity, to name just a few examples. As scholars put forth new interpretations of Christian history and tradition, they simultaneously make claims about Christianity's value and meaning for contemporary life.

In his work as theologian, historian, social theorist, and philosopher of religion, Troeltsch (1865–1923) grappled with issues concerning Christian identity that continue to vex theologians, historians, and theorists of culture and tradition today:[3] How can one conceptualize Christianity in a way that does justice to both continuity and discontinuity in its historical and contemporary forms? Do traditions have boundaries? What is the nature of Christian identity, on what is it based, and who decides? Given the relativity of knowledge, is objective reconstruction of a historical tradition possible, and can one adjudicate among competing truth claims within a tradition? What is the status of claims about the identity of Christianity, when are they authoritative, and in what way?

Examining Troeltsch's responses to these kinds of questions enables one to see him in a new light and to reassess his place in the history of modern theology. Today Troeltsch's legacy continues to be associated with a liberal theological tradition that is often summarized as "Culture Protestantism" (*Kulturprotestantismus*) and that, therefore, partakes of all the confusion and controversy attached to that term.[4] This lingering characterization of Troeltsch

---

[3] Delwin Brown argues that there is a clear connection between the issues faced by current theorists of tradition and those engaged by nineteenth-century European thinkers (including Troeltsch) who grappled with the challenge of human historicity for Christian theology. See *Boundaries of Our Habitations: Tradition and Theological Construction* (Albany, N.Y.: SUNY Press, 1994) 2. John Thiel makes a similar point in his identification of continuity and change as themes central to both nineteenth-century and current theology. See *Senses of Tradition: Continuity and Development in Catholic Faith* (Oxford: Oxford University Press, 2000) vii.

[4] A number of important works on "Culture Protestantism" demonstrate both the internal diversity among such thinkers and their shared traits with other more conservative Protestant theologians in imperial Germany. According to Friedrich Wilhelm Graf, both liberal and conservative Protestant theologians, for example, were nationalistic in some way and shared a sense that there should be a close connection between Protestant theology and general cultural values. Although Cultural Protestants can be broadly described as those who sought to extend theology beyond the purview and control of church structures and envisioned it as a cultural discipline that might ground a Protestant civil religiosity, they nevertheless were marked by a wide diversity of political opinions and theological assessments of traditionally Protestant sources of authority such as the Lutheran Reformation and Scripture. See "Protestantische

can be explained by the effects of the erstwhile dominance of neo-orthodoxy, which in the first half of the twentieth century relegated him (among others) to the exhausted liberalism of the nineteenth century.[5] It is striking that, despite the significant number of studies in the past two decades that have illuminated the nature and context of Troeltsch's thought, his overall reputation continues to be associated with an outmoded theological modernism.[6]

This way of classifying Troeltsch obscures the actual contours and concerns of his thought and fails to assess and analyze his work (whether positively or negatively) in conversation with a new set of current scholarly questions. Recent important work on Troeltsch as a cultural historian (*Kulturhistoriker*) proves immensely helpful in narrating the intellectual, cultural, and political context and driving concerns of Troeltsch's work. These contributions enable one to see significant ideological and theological diversity in the liberal Protestantisms of Troeltsch's time and in the history of religions school.[7] They also clarify the extent to which Troeltsch used his

---

Theologie in der Gesellschaft des Kaiserreichs," in *Profile des neuzeitlichen Protestantismus* (ed. Friedrich Wilhelm Graf; vol. 2, pt. 1; Gütersloh: Gütersloher Verlagshaus, 1992) 54, 69, 88. See also George Rupp, *Culture Protestantism* (Missoula, Mont.: Scholars, 1977); Gangolf Hübinger, "Confessionalism," in *Imperial Germany: A Historiographical Companion* (ed. Roger Chickering; Westport, Conn.: Greenwood, 1996) 156–84; idem, *Kulturprotestantismus und Politik. Zum Verhältnis von Liberalismus und Protestantismus im wilhelminischen Deutschland* (Tübingen: Mohr/Siebeck, 1994); Mark Chapman, *Ernst Troeltsch and Liberal Theology: Religion and Cultural Synthesis in Wilhelmine Germany* (Oxford: Oxford University Press, 2001); and Graf, "Kulturprotestantismus. Zur Begriffsgeschichte einer theologiepolitischen Chiffre," in *Kulturprotestantismus. Beiträge zu einer Gestalt des modernen Christentums* (ed. Hans Martin Müller; Gütersloh: Mohn, 1992) 21–77.

[5] Karl Barth's treatment of Troeltsch (as a representative figure in nineteenth-century liberal theology's accommodation to and legitimation of German culture) is well known and frequently cited, as is his claim that Troeltsch left theology behind when he moved to the faculty of philosophy in Berlin in 1915. (Troeltsch received the call to Berlin in 1914 and moved there in 1915.) See Barth, "Evangelical Theology in the Nineteenth Century," in *The Humanity of God* (Louisville, Ky.: John Knox, 1960) 11–33.

[6] Both John Milbank (*Theology and Social Theory: Beyond Secular Reason* [Oxford: Blackwell, 1990]) and Tomoko Masuzawa (*The Invention of World Religions: Or, How European Universalism Was Preserved in the Language of Pluralism* [Chicago: University of Chicago Press, 2005]) portray Troeltsch's theology and conception of religion as quintessentially modern and typical of an allegedly monolithic liberal Protestantism of nineteenth-century Europe.

[7] Chapman discusses the broad spectrum of (often conflicting) views held among those generally labeled "liberal theologians," as well as the diverse political opinions and conceptions of religion espoused by members of the history of religions school. See Chapman, *Ernst Troeltsch and Liberal Theology*, esp. ch. 2. Sockness's study of debates between Troeltsch

theological and historical work to engage—often in terms much more critical and complex than commonly assumed—questions about the consequences and possibilities of modernity for Christian identity and faith.

My study participates in this effort to redefine Troeltsch by uncovering and rereading important dimensions of his conception of Christianity—dimensions that link him (as I shall suggest in the conclusion) with contemporary analyses of the identity of Christianity. In the pages that follow, I identify an emerging and increasingly complex conceptualization of Christianity that Troeltsch gradually articulates and adjusts in his writings on historical method, the history of Christianity, and the philosophy of history. These writings reveal Troeltsch's continuing efforts to define the boundaries and nature of Christianity and to theorize about the relations among religious, social, political, and economic forces of historical development. Tracing Troeltsch's use of the concept "essence of Christianity" is an effective way to chart the evolution of his thinking on these issues. I suggest that Troeltsch's immersion in the study of Christian history leads him to dispense with the concept altogether. Troeltsch comes to see that no single essence could capture an historical, cultural, and religious phenomenon as pluriform and contingent as Christianity.

In this process of grappling with the possible meaning, value, and problems with the concept of an essence of Christianity, Troeltsch develops what I shall call a "theory of Christianity"[8]—that is, a conception of Christianity's nature and identity that signals (I argue) both its multifariousness as a complex

---

and Wilhelm Hermann also challenges monolithic portraits of nineteenth-century German liberal theology. See Brent Sockness, *Against False Apologetics: Wilhelm Hermann and Ernst Troeltsch in Conflict* (Tübingen: Mohr/Siebeck, 1998).

[8] I am using this term differently from the way that Gerhold Becker does in his essay, "Die Funktion der Religionsphilosophie in Troeltschs Theorie des Christentums," in *Protestantismus und Neuzeit* (vol. 3 of Troeltsch-Studien; ed. Horst Renz and Friedrich Wilhelm Graf; Gütersloh: Gütersloher Verlagshaus Mohn, 1984) 240–56. Where Becker offers a reading of Troeltsch's efforts to ground the philosophy of religion in the context of modern philosophy, I define Troeltsch's theory of Christianity as an historical, sociological, and theological construct that bears some resemblance to current theories of tradition and culture in the fields of anthropology, theology, and philosophy. My classification of Troeltsch as a theorist of Christianity is similar to Reiner Anselm's portrait of him as a "Denker des Christentums." As Anselm emphasizes, Troeltsch did not place theology primarily within the boundaries of official church tradition, but connected theology to the disciplines of cultural history and sociology. "Denker des Christentums—Ernst Troeltsch," *Mitteilungen der Ernst-Troeltsch-Gesellschaft* 17 (2004) 6–25.

historical phenomenon and its potential resources and value for modern life.[9] Troeltsch as theorist of Christianity engages simultaneously in historical and normative inquiry. As an historian of religion and culture, Troeltsch seeks to conceptualize and define historical Christianity in a way that can do justice to its internal variety and its complex relations to political, social, economic, and cultural phenomena. At the same time, Troeltsch as philosopher, theologian, and ethicist understands this historical inquiry as intimately related to the creative and normative task of shaping Christianity's meaning and structure in contemporary contexts—in his case, in the context of an increasingly modernizing society. Thus, a theory of Christianity, for Troeltsch, must portray the complex constitution of the tradition while making suggestions about its abiding relevance for the present.

The Dialogue with Modernity: Troeltsch as Historian and Theorist of Christianity

Troeltsch's theory of Christianity can be better understood by reflecting on the nature of his work and identity as an historian. Friedrich Wilhelm Graf rightly states that "Troeltsch was not an historian in the technical sense of the term. . . . Troeltsch was an historian only insofar as he was also a philosopher of culture."[10] This does not overlook the regular and important contributions that Troeltsch made to historical conversations in his day, but rather acknowledges the style and content of his historical writings. In these writings, Troeltsch did not aim chiefly to present carefully researched details arising from original observations about primary materials, but to offer, instead, a broad narrative (reliant primarily upon secondary sources) assessing the resources and limits of past and present traditions and movements for contemporary realities.[11]

---

[9] In his work as theologian and philosopher of culture, Troeltsch thought he was dealing with the realities and consequences of modernism, but in certain ways (especially toward the end of his life) he was already addressing conditions and questions concerning relativism, pluralism, and historicity that are often associated with "late modernity" or with postmodernity. See Max Stackhouse, "A Premature Postmodern?" *First Things* 106 (2000) 19–22. See also Garrett E. Paul, "Why Troeltsch? Why Today? Theology for the 21st Century," *The Christian Century* 110 (1993) 676–81.

[10] Graf, "Ernst Troeltsch: Kulturgeschichte des Christentums," in *Deutsche Geschichtswissenschaft um 1900* (ed. Notker Hammerstein; Stuttgart: Steiner, 1988) 131–32.

[11] Ibid., 132, 135. Graf offers the interesting detail that Troeltsch contributed more regularly to the *Historische Zeitschrift* than did any other nonhistorian in the first two decades of the twentieth century. According to Volker Drehsen and Christian Albrecht, Troeltsch

Troeltsch established his primary identity as a systematic theologian and philosopher of religion and culture. Particularly between 1904 and 1914, however, Troeltsch devoted himself intensively to a number of projects on the history of Christianity and Protestantism.[12] Why did the systematic theologian of the history of religions school—as Troeltsch came to be called—make this decade-long turn to history?[13] A number of recent studies of Troeltsch have helped to contextualize his writings during this period toward which I direct the bulk of my study. During his years as professor of theology in Heidelberg from 1894 to 1914, Troeltsch was among a group of liberal intellectuals who regularly discussed and assessed various forms of political, economic, and societal modernization.[14] Questions about the democratization and parliamentarization of the imperial regime, the pace of modern capitalism, the rise of a mass society, and the loss of traditional intellectual and religious narratives led to a sense among such intellectuals

---

was innovative in his efforts to direct his historical writings not only to specialists but to a broadly educated public. This is consistent with the spirit of his historical writings, which were intended to stimulate reflection on cultural challenges and conversations of the day. See "Einleitung" to *KGA* 7:3.

[12] Although the decade between 1904 and 1914 constitutes a period of intensive historical and sociological investigation for Troeltsch and thus is the major focus of this study, it should be noted that Troeltsch's interest in historical and sociological questions spanned his entire intellectual life, as is evident in the focus of his dissertation, which engaged in historical analysis of Melanchthon's thought as a way of getting at questions about the relation between Protestantism and modernity. Similarly, with his completion of the publication of his massive history of Christianity—*The Social Teachings of the Christian Churches and Groups*, on which a large portion of my study focuses—Troeltsch did not leave historical projects behind but continued them in his 1915 study, for example, of Augustine's thought.

[13] In his 1922 essay, "My Books," Troeltsch describes some of the reasons for his turn around 1903 to a range of sociological and historical projects. Troeltsch indicates that after publishing his 1902 work *The Absoluteness of Christianity and the History of Religion*, which analyzed the nature, limits, and possibilities of Christianity's claims to validity as a religion, he was moved to "further studies as to what today can be called Christianity in view of its extraordinary historical variations and its inner crisis" ("My Books," in *Religion in History*, 371; "Meine Bücher," in *GS* 4:9). He also notes that at this time he was "virtually swept back into historical studies concerning the essence and history of Christianity by certain new perspectives that now obtruded upon me," including "practical tasks of social politics, reflections on political and social affairs, the whole process of coming of age politically," as well as his encounter with the "very powerful personality" of Max Weber (*Religion in History*, 371–72; *GS* 4:11).

[14] See Graf, "Puritanische Sektenfreiheit versus lutherische Volkskirche: Zum Einfluß Georg Jellineks auf religionsdiagnostische Deutungsmuster Max Webers und Ernst Troeltschs," *ZNThG/JHMTh* 9 (2002) 42–69.

of a crisis of modern culture,[15] and prompted new research aimed at seeking new sources of orientation in such a context. Troeltsch and many of his colleagues viewed religion as a force capable of shaping culture, and therefore of influencing the quality and contours of modern societies.

Especially beginning in 1904, with the creation of the *Eranos-Kreis* (Eranos Circle), Troeltsch engaged with others in interdisciplinary exchange as a way of exploring religion's cultural significance (*Kulturbedeutung*) in the context of this rapid social change. The *Eranos-Kreis*, founded by New Testament scholar Adolf Deissmann, met monthly and consisted of fifteen scholars who represented a number of disciplines and included such intellectuals as sociologist Max Weber, jurist and legal historian Georg Jellinek, cultural historian Eberhard Gothein, economist Karl Rathgen, and philosopher Wilhelm Windelband.[16] Members of this group shared an interest in the historical analysis of religion's potential relationship to culture, and they increasingly looked to sociology as a framework for investigations into the meaning and future of modern society.[17] For these scholars, historical study of Christianity's cultural significance and complex relations to political, economic, and social institutions could provide important insight into Christianity's relation to—and possible role in—the modern world.[18]

The studies that emerged from these interdisciplinary and sociologically oriented historical inquiries were not, of course, politically or ideologically neutral, especially insofar as they raised questions about the relations among religious groups, cultural values, and political structures.[19] The stance

[15] Ibid., 43–44.

[16] See "Einleitung" to *KGA* 8:5–6.

[17] In his essay "The Cultural Significance of Calvinism" (1910), Troeltsch comments on the importance of sociology for the historical projects of the *Eranos-Kreis*. Despite how "unstable" and "chaotic" sociology is as a discipline, notes Troeltsch, he and his colleagues have found it "very fruitful for the historical and systematic disciplines." Troeltsch also speaks to the group's interest in addressing the "pressing problem" of how best to understand "the relation of the real, economic-social 'substructure' of modern development to its ideological scientific-ethical-religious 'superstructure'" ("Die Kulturbedeutung des Calvinismus," in *KGA* 8:146–47).

[18] Max Weber's *Protestant Ethic and the Spirit of Capitalism* (1904/5) should be placed in this context as well. See "Einleitung" to *KGA* 8:6.

[19] As Graf ("Protestantische Theologie," 80) states, "In a system in which the Protestant church and state were not separate, Protestant tradition was officially acknowledged as the civil religion that unified the state, the monarchical authority was religiously legitimated and many bourgeois liberal reformers sought religious grounds for their efforts at a democratization of the society through an appeal to Reformation cultural values, there was no politically

that Troeltsch took toward the question of Protestantism's relationship to modernity stood in contrast to that of many conservative Lutheran theologians who rejected modern forms of individualism and sought a strong authoritarian state with close ties to an official church.[20] As a cultural liberal, Troeltsch sought to bring modern individualism and Christian social values into mutual exchange and critique, and favored (though cautiously) modest political and societal reforms.[21]

Troeltsch's works on the history of Christianity and Protestantism, therefore, were not "pure histories" but rather explorations intended to put forth a constructive vision for the present and future. Troeltsch states this clearly in the introduction to *Protestantism and Progress: The Significance of Protestantism for the Rise of the Modern World*:[22]

> We always, either voluntarily or involuntarily, relate the course of past events to the complex of effects which lies before us in the present, and ... we are constantly drawing either special or general

neutral space for Protestant theology." In another essay ("Puritanische Sektenfreiheit," 49–50), Graf also notes that any intellectual reflection (such as that carried out by Troeltsch and his colleagues in Heidelberg) on modernity, capitalism, Western rationalism, and religion was necessarily a discussion in which "the fundamental problems concerning the political ordering of bourgeois society" were being thematized. Graf also notes that Troeltsch and his colleagues Weber and Jellinek were conscious of this feature of their work.

[20] Graf, "Puritanische Sektenfreiheit," 45.

[21] Troeltsch's political views changed toward the end of World War I, when he became a more pronounced advocate of democratization and a stronger critic of nationalism. The question of Troeltsch's political views is a complex issue that is beyond the scope of this book. On this, see Bernd Sösemann, "Das 'erneute Deutschland.' Ernst Troeltschs politische Engagement im ersten Weltkrieg," in *Protestantismus und Neuzeit* (ed. Renz and Graf) 120–44; and Ernst Troeltsch, *Schriften zur Politik und Kulturphilosophie (1918–1923)* (vol. 15 of *Ernst Troeltsch Kritische Gesamtausgabe*; ed. Hübinger in collaboration with Johannes Mikuteit; Berlin: Walter de Gruyter, 2002); and Aimee Burant, "'A Metaphysical Attitude towards Life': Ernst Troeltsch on Protestantism and German National Identity," *ZNThG/JHMTh* 14 (2007) 81–100.

[22] Ernst Troeltsch, *Protestantism and Progress: The Significance of Protestantism for the Rise of the Modern World* (1912; trans. W. Montgomery; Philadelphia: Fortress, 1986); trans. of 1911 edition of *Die Bedeutung des Protestantismus für die Entstehung der modernen Welt*, in *KGA* 8:199–316. The first edition of this work (written in 1906) also appears in *KGA* 8. Note that "Protestantism and Progress" was the title given only to the English translation. The title in German is simply, "The Significance of Protestantism for the Emergence of the Modern World." Hereafter references to this work will offer first the relevant pages from the English translation, abbreviated *PP*, followed by the pages from the German edition, abbreviated *BP*.

conclusions from the past and making use of them in our task of shaping the present with a view to the future. Subjects which do not admit of such a relation to the present belong to the antiquarian, and investigations which entirely and on principle leave such considerations out of account have value only for the virtuoso, or as work for work's sake. Even when we employ the art, so familiar to modern thinking, of tracing out evolutionary series, we do so at bottom only in order that we may be able to understand the present itself in its place in such a series. . . . Thus the understanding of the present is always the final goal of all history.[23]

One must, then, read the various historical works that Troeltsch published between 1904 and 1914[24] as explorations into the role that Christianity, and specifically Protestantism, might play in addressing the challenges of modern societies.[25] Thus, the "evolutionary series" that Troeltsch crafts in his histories of Christianity often provide clues to his assessment of institutions and thought forms in his context.

For example, in several of his historical writings, Troeltsch signals his approval of modern noninstitutional forms of spirituality by linking them to a respected legacy that, according to his construal of Christian history, originates in the individualism of "the Gospel," extends through Pauline "Christ mysticism," and includes Luther's "mystical tendencies," such as his emphasis on a mystical indwelling of Christ in the believer. In granting legitimacy to these movements in this way, Troeltsch shows his appreciation for certain kinds of religious sensibilities, such as a relative conception of truth and a support for freedom of conscience, that are well suited to modern practices and thought forms.

Troeltsch's assessment of modernity can also be detected in his historical treatment of modern "rationalistic" individualism and its relationship

---

[23] Troeltsch, *PP*, 17–18; *BP*, in *KGA* 8:204–5.

[24] Troeltsch's major historical works in this period include, for example: *Protestantisches Christentum und Kirche in der Neuzeit* (*KGA* 7), which appeared in 1906 in the first edition of Paul Hinneberg's edited volume, *Die Christliche Religion*, and which was heavily revised and expanded for the 1909 edition; *Die Bedeutung des Protestantismus für die Entstehung der modernen Welt* (1906; rev. ed. 1911) (*KGA* 8); and *Die Soziallehren der christlichen Kirchen und Gruppen* (1908–1912) (*GS* 1).

[25] Thus, according to Graf ("Ernst Troeltsch: Kulturgeschichte," 132), "Troeltsch's historical publications are properly understood in the context of his systematic theoretical program. . . . For him, all historical presentations were a function of his practical interest in the present."

to Christian individualism. In his historical narratives, Troeltsch traces the roots of this form of (modern, rationalistic) individualism to ancient rationalism, or often just to Stoicism, and thereby separates it (largely) from a Christian form of individualism, which is said to have its own unique characteristics and development. By crafting two distinct, though overlapping, historical trajectories—one for Christian and one for modern rationalistic individualism—Troeltsch reveals his own assessment that, despite the genuine affinities between these two forms of individualism, they ultimately stand in tension with each other.[26] Christianity's social philosophy, in Troeltsch's account, avoids the excesses of certain modern institutions and conceptions of human nature. It therefore ought to serve as a resource for reflection on the ideal shape of modern society in his own time.

These two examples illustrate well the appreciation and ambivalence that characterized Troeltsch's view of processes of modernization, and they help to nuance the typical portrait of Troeltsch as one who embraced modernity and recommended Christianity's accommodation to it. Troeltsch's positive portrayal of modern spiritual (and noninstitutional) movements shows his sympathy for certain modern sensibilities, while his protective effort to separate Christian from modern "rationalistic" individualism reveals his deep misgivings about other modern trends and social forms. Troeltsch generally shared Weber's pessimistic "iron cage" view of the paralyzing power of modern institutions such as capitalism and bureaucracy. In the concluding section of *Protestantism and Progress*, for example, Troeltsch wrote:

> Often enough . . . the modern organization of life becomes simply a gloomy, tyrannical fate, devouring all a man's working powers. . . .

[26] Troeltsch has a multifaceted view of the relation between Christianity and modernity. He therefore does not always use language that suggests utter incompatibility between modern and Christian individualism. In another essay he writes, "Christian individualism provided the first impulses to modern individualism." ("The Essence of the Modern Spirit," in *Religion in History*, 267; "Das Wesen des modernen Geistes," in *GS* 4:332.) In *Protestantism and Progress*, he identifies the "extraordinary extension and intensification of the thought of freedom and personality" as modernity's "most valuable feature." Yet, he also argues that this modern individualism should be based on the "strong religious and metaphysical foundation" that Christian individualism provides (*PP*, 101; *BP*, in *KGA* 8:315). Without this foundation, according to Troeltsch, modernity's growing "rationalistic" conception of individualism will continue to be opposed to the individualism springing from Christianity. For Troeltsch, Protestantism has many relationships to the modern world; his goal is to offer a complex portrait of their interrelation that shows their opposition and their compatibility, and that allows for many possibilities for collaboration and mutual critique.

Our economic development is rather tending in the direction of a new bondage, and the great military and bureaucratic states, in spite of all their parliaments, are not wholly favourable to the spirit of liberty.[27]

Troeltsch believed that certain aspects of modern society promoted a radical individualism while suffocating a more personalistic form of individualism that he associated with earlier modern and Christian ideas. Yet, despite this ambivalence toward modernity, Troeltsch did not share Weber's pessimistic attitude toward the possibility of religion serving as a fruitful and efficacious force in modern society.[28] Graf states:

> [D]espite the genetic relevance of ascetic Protestantism to the establishment of modern industrial capitalism, Weber was unable to accord any continuing social function to religious values; Troeltsch, by contrast, sought to adapt the ethical content of Christianity to modern social problems: faced with the destructive consequences of capitalist modernization, the social potentialities of religion were in this way to be rendered effective (once again) in favour of a shaping of society according to humane principles.[29]

Troeltsch's historical works contain both criticisms and affirmations of various modern institutions and values. These works explore how Christianity might contribute positively to the shape and character of modern society.

---

[27] *PP*, 91, 101; *BP*, in *KGA* 8:302, 315–16. Graf notes that Troeltsch actually radicalizes Weber's "iron cage" portrait of modernity by extending Weber's critique beyond the economic sphere and into other cultural and intellectual realms. See "Religion und Individualität. Bemerkungen zu einem Grundproblem der Religionstheorie Ernst Troeltschs," in *Protestantismus und Neuzeit* (ed. Renz and Graf) 215.

[28] See Graf and Harmut Ruddies, "Ernst Troeltsch. Geschichtsphilosophie in praktischer Absicht," in *Philosophie der Neuzeit IV* (ed. Joseph Speck; Grundprobleme der großen Philosophen; Göttingen: Vandenhoeck & Ruprecht, 1986) 138. Similarly, Ruddies shows that both Troeltsch and his contemporary Friedrich Naumann departed from Weber on the question of how religion might function in modern capitalist society. Ruddies attributes this to what he sees as the similar vocational and professional biographies of Troeltsch and Naumann. See Harmut Ruddies, "Ernst Troeltsch und Friedrich Naumann: Grundprobleme der christlichen Ethik bei der Legitimation der Moderne," in *Ernst Troeltschs Soziallehren. Studien zu ihrer Interpretation* (vol. 6 of Troeltsch-Studien; ed. Graf and Rendtorff; Gütersloh: Gütersloher Verlagshaus, 1993) 259.

[29] Graf, "Friendship between Experts: Notes on Troeltsch and Weber," in *Max Weber and His Contemporaries* (ed. Wolfgang J. Mommsen and Jürgen Osterhammel; London: Hyman, 1987) 225.

Troeltsch and his colleagues in Heidelberg were deeply concerned with understanding the roots of Western rationalism and saw this task as central to their analyses of modernity. Troeltsch joined in this project precisely by exploring the possible relations between Western rationalism and Christian (and especially modern Protestant) views of the human person. In so doing, he settled neither for simple assimilation of modern and Protestant individualism nor for their opposition, but instead tended to outline a plurality of forms of both modern and Christian individualism, all of which he then placed in complex interrelation.[30] Such a portrait enabled Troeltsch to achieve a critical distance from modernity even as he remained committed to a modern worldview and sought productive responses to its excesses. Troeltsch turned to religion as a potential source for the preservation of both individual freedom and social cohesion in the modern world.

Precisely here Troeltsch's works on the history of Christianity—as well as his theoretical reflections and writings on the essence of Christianity—gain their significance. To demonstrate religion's potential role in modern culture, Troeltsch needed concrete data about its various relations to societies and cultures in the past. The history of Christianity yielded a plurality of more or less retrievable possibilities that might contribute to the softening of Western rationalism and to the shaping of modern European culture. The study of history occupied a central position in Troeltsch's work as philosopher of culture, philosopher of religion, and theorist of Christianity.

Sources for Constructing Troeltsch's Theory of Christianity

While the bulk of my study focuses on Troeltsch's major work on the history of Christianity, *The Social Teachings of the Christian Churches and Groups* (1908–1912),[31] it begins and ends with two works separated by twenty

[30] See, for example, Troeltsch's writings on the relation between Protestantism and the modern world, especially "Die Kulturbedeutung des Calvinismus" (1910) and "Die Bedeutung des Protestantismus für die Enstehung der modernen Welt" (1906/1911), both in *KGA* 8.

[31] *Die Soziallehren der christlichen Kirchen und Gruppen* (vol. 1 of *Gesammelte Schriften*, by Ernst Troeltsch; Tübingen: Mohr, 1912); translated into English as *The Social Teaching of the Christian Churches* (trans. Olive Wyon; London: George Allen & Unwin, Ltd., 1931; repr., Louisville, Ky.: John Knox, 1992). Hereafter abbreviated in the footnotes as *GS* 1 and *ST*, respectively (see the Abbreviations and Short Titles page at the front of this book). Because the title of the English translation does not match the exact title of the German original, throughout this book I use a correct translation of the German title (*The*

years but much more closely related than generally recognized: Troeltsch's 1903 essay, "What Does 'Essence of Christianity' Mean?" (rev. ed. 1913)[32] and his 1922 volume *Historicism and Its Problems*. In both of these works, Troeltsch struggles with the two concerns that I argue are central to his theory of Christianity: 1) how to conceptualize large historical complexes in ways that do justice to their internal plurality and to their interrelation with social, political, and economic forces; and 2) how to relate this historical conceptualization to normative concerns about the proper shape of religions and cultures in the present world. By framing my study with these early (1903) and late (1922) articulations of Troeltsch's theory of tradition, and by placing Troeltsch's historical work in the middle, I show how Troeltsch's historical writings led him to develop and alter central aspects of his theory of Christianity.

In the essence essay, which is the subject of chapter 1, Troeltsch tackles the challenges of conceptualizing a religious tradition by analyzing the meaning and significance of the then-popular concept of an essence of Christianity. As he distinguishes among various dimensions of this complex philosophical concept, Troeltsch sketches a conception of Christianity that has long been celebrated for its striking continuities with current sensibilities concerning the identity of Christianity.[33] Troeltsch emphasizes diversity, problematizes

---

Social Teachings of the Christian Churches and Groups) whenever I refer to this work in the body of my text. The first portions of Troeltsch's *Social Teachings* appeared in gradual installments (from 1908–1910) in the *Archiv für Sozialwissenschaft und Sozialpolitik*, and the completed entire work appeared as the first volume of Troeltsch's *Gesammelte Schriften* in 1912. For more information on the history and publication of the *Social Teachings*, see ch. 2 of this study.

[32] The first edition of this essay ("¹WCh") was published in 1903 in *Die Christliche Welt*; the 1913 revised edition ("²WCh") was published in *GS* 2:386–451; the English translation of the 1913 edition ("Essence") is in *Writings*, 124–79. See also the list of abbreviations and short titles at the front of this book.

[33] Michael Pye has suggested that Troeltsch's essence essay contains the beginnings of a "family resemblance" conception of tradition. See "Ernst Troeltsch and the End of the Problem of 'Other' Religions," in *Ernst Troeltsch and the Future of Theology* (ed. John Powell Clayton; Cambridge: Cambridge University Press, 1976) 172–95, esp. 187. John Clayton has made a similar argument at least implicitly in his critique of theologies of correlation. He footnotes Troeltsch's essence essay when discussing the advantages of family resemblance theories of Christianity. "Was ist falsch in der Korrelationstheologie?" *Neue Zeitschrift für systematische Theologie* 16 (1974) 93–111, esp. n. 65. Norbert Witsch has related the essence essay to a new postdogmatic doctrine of the church in *Glaubensorientierung in "nachdogmatischer" Zeit. Ernst Troeltschs Überlegungen zu einer Wesensbestimmung des Christentums* (Paderborn: Bonifatius, 1997).

the category of Christian origins, and links Christianity's historical development to political, economic, and social forces. He also recognizes that the ideological interests and values of the scholar shape any definition of the essence of Christianity. As a summary of Troeltsch's reflections on the identity of Christianity, the essence essay presents claims, commitments, and insights that are central to the theory of Christianity toward which he was working in his historical and philosophical writings.

Yet, Troeltsch's essay on the essence of Christianity also leaves the reader with a host of interpretive conundrums. Notwithstanding its perceptive discussion of the complexities involved in defining any tradition, the essence essay is also littered with seemingly contradictory statements that have long puzzled interpreters. Three examples suffice to demonstrate the confusion that, along with its insightfulness, seems to mark Troeltsch's reflection in this essay. First, Troeltsch uses the term "essence" in such a variety of ways that one is hard-pressed to discern exactly how he intends to classify it. Is the essence a conceptual tool and a heuristic device—an ideal type of sorts—used by historians to summarize a large complex of data? Or is it some kind of normative claim about Christianity's uniqueness and value in the past, present, and future? Troeltsch's usage seems to reflect both conceptions, while also occasionally hinting that the essence is a metaphysical driving force moving autonomously through history. Second, Troeltsch seems to equivocate on the status of the concept of an essence of Christianity as objective and empirically verifiable, on the one hand, and as marked by "strongly subjective factors" and values of the historian, on the other.[34] Is the essence an historical description or a philosophical judgment? Finally, Troeltsch makes conflicting statements about the value and usefulness of the concept. Even as he refers to the concept of an essence of Christianity as "the crown of historical theology,"[35] so does he describe it as a concept that is "very difficult to determine," and that must be used with great caution, if at all.[36]

Stephen Sykes has noted that these inconsistencies arise in large part from changes Troeltsch made to the 1903 version of his essay when he revised it in 1913 for inclusion in the second volume of his *Gesammelte Schriften.* My study builds upon this insight by exploring in much greater detail exactly

---

[34] "Essence," 160; "¹WCh," 652; "²WCh," 428.

[35] "Essence," 164; "¹WCh," 678; "²WCh," 433.

[36] "Essence," 126; "²WCh," 388. This statement was not in the original 1903 version of the essay, but was added in the 1913 edition.

how Troeltsch's composition of his major history of Christianity, the *Social Teachings* (completed in 1912), led him not only to edit his essence essay but virtually to leave the category "essence" behind. In this and several other ways, I show the intimate connection between Troeltsch's essence essay and his *Social Teachings*.

At the same time, however, I show that the additions made in 1913 cannot explain completely the alleged contradictions in the 1903 essence essay. Thus, I analyze the 1903 essay on its own terms in chapter 1. In the first part, I locate the 1903 essay in the context of Troeltsch's engagement with interdisciplinary debates concerning the nature of historical knowledge and its relation to questions of cultural values. This treatment broadens the field in which the essay is usually understood[37] and clarifies the theoretical challenges with which Troeltsch was grappling just prior to his composition of the 1903 essay.[38] One can then understand Troeltsch's competing claims not as contradictions but as part of his effort to attend to a range of complex questions about the nature of historical objects and historical understanding, and about the relative importance of the empirical and philosophical tasks of history. Troeltsch directs these questions to the task of developing a theory of Christianity. Sketching the elements of this nascent theory, then, constitutes the second and major section of chapter 1. My analysis details the ways in which Troeltsch uses such categories as essence, origins, and development, and highlights the normative interests and concerns that drive his efforts at conceptualizing Christianity.

Troeltsch develops and pursues precisely these categories and interests in his works on the history of Christianity. In the *Social Teachings*, Troeltsch's

---

[37] The standard practice is to locate the essay in the context of the Harnack-Loisy debate. Both Wendell Dietrich, in "Loisy and the Liberal Protestants," *Studies in Religion* 14 (1985) 303–11 and Guglielmo Forni, in *The Essence of Christianity: The Hermeneutical Question in the Protestant and Modernist Debate (1897–1904)* (Atlanta, Ga.: Scholars, 1995), have made important contributions here. While this theological conversation was extremely important for Troeltsch's treatment of the question of an essence of Christianity, it constitutes only one influence on Troeltsch at this time and does not account for the interdisciplinary engagement that also shaped Troeltsch's essay.

[38] Sykes discusses briefly the influence of both Rickert and Weber on Troeltsch's 1913 edition of the essay, but does not consider the influence of Rickert on the 1903 version. See Stephen Sykes, *The Identity of Christianity* (Philadelphia: Fortress, 1984) 168–69; see also the brief allusions to Rickert that Sykes makes in his essay, "Troeltsch and Christianity's Essence," in *Future of Theology* (ed. Clayton) 149, 158. Finally, see Sykes's note on the English translation of Troeltsch's 1913 essence essay in *Writings*, 180–81.

only comprehensive history of Christianity, he undertakes a massive history of the social ethic of Christianity in its various forms and attempts to explore the different ways in which Christian groups, communities, and institutions have organized themselves and developed their doctrines in relation to society. Despite Troeltsch's own suggestions about the connection between the essence essay and the *Social Teachings*, no study has explored their interrelation. Yet, the theoretical structure of the *Social Teachings* presupposes a theory of tradition that has striking similarities to that developed in the early essence essay.

Chapters 2, 3, and 4 offer analyses of three categories that are central to Troeltsch's conceptualization of Christianity. In chapter 2, I focus on Troeltsch's view of Christian origins in order to determine what place they occupy and what authority they assume in his conception of Christianity. Chapter 3 offers an articulation of the conception of historical development that can be discerned "in between the lines" of his historical narrative in the *Social Teachings*. In that chapter, I also begin to uncover the normative agenda that informs Troeltsch's historical investigation and that shapes his portrait of Christianity's development from its beginnings to the modern period. In chapter 4, I outline the ways in which Troeltsch uses the ideal types of church, sect, and mysticism to underscore the internal variety of Christianity and to explore how Christianity might contribute to the shape and quality of modern life. I show that Troeltsch's ambivalence toward modernity is hidden in his account of the gender ethic of each type. Together, these three chapters show that one can read Troeltsch's *Social Teachings* as an implicit historical demonstration and expansion of the explicit argument found in his essay on the essence of Christianity, namely, that any conception of Christianity's "identity" or "essence" must do justice to the variety of its forms and the complexity of its historical development. As I analyze the way in which Troeltsch tells the history of Christianity and its social doctrines, I demonstrate the degree to which his historical narrative is shaped by this commitment and by his normative concerns about the relation between Christianity and society in his own day.

The third area to which this study turns for an indication of Troeltsch's theory of Christianity is his later work on the philosophy of history, *Historicism and Its Problems*. The *Historicism* volume does not deal directly with Christianity itself but, rather, with European culture. It offers, nevertheless, valuable insight into Troeltsch's view of the nature and complexity of large historical aggregates such as Christianity, and the proper way to conceptualize them and reflect on their meaning and value for the present and future. Thus, I read this work as being in continuity and critical conversation with Troeltsch's earlier efforts to achieve a sufficiently complex conceptualization of Christianity. Specifically, I show how themes that Troeltsch first addresses in his 1903 essay on the essence of Christianity are once again taken up in the *Historicism* volume, but with deeper awareness of the complexity of historical phenomena, thanks largely to his historical investigations in the *Social Teachings*.

The picture of Christianity that emerges from the *Social Teachings* is one that is even more enmeshed in large historical complexes and developments than Troeltsch had previously realized. Although he has not dispensed with the notion of Christianity as a discrete phenomenon with its own integrity and boundaries, Troeltsch, by the end of his life, has also turned his attention to the larger unit of the cultural circle. In my analysis of the *Historicism* volume, I show that the twofold concern that drives his theory of Christianity as gleaned from earlier works is also operative here: any conception of a large cultural totality must adequately represent its complex constitution while indicating its value for the present and future. Thus, the *Historicism* volume is a valuable resource for imagining what Troeltsch's theory of Christianity might have looked like toward the end of his life.

In chapter 5, I trace Troeltsch's move beyond the concept of essence to that of cultural synthesis, first by showing how the category of an essence of Christianity is repeatedly called into question and rarely appears in his writings after 1912 (the year he finished writing the *Social Teachings*), and then by examining the function that he gives to the concept of a cultural synthesis in the *Historicism* volume. I argue that Troeltsch settles on a concept (cultural synthesis) that can highlight the composite nature of historical entities while clearly serving as a normative proposal for the shape of a tradition in the present and future. To offer a sufficiently multifarious and complex conception of Christianity while also exploring its possible resources for modern life, Troeltsch moves beyond the category of essence.

Focusing on the various ways in which Troeltsch struggled to define the identity of Christianity clarifies the nature and driving concerns of his work and points to a new set of contemporary questions in relation to which one might fruitfully analyze his writings afresh. Troeltsch as theologian worked outside the typical boundaries of that field, employing tools of the historical and cultural sciences to explore the complex nature of religious traditions

as a way of engaging contemporary problems and debates about the shape
of modern society and the potential role of Christianity in it. His conception
of the essence of Christianity, his portrait of earliest Christianity, his use of
the ideal types, and his arrangement and analysis of Christian history should
all be read in this light. Doing so would provide important insights into the
history of these categories in the study of religion and might open up an
interesting dialogue between Troeltsch's views on the essence of Christianity
and current theories about Christianity's identity, boundaries, and nature as
a tradition.

CHAPTER ONE

The Essence of Christianity and Modern Historical Thinking

For Troeltsch, the quest for a theory of Christianity is intertwined with an interest in affirming the abiding value of Christianity in the modern world. Troeltsch's 1903 essay "What Does 'Essence of Christianity' Mean?"[1] is an early articulation of his insights into the nature and complexity of Christianity as an historical phenomenon. It presents Troeltsch's initial struggle with key themes, commitments, and ambiguities that will remain central to his conceptualization of Christianity in his subsequent works. It is therefore an ideal place to begin to discern the theory of Christianity that I am arguing is at the heart of Troeltsch's historical writings produced in the decade following the appearance of this essay.

Indeed, as I shall argue, the essence essay contains the elements of an emerging theory of Christianity that seeks to combine objective historical representation with normative suggestions about Christianity's possible meaning and vitality in the present and future.[2] For Troeltsch, it is the nature of modern historical thinking (*modernes historisches Denken*) to engage in both empirical (factual) and philosophical (normative) analysis of historical

---

[1] "Was heißt 'Wesen des Christentums'?" See abbreviations page at front of book for full references to the two editions of this essay (abbreviated "¹WCh" and "²WCh").

[2] In this chapter, I deal only with the original 1903 edition of this essay ("¹WCh"). Troeltsch revised and expanded the essay for its second edition ("²WCh" = *GS* 2:386–451) in 1913, when it was prepared for inclusion in the second volume of Troeltsch's *Gesammelte Schriften*. Because no standard English translation of the 1903 edition exists, wherever possible I take my quotations from the English translation of the 1913 edition ("Essence" = *Writings*, 124–79). In all cases where the 1903 text has been altered in the 1913 edition (and therefore also in the English translation of that edition), I offer my own translation.

phenomena. And it is precisely this kind of thinking, according to Troeltsch, that is to be employed when defining the essence of Christianity.

In the first half of this chapter, I discuss the context of Troeltsch's 1903 essence essay with particular attention to the ways in which Troeltsch's reception and critique of Heinrich Rickert's historical method informs his analysis of the concept of an essence of Christianity. Previous scholarly treatments of Troeltsch's essence essay focus primarily on its relation to the "essence of Christianity" debate between Adolf Harnack and Alfred Loisy.[3] While this debate certainly informs Troeltsch's essay, it cannot account for the wide range of issues that Troeltsch incorporates into his discussion of the topic. I suggest that attention to Troeltsch's 1903 review of Rickert's theory of historical knowledge provides further insight into the conceptual questions with which Troeltsch was grappling just prior to writing the essence essay that same year.

In the second part of this chapter, I identify and analyze central categories, tensions, and distinctions that together constitute the elements of a theory of Christianity that Troeltsch begins to articulate in the essence essay. Whereas much analysis of this essay focuses on particular strengths or weaknesses in Troeltsch's argumentation or constructive proposal,[4] I argue that an examination of the key terms and concepts employed in the essence essay

---

[3] For example, see Sykes, *Identity*; Witsch, *Glaubensorientierung*; Forni, *Essence of Christianity*. Sykes discusses briefly the influence of both Rickert and Max Weber on Troeltsch's 1913 edition of the essay, but not on the 1903 version treated here. See note 38 of my Introduction, above. Walter E. Wyman, Jr., offers an illuminating discussion of the influence of Rickert's philosophy on Troeltsch's understanding and formulation of the essence of Christianity. Specifically, Wyman identifies a Rickertian influence in the "subjective, individualistic strand" of thought (as opposed to the "objective strand") that can be discerned in Troeltsch's reflections on the concept of Christianity's essence. See Walter E. Wyman, Jr., *The Concept of* Glaubenslehre: *Ernst Troeltsch and the Theological Heritage of Schleiermacher* (Chico, Calif.: Scholars, 1983) 82–90.

[4] Sykes (*Identity*, 172–73) judges Troeltsch's approach ultimately too self-confident and elitist, separating Christian identity from the church and leaving the definition of its essence to the experts. Witsch (*Glaubensorientierung*, 267–93) retrieves Troeltsch's principles of essence definition for a contemporary understanding of Catholic tradition and church. Witsch takes particular interest in the relevance of Troeltsch's theory for current theological reflection on issues of unity, diversity, and pluralism within the Christian church (see, for example, 21, 252). Michael Pye ("Troeltsch and the Science of Religion," in *Writings*, 247) applauds Troeltsch's treatment of the question of an essence of Christianity as "the classical statement of what it means to interpret a religious tradition on the basis of an uncompromisingly modern historical perspective."

points to a theory of Christianity that informs Troeltsch's historical work in *The Social Teachings of the Christian Churches and Groups.*

By situating Troeltsch's treatment of the concept of an essence of Christianity both in the context of the interdisciplinary debates of his time and as a conceptual precursor to the *Social Teachings*, I propose a new interpretation of the essence essay. Specifically, I show that the essence essay represents Troeltsch's early effort to conceptualize Christianity in a way that can do justice to its complex historical constitution while exploring its continuing value and vitality for modern life. As I argue throughout this study, Troeltsch continues to develop and adjust this conception in his works on the history of Christianity and Protestantism and into his late work on the philosophy of history.

The Background and Argument of Troeltsch's Essay

Troeltsch first wrote his essay on the essence of Christianity in 1903, in the wake of the interest and debate sparked by Adolf Harnack's published lectures, *Das Wesen des Christentums.*[5] In these lectures, Harnack sought to provide what he called a "purely historical" (*rein geschichtlich*) account of the essence of Christianity.[6] This essence, or "kernel" (*Kern*), he describes as a simple, threefold message of the gospel as uttered by Jesus—"the fatherhood of God, the brotherhood of man, and the ethical commandment of higher righteousness"—and preserved in certain forms of Christianity since that time.[7] In contrast to this "kernel," Harnack identifies as the husk

[5] *Das Wesen des Christentums* (Academic edition; Leipzig: Hinrichs, 1902). Harnack's lectures were delivered at the University of Berlin during its winter semester in 1899–1900. They were published in 1900 and translated into English that same year under the title *What Is Christianity?* In his introduction to the 1957 English edition, Rudolf Bultmann notes that in the United States this work had an enormous influence "not only on the rising generation of theologians but also on the educated classes" during the beginning of the twentieth century. See "Introduction" to Harnack, *What Is Christianity?* (trans. Thomas B. Saunders; repr. Gloucester, Mass.: Peter Smith, 1978) vii.

[6] Harnack (*What Is Christianity?,* 6; *Das Wesen des Christentums,* 4) defined a "purely historical" (*rein geschichtlich*) approach to the essence of Christianity as an exploration of the main ideas of Christianity based not on apologetic or abstract philosophical claims, but on an employment of historical methods and a study of what he called "the actual course of history." Later in this chapter, I discuss Troeltsch's understanding of the term "purely historical" (which Troeltsch formulates as *"rein historisch"*).

[7] Harnack argued that the essence of Christianity was preserved in the apostolic community, Paul's message, the early church, the Reformation, and modern Protestantism.

(*Schale*) all of the historical circumstances and contingencies that attached themselves to the kernel. These contingencies often distort the kernel or join with it temporarily and fortuitously but never bear any intrinsic, essential relation to the eternal, transhistorical gospel.

Among the various critical responses to Harnack's lectures, Troeltsch found most impressive and important that produced by French Roman Catholic modernist Alfred Loisy. In *The Gospel and the Church*,[8] Loisy responded to Harnack's thoroughly Protestant account of the essence of Christianity[9] by presenting an organic, developmental view of Christianity. For Loisy, the main Protestant feature of Harnack's presentation was its appeal to an original message of the gospel as an unchanging expression of true Christianity and therefore as the criterion for all forms and periods of Christianity.[10] In this way Harnack could characterize the development of the Catholic church as contrary to the essence. Loisy denied the existence of any essence of Christianity and instead presented a view in which the meaning

---

Both Orthodox and Catholic Christianity are seen by Harnack as distortions of the essence of Christianity.

[8] In 1902, Loisy, a French Catholic modernist and biblical scholar influenced by the history of religions school, wrote *L'Évangile et l'église* (ET: *The Gospel and the Church* [1903; trans. Christopher Home; repr. Philadelphia: Fortress, 1976]) in response to Harnack's *Wesen des Christentums*. Although Loisy defended the church as the major site of the gospel's development, his view of the church and its need to adapt to the modern world resulted in his excommunication in 1908.

[9] Loisy makes two main criticisms of Harnack's treatment of Christian origins and account of the gospel. First, Harnack reconstructs Jesus' message in a way that does not do justice to his historical context and instead projects back onto Jesus a modern Protestant sensibility. In addition, Harnack appeals to an unchanging essence of the gospel and denies that any message or truth must continually be expressed and developed according to the situation and circumstances of each age. See Loisy, *The Gospel*, 65–66, 87, 97–98, 109–10, 115, 139, 166, 169. Another obviously Protestant feature of Harnack's interpretation of the essence is its privileging of Luther and the Reformation.

[10] Wendell Dietrich ("Loisy and the Liberal Protestants") offers an illuminating account of Loisy's relation to and possible dependence on the thought of German liberal Protestant biblical scholars and theologians, focusing particularly on Loisy's relation to Johannes Weiss and Troeltsch. Dietrich emphasizes that Loisy based his views "on his own independent research" but came to strikingly similar positions as Weiss on issues of Jesus' eschatology (304–5), and also shared Troeltsch's interest in the implications of "the modern historical conception of truth" for theology (306). Dietrich argues that "There is no doubt that Loisy was very much in touch with late-nineteenth-century Protestant scholars' exegetical results (especially Weiss and the history of religions school) and theological resources (Sabatier and the French Ritschlians). . . . But it is also clear that the Modernist Loisy transferred these borrowings into a Catholic intellectual structure" (311).

of the gospel develops over time throughout the history of Christianity and reaches its fullness in the continued growth and adaptations of the church.

In his contribution to the essence of Christianity debate,[11] Troeltsch wishes not to define the actual essence of Christianity,[12] but to reflect on the nature of such a concept, teasing out its methodological presuppositions and goals. Troeltsch makes three broad contributions to the discussion that are also central to his emerging conception of Christianity. First, Troeltsch articulates the presuppositions implied in the concept of an essence of Christianity and argues that such a concept[13] is a product of "modern historical thought" (*modernes*

---

[11] Troeltsch's essay was published over a period of two months, in six separate issues of *Die Christliche Welt*. It is likely that Troeltsch wrote the essay gradually during this period, and not in its entirety beforehand. This may contribute to the common observation—also under consideration in this chapter—that Troeltsch's essay contains many inconsistencies and tensions that are not worked out systematically. *Die Christliche Welt* was a journal created by Martin Rade to address a range of political, theological, and social questions among a large variety of liberal Protestant scholars, pastors, and lay people. Drescher notes that Troeltsch's decision to present the article in *Die Christliche Welt* (whose subtitle was "Evangelisches Gemeinblatt für Gebildete aller Stände" [ET: "Protestant Journal for Cultured People of All Classes"]) suggests that Troeltsch desired to pose the discussion as "a basic problem going beyond academic theology, one which also involved his educated contemporaries." See Hans Georg Drescher, *Ernst Troeltsch: His Life and Work* (1991; trans. John Bowden; Minneapolis: Fortress, 1993) 171. For more on *Die Christliche Welt* and the participation of liberal theologians in public debates during the Wilhelmine period, see Mark D. Chapman, *Ernst Troeltsch and Liberal Theology*, 5–6. See also Hübinger, *Kulturprotestantismus*, esp. 129–42.

[12] Throughout his essays, Troeltsch rarely offers a definition of the essence of Christianity. One instance is found in "The Dogmatics of the History-of-Religions School," where he states, "The definition of the essence of Christianity I would put as the basis of dogmatics reads as follows: Christian religious faith is faith in the rebirth and higher birth of the creature who is alienated from God—a regeneration effected through the knowledge of God in Christ. The consequence of this regeneration is union with God and social fellowship so as to constitute the kingdom of God" ("The Dogmatics," in *Religion in History*, 97; "Die Dogmatik," in *GS* 2:512).

[13] Although Troeltsch links the concept of an essence of Christianity in part to German Idealism, he does not understand the term "concept" here in the sense of a Hegelian *Begriff*. Although there are Hegelian aspects of Troeltsch's account of Christianity's essence, and although he sometimes speaks of the essence in metaphysical terms (as I discuss further below), Troeltsch states several times that the term "essence of Christianity," in the sense in which he is using it, no longer has the strict Hegelian resonance wherein "the historical reality" can be "deduce[d] . . . quite necessarily out of a basic idea, once the essence was grasped as the principle" ("Essence," 131; "'WCh," 484). Wyman (*Concept*, 87) states that Troeltsch's own use and treatment of the term "essence of Christianity" attempts to provide "a third alternative" between what could be called Hegelian and Rickertian (or neo-Kantian)

historisches Denken), a set of assumptions, commitments, and modes of understanding prepared for by the Enlightenment and deeply shaped by German Idealism and German Romanticism.[14] Troeltsch often defines modern historical thinking by contrasting it with what he calls a dogmatic approach to determining Christianity's fundamental meaning.[15] Whereas dogmatic

ways of thinking about an essence of Christianity. Later in this chapter, I discuss the ways in which Troeltsch's view of the "essence" includes Rickertian moments.

[14] "Essence," 131; "¹WCh," 485. Troeltsch defines Idealism as "the metaphysical theory which, as regards the primary and most certain datum of experience, takes its stand upon consciousness and its contents. . . . Idealism implies that the relation of subject and object is one of the essential starting points of philosophy, and in its view of that relation it lays down the decisive principle that objects can exist only for a subject, and that the subject which carries the objects within itself is the higher category, and as such must determine the process of philosophic thought." "Idealism," *Encyclopaedia of Religion and Ethics* (ed. James Hastings; New York: Scribner, 1914) 90.

[15] In his critiques of dogmatic (vs. historical) methods in theology, Troeltsch has in mind not simply conservative Protestant theologians, but actually the work of many of his liberal colleagues associated with Ritschl, including, to some extent, Harnack. Troeltsch came to believe that Ritschlian theology isolated a particular conception of Jesus' message and Scripture from rigorous historical and comparative analysis. (For more on Troeltsch's break with Ritschlianism, see Sarah Coakley, *Christ Without Absolutes: A Study of the Christology of Ernst Troeltsch* [Oxford: Oxford University Press, 1998] ch. 2). For Troeltsch, Harnack's commitment to historical methods was compromised by his insistence on the gospel as unique, eternal, and beyond comparison. See Chapman, *Ernst Troeltsch and Liberal Theology*, ch. 3. As I suggest further on, the distinction between historical and dogmatic methods in theology was intimately connected, for Troeltsch, to the question of Christian theology's possible participation and place in the shaping of modern society. Chapman explains Troeltsch's concern as follows: "Only if theology was open to criticism could it hope to maintain its status in the modern world. A haughty disregard for the rest of learning would threaten its very existence" (Chapman, *Ernst Troeltsch and Liberal Theology*, 55). On this point see also Graf ("Protestantische Theologie," 69–79), who locates the historical-dogmatic debate in the political context of imperial Germany, where debates over theological method were intimately linked to competing conceptions of state, society, and church. According to Graf, liberal and conservative Protestants shared the conviction that Christian theology should serve as the basis of cultural values and should preserve the Christianness of the state and society (69). They disagreed, however, on what this meant in practice. For liberals, only a free scientific approach to theology could help scholars understand the "cultural meaning of Christianity" (71). For conservatives, however, such a "radically historicizing" approach to theology was counterproductive (70); they sought to preserve a Christian culture through "strict binding to Holy Scripture and traditional church knowledge" (72) and through a defense of the church's role in the appointment of university theologians (73). Graf also notes that orthodox theologians often prevailed in disputes with liberals over university appointments, especially in Prussia, and often against the will of the faculty majority (74). Thus, questions about an historical or a dogmatic method in theology had poignant and immediate political resonances.

approaches appeal to authoritative scriptural or institutional traditions for a definitive account of Christianity, modern historical approaches determine the nature of Christianity by treating it like any other historical phenomenon.[16] From the numerous historical details, one constructs a conception of the essence of a phenomenon, represents it, and thereby makes its complicated reality and unique identity comprehensible. Thus, for Troeltsch, the essence is a concept uniquely linked to modern historical sensibilities, rooted not in miraculous or supernatural claims but in the presuppositions of historical-critical methods of investigation. These modern historical sensibilities, however, are in no way unconcerned about the meaning, value, and future of Christianity. On the contrary, for Troeltsch, as I shall suggest later in this chapter, the adoption of a modern historical worldview and method entails a set of values and an interest in the contributions of religion to the development of society and culture.

Second, Troeltsch further complexifies the concept of an essence of Christianity by distinguishing three dimensions intrinsic to such a concept. Not emerging simply from an all-encompassing survey or summary of the facts of Christianity,[17] the essence is at once a critical, developmental, and ideal concept. As a *critical* concept, its formation entails judgment (and not simply acceptance or comprehensive presentation) of the various historical forms and events in Christian history. Given the vast array and heterogeneous mass of events, expressions, and tendencies that constitute Christianity's history, the historian must select or privilege certain elements of the historical data, omit others, and thereby discern which developments best express and reflect Christianity's true nature and which do not. Troeltsch implies here his critique of Loisy, whose organic-developmental approach to understanding the identity of Christianity (in Troeltsch's view) regards the development and rise of Catholicism as evidence of its normativeness.[18] Instead of accepting historical developments as indications of what is normative in Christianity, Troeltsch argues that one ought to *evaluate* historical events and forms as either consistent with or contrary to "what ought to have been."[19] This evaluation

---

[16] Troeltsch states that "the whole expression 'essence of Christianity' is linked to modern, critical and evolutionary history. Catholic theology would never have used it. It would have said 'the faith of the church'. . . . Nor would orthodox Protestantism have used it. It would have said 'the revelation of the Bible'" ("Essence," 128; "'WCh," 483).

[17] "Essence," 140; "'WCh," 533–34.

[18] "Essence," 134, 145; "'WCh," 486, 536.

[19] "Essence," 145; "'WCh," 536. Here Troeltsch describes the task of essence definition

aims at objectivity, or at least at what Troeltsch calls an absence of "partisan spirit" (*Parteileidenschaft*) insofar as it proceeds according to a principle of immanent criticism, attempting to perceive "historical formations in terms of the ideal which lies in their main driving force."[20] That said, this criticism also inevitably involves the historian's "personal considerations" (*persönliche Betrachtungen*).[21] The inclusion of such subjective considerations cannot be avoided, however, if one accepts that historical work involves making "distinctions of principle" concerning the historical material.[22]

Troeltsch recognizes, however, the difficulty of determining the criteria for these distinctions. Here he criticizes Harnack's biblicism, which takes a view of the gospel in its alleged original form (that is, Jesus' preaching) as normative for all of Christianity.[23] Troeltsch argues that if one takes historical criticism seriously, one will admit that Christianity's origins are not as pure, simple, or singular as some historians and theologians suggest. Further, Troeltsch insists that one must view features from the *entire* history of Christianity (and not simply from its earliest period) as "contained within the essence" as well.[24] The essence, then, is also a *developmental* concept, and

in a way that echoes Harnack's efforts to distinguish the "kernel" of Christianity from those developments that distorted or corrupted it ("Essence," 139–40; "¹WCh," 533–34).

[20] "Essence," 142; "¹WCh," 534. Troeltsch explains what this process of immanent criticism looks like when he writes, "the historical is measured by the historical, the individual formation is measured against the spirit of the whole conceived intuitively and imaginatively" (ibid.).

[21] "Essence," 142; "¹WCh," 534.

[22] "Essence," 145; "¹WCh," 578.

[23] In fact, Harnack does not do this exactly. While he clearly draws heavily on the origins of Christianity for the determination of its kernel, Harnack does not believe the kernel was present absolutely in its best form during the time of Jesus. This is evident in the fact that Harnack describes Paul as having actually improved on aspects of Jesus' message. Thus, while Harnack *generally* appeals to a static criterion (i.e., the gospel, found in the origins of Christianity) as normative for all other developments, which are seen primarily as corruptions of the original form, he also suggests that certain developments are fortuitous for the kernel, carrying it forward, and in the case of Paul, improving on it.

[24] This view corresponds to Troeltsch's notion of progressive revelation, wherein revelation cannot be confined to the origins of Christianity but must be seen throughout its history. In his *Glaubenslehre*, Troeltsch uses the term "progressive revelation" in two ways. First, he employs it broadly to signify the need to view sources and traditions beyond the Bible as revelation. He writes, "There is another revelation that stands alongside the Bible, a subjective element to which the doctrine of the Holy Spirit attests. Hence we must recognize other sources of revelation besides the Bible. We are heirs to a tradition that extends throughout the whole of history down to our own day, a day whose life also flows

here Troeltsch approves of Loisy's approach over Harnack's.[25] The essence must be conceived as "an entity [*Größe*] with an inner life and flexibility, and a productive power for new creation."[26] Not simply the original period of Christianity nor just the preaching of Jesus, but all of the subsequent historical developments must, too, be part of the material from which an essence is constructed. One must also conceive of the diversity within Christianity's history, then, as part of the continuum of possibilities that together make up the essence of Christianity. This continuum must even include opposing tendencies.[27] No simple concept of continuity will do.

Because it involves both historical research and normative evaluation, the formation of a concept of the essence of Christianity is a task at the boundary between empirical-historical and philosophical-historical work.[28] Thus the concept of an essence of Christianity is also an *ideal* concept. It is grounded in careful historical analysis, but it is shaped by a vision of Christianity's future. The essence therefore requires for its formulation an ethical decision about what Christianity *ought* to be and with which norms and values it is best and most accurately connected. These assessments also inform the articulation of the essence. Hence, Troeltsch makes his well-known statement that "to define the essence is to shape it afresh."[29]

Third, Troeltsch lends clarification and sophistication to the essence of Christianity debate by raising questions about the epistemological status

---

from God. We hold to the concept of *progressive* revelation." *The Christian Faith: Based on Lectures Delivered at the University of Heidelberg in 1912 and 1913* (trans. Garrett E. Paul; Minneapolis: Fortress, 1991) 45. In addition, Troeltsch defines progressive revelation more narrowly as one of three kinds of revelation: foundational and central revelation (the Bible and "the history to which it witnesses"), progressive revelation (the history of the church and "the modern world of religious feeling"), and contemporary revelation ("contemporary religious experience," ibid., 40).

[25] In a letter to von Hügel dated 10 March 1903, Troeltsch expresses his admiration for Loisy's book, *The Gospel and the Church,* including its critique of the limitations of Harnack's presentation of Jesus. Troeltsch writes, "[Loisy's work] is the most intelligent and beneficial critique of Harnack that has come into my hands." Troeltsch, *Briefe an Friedrich von Hügel* (ed. Karl-Ernst Apfelbacher and Peter Neuner; Paderborn: Bonifacius Druckerei, 1974) 63.

[26] "¹WCh," 581. Troeltsch altered this sentence slightly for the 1913 (second) edition. He wrote, "In reality however the essence has to be an entity with an inner, living flexibility, and a productive power for new creation and assimilation" ("Essence," 151; "²WCh," 418).

[27] "Essence," 152–54; "¹WCh," 582–83.

[28] "Essence," 134; "¹WCh," 486.

[29] "Essence," 162; "¹WCh," 654.

of any given definition of the essence. Are such definitions objective or subjective, products of empirical-historical reconstruction or philosophical-historical speculation? Troeltsch argues that both sets of classification apply. A claim about the essence of Christianity is objective insofar as it is grounded in a rigorous immersion in empirical-historical data; it is subjective insofar as it entails the creative judgment, evaluation, and recommendation of the inquirer. Although Troeltsch seeks strategies for managing or checking the subjectivism inherent in any construction of the essence, he denies that such an element will ever disappear. Instead, Troeltsch insists that the relation between objectivity and subjectivity in the definition of the essence will always be a "knotty problem" whose strands cannot be untangled but must be united in the conscientious "living act" of the historian.[30] For Troeltsch there is no way—and no need—to do away with the subjective element in all historical investigation, analysis, and judgment. Therefore he asserts:

> If [subjectivism] is an unavoidable matter of fact however, it is better not to try to deny it but rather to recognise it freely and openly. The less effort one spends in self-deceit, trying to find a theoretical escape from subjectivism, the freer one's hands are to set practical limits to it and defuse the danger.[31]

Insofar as history should serve the present, the effort to root out all subjective elements in historical analysis is wrong-headed. Insofar as history should also aim to provide responsible and relatively objective accounts of historical phenomena and events, it should find strategies for tempering the inevitable subjectivism in all historical reconstruction through the articulation of careful methods and means of analysis.

By relating the question of an essence of Christianity to theories of history, historical development, and historical knowledge, Troeltsch alludes to a wide range of issues beyond the Harnack-Loisy debate. While this debate may have been the occasion for Troeltsch's essay, the grounds and scope of his own response touched on much broader interdisciplinary questions and cultural concerns that were of great interest to Troeltsch and his colleagues in the Eranos Circle during his Heidelberg years. These concerns extended beyond the usual purview of biblical studies, history of Christianity, and Christian theology into the realms of philosophy of history and the

---

[30] "Essence," 160; "¹WCh," 653.
[31] "Essence," 167; "¹WCh," 680.

emerging field of sociology. At stake in Troeltsch's and his colleagues' interdisciplinary endeavors during this time were questions about the possible contributions of the historical and cultural sciences to the pressing challenges of modernization.

A review essay written by Troeltsch in the early months of 1903 provides an invaluable glimpse into the nontheological sources of Troeltsch's position on the essence of Christianity. In "Modern Philosophy of History,"[32] published in the *Theologische Rundschau* in January through March of 1903, Troeltsch gave an enthusiastic review of Heinrich Rickert's 1902 work, *The Limits of Concept Formation in Natural Science.*[33] In this book, Rickert attempted to make a case for the validity, objectivity, and indispensability of the kind of knowledge pursued in the historical sciences. Troeltsch's enthusiasm for and criticism of Rickert's approach to the historical method reveal much about the range of historical and philosophical issues he was addressing as he wrote his essay on the essence of Christianity. Hence, more than has been acknowledged in Troeltsch scholarship, a close examination of Rickert and Troeltsch's response to him is vital for an understanding of the essence essay.

Heinrich Rickert and the Study of History

Rickert belonged to the Baden, or southwest German, school of neo-Kantianism, led by his teacher Wilhelm Windelband (1848–1915), who was Troeltsch's colleague in Heidelberg. The members of this school wanted to offer a theory of historical knowledge—its nature, objects, and goals—and its relation to values (*Werte*).[34] They argued that the historical sciences were

---

[32] "Moderne Geschichtsphilosophie," *Theologische Rundschau* 6 (1903) 3–28, 57–72, 103–17. This essay was revised for the second volume of Troeltsch's *Gesammelte Schriften* in 1913 (*GS* 2:673–728). ET of this revised 1913 edition is "Modern Philosophy of History," in *Religion in History*, 273–320. Hereafter references to this essay offer first the relevant pages from the ET, then the page numbers from the 1913 German edition in *GS* 2, followed by the page numbers from the original 1903 version.

[33] Heinrich Rickert, *The Limits of Concept Formation in Natural Science: A Logical Introduction to the Historical Sciences* (trans. from rev. 1929 edition by Guy Oakes; Cambridge: Cambridge University Press, 1986) 40.

[34] My exposition of Baden neo-Kantianism and of Rickert's philosophy is indebted to Guy Oakes, *Weber and Rickert: Concept Formation in the Cultural Sciences* (Cambridge, Mass.: MIT Press, 1988). For more on neo-Kantianism as a movement, see Thomas E. Willey, *Back to Kant: The Revival of Kantianism in German Social and Historical Thought, 1860–1914* (Detroit, Mich.: Wayne State University Press, 1978).

distinct from the natural sciences, but were equally capable of yielding the
"rational" and "objective" results that were generally credited to the latter.[35]
The historical sciences, they argued, concerned themselves with the same
objects or reality as did the natural sciences, but did so according to distinct
interests, goals, and methods. Theirs was, then, an epistemological approach
to defining the distinctiveness of the historical sciences, and not an ontological
one.[36] The following assumptions were central to the Baden school's view
of history and the objects of history.[37] First, members of the Baden school
argued that the individual is the most basic unit of reality. That is, reality
itself is composed of an infinite mass of individual, irrational, unique, and
unrepeatable events and units, all carrying their own value.[38] Second, history
as a science, they argued, is interested in knowledge of these individual units
and their value and significance, both for historical agents themselves and for
scholars of the cultural sciences.[39] The natural sciences, on the other hand,
are interested not in individualities but in generalities. They therefore seek
not to gain knowledge of the quality or nature of these individual elements
that constitute concrete reality, but rather to understand the universal laws
that govern reality. Third, because reality is composed of an intricate and

[35] Although Rickert and other members of the Baden school of neo-Kantianism often used
the term "cultural sciences" (*Kulturwissenschaften*) as the counterpart to natural sciences,
I shall use the term "historical sciences" (*Geschichtswissenschaften*) in my discussions of
Rickert's approach to history, since that is the term Troeltsch most commonly employs and
the term used by Rickert in *The Limits*.

[36] An ontological approach would argue that history and natural science deal with
fundamentally different objects.

[37] For elaboration on these and other central concerns of the Baden school, see Oakes,
Weber and Rickert, 41–42.

[38] Individuality is a concept commonly associated with historicism. It does not refer
simply to human individuals, but rather to the nature of reality as composed of an endless
plurality of individual events, units, and particularities. Georg Iggers identifies the concept
of individuality as one of the key elements of what he calls a tradition of historicism in
Germany reaching from Wilhelm von Humboldt to Gerhard Ritter. Developed by Johann
Gottfried Herder in opposition to natural law philosophy, the idea of individuality "assumes
that all cognitions are historical and individual." Reality, then, is comprised of unending and
fleeting individualities. Because value comes to be seen only in these individualities (these
particulars of history), all history is simply "value-filled diversity." See Georg Iggers, *The
German Conception of History* (rev. ed.: Middletown, Conn.: Wesleyan University Press,
1983) 30, 35.

[39] This is called an "idiographic" interest (that is, the science of history's interest in individualities), which is distinguished from natural science's "nomological" interest in abstract
generalizations about conceptual relations, regularities, and laws that govern reality.

infinite array of objects or individuals, it cannot be known directly or exhaustively. Knowledge is acquired through the formation of concepts that enable one to organize, capture, or judge some dimension of reality. Fourth, the natural sciences are particularly inadequate for producing knowledge of the individual entities and infinite details that make up concrete reality, since these could never be captured by universal laws or broad generalizations. The distinctiveness and importance of the historical sciences, then, consist in their efforts to "know" these individualities by forming concepts that select the most individual and unique (or essential) realities that can illuminate the individuality and value of the whole.

These four assertions enabled the Baden school to argue that natural scientific methods and concepts simply cannot serve the historical or cultural sciences, which, as disciplines in their own right, have their own legitimate (and equally scientific) interests, methodologies, goals, and outcomes. This argument hinged on demonstrating the limits of natural scientific knowledge so as to defend the value and need for cultural or historical sciences as well. The Baden school, therefore, attempted to show that there could be a type of concept formation that is distinct from that of the natural sciences but with equal scientific authority.

The Baden neo-Kantians approached this issue by pointing out that all knowledge, whether historical or natural-scientific, depends on concepts that enable one to organize and to do something with reality, which is irrational and infinitely complex.[40] Rickert, among others, argued that cultural sciences use concepts that *individualize*, while those of the natural sciences *generalize*. According to Rickert, concept formation in the cultural (or historical) sciences proceeds by selecting the essential and unique from the rich, irrational, and infinitely individuated mass of reality. These concepts synthesize and recast reality, abstracting from it only the part that is identified as uniquely valuable and individual. This abstraction does not duplicate reality but provides an artificial conception of its most essential features.

In this process of concept formation in the historical sciences, the human capacity for judgment is active and determinative. The selection of that which is essential and uniquely individual is always a judgment of the historian. Indeed, knowledge of the kind sought by the historical sciences would be impossible without this judging and selecting of the essential and important.

---

[40] For Baden neo-Kantians, knowledge is the formation of concepts that organize reality according to a specific interest, whether idiographic or nomothetic.

Reality itself is infinitely complex quantitatively and qualitatively. Knowledge of reality, therefore, is only possible through simplification and representation by a concept whose individuality and value are unique and authoritative. How does one know that the concepts of historical science are objective and not simply the random or subjective judgments and selections of individual historians? Rickert's book attempts to address this challenge. Therefore, he shows an interest in the criteria or principles by which certain individualities are selected and conceptualized in the historical sciences. According to Rickert, concept formation in the historical sciences proceeds by selecting the uniquely individual (*Individuum*) from the mass of individuals that make up reality.[41] Rickert organized his account of history according to historical centers, those unique individuals with which or with whom certain values are associated and sustained. Thus something becomes an object of historical conceptualization when it stands in relation to values. This is Rickert's theory of value relevance (*Wertbeziehung*). As Rickert describes it, "This view singles out from the infinite manifold only that which stands in some sort of relation to values, so that it somehow makes a difference with respect to values."[42] For Rickert, the value associated with these centers must be of a general sort. This means that this value is not simply the subjective opinion or personal value of a single person, but is rather a value acknowledged by the larger culture under investigation. Moreover, these general values must not be simply *held* by all people in the culture, but actually felt as a demand by all in the culture; that is, these cultural values have a general normative status.[43]

The historian seeks to identify, therefore, the historical centers and values of the culture or period under question and uses these as the organizing concepts for her or his historical study. Although the historian must have at least some *interest* in the values held by the period under question, the historian's work is guided not by his or her own values, but rather by those of the culture under investigation. For Rickert, the historian has a *theoretical interest* in the values, corresponding to the theoretical relation that historical individuals have with certain values. Rickert distinguishes theoretical interest from practical and evaluative interest. Thus, the importance of the historian's

---

[41] The concept of individuality here includes historical creations (such as the state or works of art), historical events, and individual human beings. Goethe was a favorite example of an "historical individual" among many German intellectuals of Rickert's period.

[42] Rickert, *Limits*, 92.

[43] Oakes, *Weber and Rickert*, 81–83.

interest and the historical individual's value-relevance being *theoretical* has to do with the need for both to be objective.

Rickert knows that reality—infinitely complex as it is—offers the possibility of many historical centers and the identification of many contradictory or contrasting historical centers, whether in the same culture or among different cultures. Thus Rickert addresses the problem of how to choose among the various possibilities of value relations that may be said to inhere in a culture. Lest historical work be proven nonscientific and merely subjective or idiosyncratic, Rickert theorizes about how to defend the historian's choice according to some kind of objective principle.

Rickert approaches the problem of a variety of conflicting and seemingly equally valid or defensible values[44] by making a transcendental argument for the existence of objective values whose content we do not know but on which we rely for our conception of the world. Rickert makes these formal values analogous to Kant's categories, that is, they are irreducible and unanalyzable, beyond the sphere of subject and object.[45] Rickert argues that because humans can arrive at conflicting value judgments of historical phenomena and can argue about these conflicts, their conception of the world rests on there being objective values. Moreover, Rickert asserts that if cultural science *must* proceed by forming conceptions of historical individuals and their value, then there must be some values that are unconditionally valid. All the various value positions then stand in relation to these unknown but objective values.[46] As Rickert writes:

> Thus if historical science claims that its problem is a scientific necessity, it must assume that in the domain of value as well, it is not *only* a question of the caprice of many or all persons. This, in fact, implies the metaempirical presupposition that *some* values are *unconditionally* valid and that all human value positions stand in a more or less proximate *relation* to them that is defined as more than capricious. If this were

---

[44] For Rickert, this problem would result unhappily in an utter relativism of, or skepticism about, values. The kind of relativism that Rickert (and Troeltsch) wants to avoid can be classified as that which Sarah Coakley (*Christ Without Absolutes*, 17) calls a "criterial value relativism" or "strong epistemological relativism," wherein there are no criteria for truth—and possibly no such thing as "truth" at all—beyond those stemming from the particular framework within which each truth claim is articulated.

[45] See Oakes, *Weber and Rickert*, 101–2.

[46] See ibid., 104–6.

not so, purely scientific history with a value-relevant, individualizing concept formation could never be written.[47]

With this discussion, however, Rickert knows that he is at the boundary between empirical history and philosophical history. He is fully convinced that the former can be shown to proceed objectively and scientifically. The latter, philosophy of history, is a much more difficult project, but one that can and must proceed in conversation with, and based upon, this logic of the historical sciences that Rickert and his colleagues have set out to articulate.

Troeltsch's Reception and Critique of Rickert's Historical Method

There are some striking continuities between Rickert's view of concept formation in the historical sciences and Troeltsch's analysis of the concept of an essence of Christianity. Troeltsch uses the essence as a concept for arriving at knowledge of both the distinctiveness and the value of Christianity. The essence is an abstraction constructed by the historian, who selects from Christianity's history the most important events, developments, continuities, and innovations. These then represent the individuality of the larger whole and thus make sense of and hold together its diverse components. Like Rickert's account of concept formation and the selection of historical centers, the definition of the essence for Troeltsch is achieved only by the most careful empirical-historical work, undertaken without regard for the historian's own values, but rather with an objective approach. The criteria for the selection of the essential arise both from the historical data and from the conscience of the historian. This leads Troeltsch to the problem of objectivity and subjectivity in the construction of concepts such as the essence of Christianity—a theme that also troubled Rickert.

References to Rickert's work occur throughout Troeltsch's corpus; indeed, the two were in many ways lifelong conversation partners.[48] On the one hand, Troeltsch consistently saw certain problems with Rickert's strict

---

[47] Rickert, *Limits*, 205.

[48] Although professors at different universities, Troeltsch and Rickert (1863–1936) interacted in the early 1900s at regional philosophical meetings and lectures. They maintained occasional correspondence throughout their lives. Troeltsch's (extant) letters to Rickert have been compiled and annotated in "Ernst Troeltschs Briefe an Heinrich Rickert," in *Mitteilungen der Ernst-Troeltsch-Gesellschaft* VI (ed. Graf; Augsburg, 1991) 108–28.

neo-Kantianism and ultimately determined that, as he would write in a 1921 letter to Rickert, "my philosophical blood is certainly different [from yours]. That has become increasingly clear to me."[49] Yet, Troeltsch preceded this comment with the statement, "I have learned and always continue to learn an extraordinarily great deal from you."[50] Despite the clear philosophical differences that gradually separated him from Rickert and from Baden neo-Kantianism in general, Troeltsch nevertheless appreciated certain features of Rickert's historical method (and its emphasis on the concept of individuality), and associated himself loosely with Baden neo-Kantianism in the early years of the twentieth century.[51] Certainly in 1903—the year he published both his review of Rickert and his essence essay—Troeltsch responded favorably to certain aspects of Rickert's understanding of the historical sciences and the nature of historical knowledge. As Troeltsch himself would later state, in a passage revised for the 1913 edition of his review of Rickert:

> My studies of "The Absoluteness of Christianity" and of the concept of "The Essence of Christianity" have accordingly made use of Rickert's philosophy of history, and in particular of its teaching on the connection between empirical historiography and philosophy of history as the most important means for the solution of what we felt to be serious problems.[52]

[49] Letter to Heinrich Rickert, 22 December 1921, in ibid., 124.

[50] Ibid.

[51] Drescher periodizes Troeltsch's intellectual development into three phases and asserts that Troeltsch's engagement with Rickert, and with neo-Kantianism in general, was one of several central features of the second phase (1902–1914). See Hans Georg Drescher, "Ernst Troeltsch's Intellectual Development," in *Future of Theology* (ed. Clayton) 14, 15, 27. Both editions of the essence essay (1903 and 1913) stand within this second phase of Troeltsch's intellectual development, and both exhibit an appreciation of Rickert. It is notable that, in a letter to Rickert in 1915, shortly after the death of Windelband, Troeltsch refers to himself as "a member of your [Rickert's] group," and again uses the phrase "our group" at the close of the letter. Letter to Heinrich Rickert, 22 November 1915, in "Ernst Troeltschs Briefe an Heinrich Rickert," (ed. Graf) 113.

[52] "Modern Philosophy of History," 308; *GS* 2:716. See also *Theologische Rundschau* 6 (1903) 106. Troeltsch makes a very similar comment in a footnote in *Die Bedeutung des Protestantismus für die Entstehung der modernen Welt*. Commenting on the challenges of defining large historical phenomena such as "Protestantism," Troeltsch points to the necessity of generating abstract, ideal conceptions that capture something of the historical whole (in this case, "Protestantism") without claiming to give an exhaustive empirical account of it. In the footnote he writes, "On the character of such 'historical general-conceptions,' see my article, "Was heißt 'Wesen des Christentums'?" in the *Christliche Welt* for 1903. Everyone

I would like to suggest that Troeltsch develops his conception of the essence of Christianity by drawing upon at least four resources he discovers in Rickert's 1902 work.

First, Troeltsch appropriates Rickert's tools for conceptualizing complex historical phenomena such as Christianity. According to Rickert, historical thinking takes place when one forms general concepts "to master the infinite diversity" of historical reality and structures these concepts according to that which is "characteristic and interesting in these diversities."[53] Troeltsch agrees with Rickert that the concepts formed in historical work are not organized according to a concept of a law, but rather by means of a concept that synthesizes the various individualities into a coherent whole. This synthesis is done according to "the concept of the value they possess for the human consciousness that becomes aware of them."[54] This concept of the value of a particular historical complex arises not from the historian's personal or subjective valuations. Instead, the historian forms the data of history into "value units" that have been influential and effective historically.

Second, Troeltsch finds in Rickert's work a potential model for discerning the continuity or coherence of complex historical phenomena. While both Rickert and Troeltsch reject a Hegelian notion of lawful historical development, they point to a teleological principle by which values are related and organized. The work of historical conceptualization integrates the plurality of objects and facts by selecting from them a center around which everything is organized and integrated with respect to values and norms. As Troeltsch explains:

> The task is to structure the flow of unique events according to the objective-teleological principle of linking these events together into value units that are ever new, that form ever unique combinations and that are felt to be such, either directly or indirectly, by the historical center around which history revolves.[55]

This work is done only by immersion in the details of history and by seeking a knowledge of value units as they are found in history. For both Troeltsch

---

who is familiar with the subject will recognize that my formulation of the concept is based on Rickert's *Methodenlehre*" (*PP*, 104 n. 1; *BP*, in *KGA* 8:225 n. 4).

[53] "Modern Philosophy of History," 288; *GS* 2:691; *Theologische Rundschau* 6 (1903) 21.

[54] Ibid.

[55] "Modern Philosophy of History," 289; *GS* 2:693; *Theologische Rundschau* 6 (1903) 23.

and Rickert, therefore, one can discern the continuity of a complex historical phenomenon while also making a strong case for the objectivity of historical research at this empirical level.

Third, Troeltsch appreciates Rickert's contribution to the question of whether and where values and norms have a place in historical work. In fact, Troeltsch applauds Rickert's approach in his 1902 work as an important step toward the solution of the problematic relation between norms and history. According to Troeltsch, Rickert sees the need for articulating a philosophy of history but makes the appropriate move by looking *first* to the interests, goals, and methods of the empirical study of history vis-à-vis those of the natural sciences. Troeltsch fully agrees with this starting point and with Rickert's efforts to deduce the methodologies of the historical sciences from a view of their objectives. This shows that there is no universal scientific methodology and that the natural sciences cannot yield the kind of knowledge sought by the historical sciences.[56] Thus Rickert's epistemological starting point[57] recognizes the uniqueness of history (and its relation to norms and values), but establishes this uniqueness without all the problems of rival attempts, which for Troeltsch are either too naturalistic, positivistic, relativistic, or deterministic in the Hegelian sense.[58] For Troeltsch, Rickert's approach to history (both at the empirical and philosophical levels) clearly distinguishes

---

[56] "Modern Philosophy of History," 280; *GS* 2:681–82; *Theologische Rundschau* 6 (1903) 11–12.

[57] Although he appreciates many features of Rickert's epistemological starting point, Troeltsch ultimately rejects such an approach. This is evident already at the end of the essay currently under discussion ("Modern Philosophy of History") and is developed and reiterated in other works, including *Historicism and Its Problems* (= *GS* 3).

[58] Troeltsch is opposed to philosophies of history that do any of the following: 1) subject historical sciences to the criteria and methods of the natural sciences, thus admitting ultimately only one kind of scientific method that does not concern or recognize values (positivistic approaches); 2) construct the distinction between the historical and natural sciences as an ontological one, thus resulting either in a naturalism that acccepts the dominance of the natural scientific view or in a metaphysic that places historical and natural scientific objects on parallel paths with no overarching unity (psychological approaches); 3) recognize the difference between natural sciences and historical sciences, but find no path to secure objectivity in history and, therefore, abandon history to Dilthey's "anarchy of values" (relativistic approaches); or 4) establish a relation between history and a system of absolute values, but only with the destruction of the individual by means of a deterministic system in which all individuality is traced to the movement of absolute spirit (deterministic Hegelian approaches).

the historical sciences from the natural, while also relating the values conceptualized in empirical history to an "ideal system of values."[59] Fourth, Troeltsch sees in Rickert's work a method for reflecting on the ultimate, enduring validity of norms encountered in history. Troeltsch applauds Rickert's effort, despite its limited success, to suggest how the individual value units conceptualized in empirical-historical work might have validity or objective value beyond their own context. According to Troeltsch, Rickert rightly classifies this kind of inquiry concerning the normativity of historical values as a task for philosophy of history. Although Troeltsch does not accept Rickert's attempt to defend the reality of formal (transhistorical) objective values to which all particular historical value units are somehow related, he nevertheless applauds this attempt as a step in the right direction.[60]

By noting these four ways in which Troeltsch draws upon Rickert's historical method, we also gain a glimpse of the kinds of questions and possibilities Troeltsch considered as he composed his essence of Christianity essay. These questions cluster into two broad sets of issues. First, in order to explore how to arrive at a sufficiently complex conception of historical phenomena such as Christianity, Troeltsch asks such questions as: How can one organize and conceptualize the diversity of historical data and events? What is the nature of the concept of an essence of Christianity? Can it be shown to be a valid and "objective" empirical-historical concept? How can one adequately construe historical development so as to grasp the complex relations among various historical forces? Second, in order to explore how one might legitimately demonstrate the value of a complex historical phenomenon such as Christianity, Troeltsch asks such questions as: In what ways might one make room for value judgments in the construction of historical concepts? How can one affirm the abiding value of historical complexes for the present and future?

By drawing on his conversations with colleagues such as Rickert, and by bringing such questions to the essence of Christianity debate, Troeltsch broadened the discussion and related it to important issues in the fields of historiography and philosophy of history. His interest in the historical and cultural sciences related intimately to his desire to address contemporary challenges facing imperial German society. As I have noted in the introduction

    [59] "Modern Philosophy of History," 278; *GS* 2:679.
    [60] "Modern Philosophy of History," 295, 298, 315–16; *GS* 2:700, 703, 726–27; *Theologische Rundschau* 6 (1903) 59, 62, 115–16.

to this study, Troeltsch and his colleagues in Heidelberg turned to historical studies as a way of exploring possible sources of value and orientation in a rapidly changing culture. Questions about the nature of the historical and cultural sciences and about the *Kulturbedeutung* (cultural significance) of historical phenomena were deeply connected to efforts among intellectuals to address the perceived "crises of modernity" facing German society at this time.[61] This interdisciplinary dimension of Troeltsch's treatment of the concept of an essence of Christianity points not simply to the range of scholarly conversations in which Troeltsch participated, but also to the nature of the concerns that were at stake for him in this debate—concerns that reached beyond the traditional confines of church history and into complex questions about the possible meaning and value of Christianity in a modernizing society.

Equipped with these insights into the range of questions that informed Troeltsch's treatment of the essence of Christianity, I now offer my own analysis of "What Does 'Essence of Christianity' Mean?" As I provide new readings of central terms and tensions in the essay, I direct my analysis to the two main themes that I argue are central not only to this essay, but also to Troeltsch's nascent theory of Christianity that he will continue to develop in his *Social Teachings* and *Historicism* volumes: first, the importance of formulating a sufficiently complex conception of Christianity as an internally diverse historical phenomenon with multiple and overlapping relations to other spheres of culture; and second, the intrinsic relation between this effort at historical conceptualization and the desire to illuminate the potential value of Christianity for modern society.

---

[61] Graf, "Puritanische Sektenfreiheit," 46. For more on the political, social, and intellectual context of neo-Kantianism, see Willey, *Back to Kant*, esp. chs. 1, 5, 6. For an account of the intellectual and cultural situation in which debates over history as a science took place, see Otto Gerhard Oexle, "Troeltschs Dilemma," in *Ernst Troeltschs Historismus* (vol. 11 of Troeltsch-Studien; ed. Graf; Gütersloh: Gütersloher Verlagshaus, 2000) 23–64. Oexle shows how such debates (especially after World War I) were concerned to refute Friedrich Nietzsche's diagnosis of modern culture and critique of history as a science, and to show how the discipline of history might be redefined to address the perceived spiritual crises of the time (33–34).

What Does "Essence of Christianity" Mean for Troeltsch?

As the previous section indicates, for Troeltsch the term "essence of Christianity" calls up a variety of questions and interdisciplinary debates related to historical knowledge, historical development, and the meaning, value, and authority of an historical complex like Christianity and its possible contribution to and place in modern (German) culture. Because Troeltsch uses the concept of an essence in a variety of ways that are often seen as confusing or self-contradictory, sorting out these diverse dimensions of the term "essence of Christianity" is an important step in interpreting the essay. I argue that Troeltsch employs the term "essence of Christianity" as a complex notion with four distinct but interrelated aspects or meanings. The internal tensions and contradictions highlight the multifaceted nature of his view of Christianity. Understanding the variety and scope of issues and questions that inform Troeltsch's use of the concept "essence" helps to sort out the ways in which he is seeking to devise and ground his emerging conception of Christianity.[62]

Troeltsch often employs the term "essence of Christianity" as a general concept of historical science. In this first use of the term Troeltsch treats the essence simply as an abstraction in the Rickertian sense, or as an ideal type in the Weberian sense.[63] Here the essence is a tool that enables one to conceptualize and organize the vast, complicated data of history. Such conceptualization requires careful historical analysis and aims to be as objective as possible. By means of such an abstraction, one can either: 1) conceptualize all of Christianity under one essence, 2) conceptualize diverse forms of Christianity as corresponding to different versions of the essence of Christianity, or 3) conceptualize different forms of one kind of Christianity. Conceptualizations

---

[62] Troeltsch himself was well aware that the term "essence of Christianity" invoked a variety of meanings and issues. This is seen clearly in his distinctions between the essence as a critical, developmental, and ideal concept. He writes, "It is indeed true to say that the definition of the essence is an extremely complicated undertaking which is conditioned by many points of reference. The essence is an intuitive abstraction, a religious and ethical critique, a flexible developmental concept and the ideal to be applied in the work of shaping and recombining for the future" ("Essence," 164; "'WCh," 678).

[63] In his revised (1913) edition of "Modern Philosophy of History," Troeltsch explicitly calls the concept of an essence of Christianity an ideal type (313; *GS* 2, 723). Weber also views conceptions of the essence of Christianity as ideal types. See " 'Objectivity' in Social Science and Social Policy," in *The Methodology of the Social Sciences* (trans. and ed. Edward Shils and Henry Finch; New York: Free Press, 1949) 97.

of the first type enable one to compare Christianity phenomenologically with other religions or philosophical traditions in such a way that the essence of Christianity would be contrasted with the essence of Buddhism or the essence of Stoicism. Conceptualizations of the second kind enable one to distinguish and compare the various confessional forms of Christianity itself, such that the essence of Christianity in modern Protestantism would be compared to the essence of Christianity in modern Catholicism. Finally, different forms of a single type of Christianity can be conceptualized as they appear in different historical periods or cultural locations, so that one may compare the essence of late-medieval Protestantism to the essence of modern Protestantism. Each of these concepts lends great clarity to the complicated historical material that one confronts in an examination of Christianity's history. When Troeltsch uses the term "essence of Christianity" in this ideal-typical way, he often emphasizes the objectivity of the concept and insists on formulating it apart from the subjective convictions of the historian. Further, this ideal-typical conception, when employed in the second, intra-Christian sense mentioned above, leads Troeltsch to emphasize the diversity within Christianity, and therefore to suggest that there is no one essence of Christianity, but rather many versions of it.

Troeltsch uses the term "essence of Christianity," second, to denote the distinctive identity or features of Christianity, so that essence here refers to uniqueness. Where the first ideal-typical use of the term "essence of Christianity" serves primarily to organize and compare historical phenomena for the sake of furthering historical research and knowledge, this more normative use of the term aims to affirm something unique in Christianity—a distinctive identity that makes it valuable and distinguishable from other religions or from other forms of Christianity. Thus, this use most closely resembles Harnack's sense of the essence of Christianity as a shorthand for Christianity's uniqueness. This uniqueness does not derive from other sources, and it forms the basis of Christianity's value and fundamental meaning.

Troeltsch uses the term "essence of Christianity," third, to allude to a spiritual principle inherent in the process or development of Christian history itself.

> The essential is no more and no less than the epitome of fundamental religious ideas which makes itself clear from within its own manifestations in history, which determines consciously and unconsciously its own development, which stands at the center of its own thinking and

willing, and which is never complete and closed as long as it belongs to history in a living way.[64]

Thus, in contrast to the first use of the concept, which is clearly an ideal type and therefore an abstraction constructed by the historian, in this third sense, the essence comes more directly from history (*Geschichte*) itself.[65] Thus Troeltsch also refers to the essence of Christianity as "the principle which reveals itself in the whole."[66]

Troeltsch does not want to say that the essence of Christianity is *equivalent to* its history of development. If that were the case, Troeltsch argues, then "all the forms of Christianity . . . would have to be considered as being, each in its own context, necessary, and indeed teleologically and not just causally necessary revelations of the essence."[67] Troeltsch's notion of the essence as a critical concept—a concept formed by evaluating and judging Christianity's development, distinguishing the essential from the nonessential, the positive from the negative developments—rules out such a strict equation of historical development and essential identity.

Yet Troeltsch also does not want to relegate the notion of an essence of Christianity completely to the conceptual level so that it is merely a construct of the historian with no confirmation in history.[68] Nor does he want to appeal to an essence that corresponds to a truth outside of history (whether

---

[64] "Essence," 132; "¹WCh," 485.

[65] My distinction between Troeltsch's first and third uses of the term "essence" is very similar to Wyman's distinction between an "empirical motif" and an "idealistic strand" in Troeltsch's concept of an essence of Christianity. Where Wyman sees a "two-sidedness" in Troeltsch's concept of an essence, I identify four distinct dimensions of Troeltsch's use of the essence of Christianity. See Wyman, *Concept*, 74.

[66] "Essence," 132–33; "¹WCh," 485.

[67] "Essence," 138; "¹WCh," 533. In other places, and especially in the *Social Teachings*, Troeltsch draws on Ranke's view that "every historical epoch has its own direct significance in the sight of God" (*ST,* 207; *GS* 1:186). He suggests, therefore, that every epoch or form of Christianity is somehow teleologically necessary, and does not make a distinction between teleological and causal necessity. In this way Troeltsch fluctuates between a view of Christianity in which certain epochs are seen as contrary to its essence and a view that accepts all historical manifestations as valid and legitimate expressions of Christianity.

[68] This is precisely where Troeltsch breaks with Rickert, and with neo-Kantianism in general. Notwithstanding his recognition of the advantages of a neo-Kantian conception of historical knowledge, Troeltsch cannot ignore what he sees as the limits of an epistemological grounding of history, namely, that its concepts (such as the historical individual) remain concepts in the historian's mind and thus somewhat thin metaphysically.

philosophical or supernatural-miraculous). Thus he affirms that the course of history, when viewed and evaluated from a rigorous historical perspective, will show that there is a principle or teleology to Christianity's historical life. Troeltsch insists that the presupposition for defining the essence of Christianity is that Christianity's essence "is not fragmented into countless configurations each of which represents only a partial thought."[69] Instead, one assumes that the essence "separated off unbalanced and alien elements which appear in all these formations, in order to arrive at the kernel, and only then is to be conceived as a complete and unified principle."[70] Troeltsch often draws on this aspect of the term "essence of Christianity" when he seeks to establish or to defend the continuity of Christianity, or when he emphasizes that any conception of the essence of Christianity must be confirmed by and grounded in history itself.[71]

Finally, Troeltsch uses the term "essence of Christianity" to refer to a concept belonging ultimately to ethics and the philosophy of history. Troeltsch states that any conception of the essence of Christianity "changes quite automatically from being an abstracted concept to being an ideal concept."[72] In this sense the essence of Christianity is a provisional concept constructed by the theologian-historian who is concerned about and committed to Christianity and who wishes to articulate a vision for its present and future. Although construed only after thorough consideration of the historical details, all ideal conceptions of the essence of Christianity involve a measure of subjectivity. In fact, Troeltsch insists that one's personal attitude to Christianity will always shape one's definition of the essence, so that one who believes Christianity has a future will articulate its essence in a much different way than one who does not.[73] Defining one's own position with respect to "the value and truth of Christianity," therefore, is a prerequisite for reflecting on its essence.[74] The essence of Christianity thus becomes an ideal concept emerging from

---

[69] "Essence," 138–39; "¹WCh," 533.

[70] Ibid. As the next two chapters will show, this position becomes increasingly difficult for Troeltsch to defend. His historical writings convince him more and more of the complexity of Christianity and its historical development, as well as its involvement in a complex web of economic, cultural, social, political, and religious causal forces. Thus Troeltsch leans more and more toward a conception of Christianity as encompassing and displaying many diverse and disparate, though certainly related, essences.

[71] See, for example, "Essence," 142; "¹WCh," 534.

[72] "Essence," 158; "¹WCh," 651–52.

[73] "Essence," 156–57; "¹WCh," 650–51.

[74] "Essence," 158; "¹WCh," 651.

a creative act in which the historian combines knowledge from historical research with a vision for Christianity's future.[75] The fourth way in which Troeltsch uses the term "essence of Christianity," therefore, draws attention to the ethical nature of the acts of naming and identifying Christianity and of articulating its boundaries, core ideas, and goals.

These four aspects or meanings of the term "essence of Christianity" overlap and contradict in many ways.[76] Nevertheless, distinguishing these four dimensions of the term lends clarity to Troeltsch's text and aids in the identification of key issues and problems that inform Troeltsch's attempt to offer a sophisticated conceptualization of Christianity. Three examples will suffice to illustrate how these distinctions help make sense of Troeltsch's contradictory statements about the essence of Christianity.

First, throughout the essay Troeltsch appears to make two conflicting statements about the source of the essence of Christianity. On the one hand, Troeltsch states that the essence is a construct deriving from the mind of the historian and not necessarily from the course of events and phenomena that constitute "history." He writes, "The unified idea of the essence only exists after all in the thought of the historian summarizing the material. Reality nowhere displays the essence as the result of the process."[77] On the other hand, Troeltsch also defines the essence as "the epitome of fundamental religious ideas which makes itself clear from within its own manifestation in history."[78] This clearly suggests that the essence is a concept or idea deriving more directly from historical data, or from the givenness of history, and not from the imagination of the historian. In making the former claim, Troeltsch is using the term "essence of Christianity" in the first sense outlined above, that is, in an ideal-typical sense that highlights the constructed nature of historical concepts or abstractions. In making the latter claim, Troeltsch is concerned less with the nature of historical concepts and more with his conviction that historical concepts, though abstractions of the historian, must be rooted in historical reality.[79] That is, they must derive from what

---

[75] "Essence," 160, 166; "'WCh," 653, 680.

[76] The second and fourth uses, for example, underscore the statement of value that is contained in all formulations of the essence of Christianity, while the first and third uses both identify the essence as an objective (i.e., value-free) construct of the historian.

[77] "Essence," 141; "'WCh," 534.

[78] "Essence," 132; "'WCh," 485.

[79] In making this claim, Troeltsch exhibits the way in which his view of the nature of traditions differs from that promoted by postmodern constructivist views today. Despite his

Troeltsch in other places calls a sympathy (*Nachfühlen*) with the historical material,[80] which suggests that this material itself provides the basis for the historian's claims.

The second example concerns Troeltsch's emphasis on the ineradicable diversity of Christianity's history on the one hand, and his suggestion that there is a continuity or coherence to the historical whole on the other. Troeltsch's ideal-typical use of the term "essence of Christianity" implies that reality itself is much more diverse and complicated than historical abstractions and narratives often suggest, and that the many different "types" of Christianity demand analysis in their own right. Yet Troeltsch's use of the essence as an historical force that in some way "drives" the historical object in a certain coherent direction (the third use of the term) tends to emphasize the continuity that can be observed in large historical complexes like Christianity. Thus, distinguishing the ideal-typical sense of the term "essence of Christianity" from its sense as an historical reality or principle helps one to see how Troeltsch can make confusing claims about the status of historical concepts and the nature of historical reality. Further, this distinction suggests that Troeltsch was addressing a much broader range of concerns than had been at stake in the Harnack-Loisy debate. Troeltsch engages in and draws upon conversations among historians and philosophers about the nature of history and historical knowledge.

The third example concerns the question of the objectivity or subjectivity of conceptions of the essence of Christianity. Is the term "essence of Christianity" a neutral historical abstraction used simply to further historical research, or is it an evaluative concept? Troeltsch confusingly argues both points. According to my fourfold division, the ideal-typical sense of the term enables Troeltsch to argue for the neutrality of historical constructs such as the essence of Christianity, while the second and fourth uses of the term suggest that there is an evaluative element to all conceptions of Christianity's essence.[81] In making these tension-filled claims, Troeltsch engages questions

---

affinities (which are significant) with current theorists who argue that traditions are constructed and adjusted according to specific interests and situations, Troeltsch maintains a stronger sense of the authority of the past and the "given" than do such theorists.

[80] *ST*, 349; *GS* 1:383. See also *GS* 3:38.

[81] The second use emphasizes the claim to uniqueness that can be intrinsic to the concept "essence of Christianity," while the fourth use points to the subjective factors and ideals that shape any historian's formulation of the essence of Christianity. Thus, both involve explicit evaluative elements.

about the nature of historical inquiry and the relation between empirical history and philosophy of history. His statements reflect what gradually becomes and remains Troeltsch's position on these questions, namely, that although the empirical and philosophical dimensions of historical inquiry have their own integrity and tasks, the two cannot and should not ultimately be completely severed.

My identification of four uses of the term "essence of Christianity" makes sense of the conflicting claims that otherwise threaten the coherence of Troeltsch's essay. By problematizing the meaning, nature, and status of the term "essence of Christianity" and putting it to a variety of uses, Troeltsch reveals his conviction that any conception of Christianity must be sufficiently complex, coherent, and related to questions about its meaning for the present and future. Troeltsch's efforts to stretch the concept of an essence in four directions also suggest that he is becoming dissatisfied with the concept as a tool for conceptualizing complex historical phenomena such as Christianity. His arduous efforts to get as much as possible out of the concept "essence" make it no surprise that he will later look for other concepts, such as "synthesis," as he seeks to conceptualize and reflect on the nature and value of large historical complexes.

The Nature of "Purely Historical" Inquiry

The construction of an essence of Christianity raises complicated questions about historical method. How does Troeltsch conceive of the work of historical inquiry in this essay? As I have noted, in the essence essay Troeltsch makes use of a distinction (which he employs in other works as well) between empirical-historical and philosophical-historical tasks. The former refers to the reconstruction of past events and phenomena in the most accurate and nonpartisan way possible. The latter moves from this careful historical work to a philosophical and ethical inquiry concerning the normativity and validity of historical formations, expressions, and values. Roughly speaking, Troeltsch regards empirical-historical inquiry as more objective than philosophical-historical construction or evaluation, which necessarily entails the personal evaluations, value judgments, and attitudes of the historian.

Troeltsch's distinction between empirical- and philosophical-historical work is sufficiently straightforward, even though Troeltsch himself argues that it cannot ultimately be sustained.[82] The term that introduces more confusion into Troeltsch's discussion of historical inquiry—and ultimately into his work as a theorist and historian of Christianity—is "purely historical" (*rein historisch*). Troeltsch refers to Harnack's investigation as a "purely historical" one, and Troeltsch also adopts this terminology in certain places in his own essence essay, referring, for example, to a "purely historical" view of the origins of Christianity and a "purely historical" approach to the definition of the essence.[83] In using the phrase "purely historical," does Troeltsch suggest that he seeks an objective account of Christianity's nature, or that he thinks such an account even possible or desirable? These are important questions, as they get at the nature of Troeltsch's historical and theoretical efforts to conceptualize Christianity as a tradition. As I shall argue immediately and elsewhere below, Troeltsch understands his mode of inquiry as located in and directed by a tradition of historical thinking that has particular values and commitments. His conception of Christianity, then, is infused with and directed toward normative concerns.

At first glance, the term "purely historical" appears to be a synonym for empirical-historical inquiry, insofar as "purely" might suggest "objective" or "without philosophical or normative elements." Indeed, Troeltsch occasionally appears to use the term in this way. For example, he contrasts theoretical concerns with "purely historical, empirical questions."[84] He also asks how one can reconcile the "strongly subjective factors" involved in any definition of the essence with "the starting point of a purely historical" approach, suggesting that such a starting point is objective.[85] Similarly, Troeltsch suggests in one passage that purely historical inquiry focuses on the past, while normative judgments relate to present and future goals and concerns.[86] Finally, it is noteworthy that Troeltsch equates purely historical inquiry with empirical history in his article on historiography in the *Encyclopaedia of Religion and Ethics*.[87]

---

[82] Although empirical research is generally more "objective" than philosophical evaluation for Troeltsch, the former is informed by the historian's values, and the latter is not doomed to mere random subjectivism. Troeltsch is not in favor, therefore, of seeing either as wholly objective or subjective.

[83] "Essence," 124, 131, 133, 146, 147; "¹WCh," 443, 484, 486, 579.

[84] "Essence," 128; "¹WCh," 445.

[85] "Essence," 159–60; "¹WCh," 652.

[86] "Essence," 161; "¹WCh," 654.

[87] See "Historiography," *Encyclopaedia of Religion and Ethics* (ed. James Hastings; New

A closer reading, however, shows that the term "purely historical" also implies a range of much broader claims and meanings that are central to Troeltsch's essay and, indeed, to his work as a historian and theorist of Christianity. Specifically, Troeltsch uses the term "purely historical" in three important ways that reflect his dual desire to employ historical methods that can yield a sufficiently complex conception of Christianity as a historical phenomenon like all others on the one hand, and to demonstrate and defend the value of Christianity in the modern world on the other.

The first way Troeltsch uses the term "purely historical" is to distance his own method from dogmatic approaches to church history and theology. This distinction echoes that made by Troeltsch in his essay "Historical and Dogmatic Method in Theology."[88] While a dogmatic method involves a presentation or defense of doctrinal truths and uses history only selectively, sheltering certain elements of tradition from critical historical scrutiny, an historical method applies historical standards to all periods and elements of a tradition's history. It approaches the analysis of Christianity as it would that of any other historical object. It judges events by means of historical criteria and tools of analysis and not with regard to self-authorizing claims to revelation or miracle. It examines Christianity in the broadest sense, not focusing simply on the dogmas of the church, but on the entire historical life of the tradition, including its involvement in economic, cultural, social, and political developments. Thus, "purely historical" functions rhetorically here to counter dogmatic approaches to history and to defend a different way of engaging in Christian history. Troeltsch writes:

> A treatment of Christianity which seeks the essence of Christianity purely historically includes *a series of the most important and ultimately decisive presuppositions* which we affirm in connection with modern historical thought in general. It is in short the renunciation of the dogmatic method considered valid until the eighteenth century and the taking over of the historical method prepared by the Enlightenment and conceived in principle by German Idealism, or more precisely, the renunciation of a history possessing dogmatic, ready-made criteria and the assumption of a history which produces its basic concepts out of its own work. A firmly delimited normative truth, presented as available

---

York: Scribner, 1913) 718 col. 2; 719 col. 1; and 721 col. 2.

[88] "Historical and Dogmatic Method in Theology," in *Religion in History*, 11–32; "Über historische und dogmatische Methode in der Theologie," in *GS* 2:729–53.

in the Bible or in the church, and both accredited and recognizable on the basis of divine authority, is dispensed with.[89]

The point is not that historical approaches are objective while dogmatic approaches are subjective. On the contrary, although for Troeltsch a purely historical method takes empirical-historical data more seriously than does a dogmatic method, the former also concerns itself with an affirmation of Christianity's value. The distinction is that a purely historical method turns to history to demonstrate that Christianity is a vital historical force with continuing potential in the modern world, while a dogmatic treatment of Christianity turns first to the supernatural authority of the church and its doctrines, and then to history only secondarily.

The second way Troeltsch uses the term "purely historical" is to distinguish it from, and therefore to criticize, abstract philosophical ways of construing history and Christianity.[90] Troeltsch associates a philosophical approach to the essence of Christianity with a certain kind of Hegelianism that formulates a generic rational concept and then deduces Christianity's historical reality and validity from it. In a historical approach, one seeks the essence of Christianity and the normative principle for discerning Christianity's essence in history itself[91] and not in philosophical ideas or abstractions.[92] Troeltsch writes:

> To wish to learn to recognize the essence of Christianity in the history
> of Christianity means to seek the organizing and creative principle of

[89] "Essence," 131 (italics in original); "¹WCh," 484–85. For distinctions between dogmatic and historical methods, see also "Essence," 135–36; "¹WCh," 487–88.

[90] In polemically distinguishing a "purely historical" method from both dogmatic and philosophical methods for construing Christian history, Troeltsch is taking up a line of argumentation similar to that which Harnack followed in his first lecture in *Das Wesen des Christentums* (ET: *What Is Christianity?*). There Harnack distinguished his purely historical approach from an apologetic one and a philosophical (Hegelian) one. Harnack's label "apologetic," however, is not precisely the same as Troeltsch's label "dogmatic." While Harnack describes "apologetic" approaches to the essence of Christianity as including dogmatic (supernatural, authoritative) ones, he also uses "apologetic" to classify a variety of positions that equate the essence of Christianity with some particular social program or try to "dress up religion in fine clothes." Here Harnack, unlike Troeltsch, suggests that a purely historical approach is more simple and objective than these apologetic ones (Harnack, *What Is Christianity?*, 6–9; *Das Wesen des Christentums*, 4–6).

[91] Troeltsch states that a "purely historical" criterion for judging historical formations is one based on "immanent criticism," or "a criticism of historical formations in terms of the ideal which lies within their main driving force" ("Essence," 142; "¹WCh," 534).

[92] "Essence," 133; "¹WCh," 485.

the fullness of the living phenomena which we call Christianity, only more realistically and in a new way not tied to the Hegelian dialectic of progress and logical categorization of reality.[93]

Here Troeltsch expresses a view similar to that articulated in his 1902 work *The Absoluteness of Christianity and the History of Religions*.[94] Finally, Troeltsch uses "purely historical" to designate and defend something unique and valuable about history and "the historical" itself.[95] This will become a particularly prominent theme in Troeltsch's later work *Historicism and Its Problems* (1922), where he portrays the discipline of history as that which has unique access to historical phenomena precisely because it focuses on individualities in their unrepeatable uniqueness. Social sciences, natural sciences, and psychology cannot grasp historical objects in this deeper way.[96] Such a perspective appears in the essence essay as well. Troeltsch refers, for example, to a unique, "purely historical" notion of causality that seeks to illuminate the connections between diverse or related historical phenomena without falling into a reductionistic explanation of them.[97] Here Troeltsch carves out a privileged place for a historical perspective and a historical science presumably distinct from both natural-scientific and social-scientific ways of conceptualizing historical phenomena and their relations. In Troeltsch's view, therefore, a purely historical method is uniquely connected to historical phenomena and capable of reflecting on their value. Consequently, the discipline of history intrinsically involves a consideration

---

[93] "Essence," 131; "¹WCh," 484.

[94] *Die Absolutheit des Christentums und die Religionsgeschichte (1902/1912) mit Thesen von 1901 und den handschriftlichen Zusätzen* (vol. 5 of *Ernst Troeltsch Kritische Gesamtausgabe* [*KGA* 5]; ed. Trutz Rendtorff in collaboration with Stefan Pautler; Berlin: Walter de Gruyter, 1998); ET of 1912 edition: *The Absoluteness of Christianity and the History of Religions* (trans. David Reid; Richmond, Va.: Knox, 1971).

[95] Here there is perhaps a link to Ranke, whose faith in history as a meaningful domain and process was an influential element in Troeltsch's philosophy of history. On this dimension of Ranke's thought, see Iggers, *The German Conception of History*, 66–80.

[96] Troeltsch argues that while psychology and sociology, for example, can provide valuable analyses of historical phenomena, they cannot explain such phenomena without reducing them to some other, more basic phenomenon. "It is the historian who shows the fundamental objects [*Urphänomene*] of history to the psychologist and sociologist, and not vice versa" (*GS* 3:45–46).

[97] "Essence," 133–34; "¹WCh," 486.

of such matters as the essence of Christianity insofar as it ultimately demands a connection between the normative and the empirical.[98]

Broadly speaking, Troeltsch uses the term "purely historical" simply to refer to the adoption of an historical method or to the act of engaging and giving an account of something by means of concepts, abstractions, questions, dynamics, and criteria generally employed by modern historical sciences.[99] Accordingly, "purely historical" accounts of the essence of Christianity follow "the general principles of critical history and [apply] the unavoidable process of abstraction with concerted energy to Christianity as a whole."[100]

For Troeltsch, then, a "purely historical" method "entails a whole worldview."[101] It is a method informed by and bound up with what he calls a modern (and particularly a German Romantic and Idealist) perspective on historical development and historical causality.[102] While this view of history is not monolithic,[103] it is expressed in German Idealism's view that

> large coherent complexes of historical events are the development of an idea, a value, or a line of thought or purpose, which gradually develops in detail and consequences, which assimilates and subordinates alien materials and which continually struggles against aberrations from its

[98] Troeltsch writes, "History demands the step from the detailed account to the concept of the essence to be taken, regardless of the extent to which the latter may in fact coherently emerge. If we really want to be clear about Christianity in historical terms we cannot avoid proceeding from detailed historical work to a concept of the essence, however this concept then turns out" ("Essence," 134; "¹WCh," 486–87).

[99] "Essence," 133; "¹WCh," 485–86.

[100] "Essence," 134; "¹WCh," 486.

[101] "Essence," 133; "¹WCh," 486.

[102] "Essence," 133–34; "¹WCh," 486. In general, Troeltsch defines a "modern historical worldview" according to a German Romantic and Idealist conception of history. Ringer shows that Troeltsch's view is typical of German "mandarin" historians during the late-nineteenth century. He thus equates an "historical approach to man's experience" with the "German historical tradition," which he then traces to "the great German Idealists and Romantics." Ringer also demonstrates that Troeltsch distinguished this German historical approach from French and English views of history, which he viewed as either positivistic or ultimately reducible to natural science. See Fritz K. Ringer, *The Decline of the German Mandarins: The German Academic Community, 1890–1933* (1969; repr., Hanover, N.H.: University Press of New England, 1990) 341–42.

[103] It is articulated by German Romantics, German Idealists, and by representatives of the historical school in general. Troeltsch often includes in an "historical worldview" all German conceptions of history since Kant.

leading purpose and against contradictory principles threatening from
without.[104]

The main features expressed in this view of history are that history itself
contains meaningful individualities and that there are meaningful connections,
but not lawful causal necessities, that can be drawn between or among such
individualities.[105]
"Purely historical" attempts to define the essence of Christianity reflect this
worldview, wherein meaning can be found in the dynamics, individualities,
and development of history. Accordingly, "purely historical" inquiry includes
a philosophical or normative element that is articulated by means of an
"immanent criticism" that measures the historical by the historical.[106] Thus
one cannot simply equate a "purely historical" method with "objective"
empirical-historical inquiry, as it appeared in the several cases enumerated
at the beginning of this section. Troeltsch's defense of Harnack's project
as "purely historical," even given its normative dimension, illustrates my
point well. In discussing Harnack's treatment of the essence of Christianity,
Troeltsch acknowledges freely that it contains normative judgments. Yet
Troeltsch emphasizes that the presence of Harnack's own normative position
in his construction of Christianity's "essence" does not undermine the "purely
historical" status of Harnack's work, since "purely historical" does not
mean "positivistic" or "value-free" history. Rather, it refers to the adoption
of the perspectives and tools of an historical method and the acceptance of
an historical worldview. Troeltsch states in response to Harnack's dogmatic
opponents:

> For these reasons those opponents are quite right who say that Harnack's
> essence is not a purely empirical-inductive piece of work, but that it
> includes and is deeply influenced by important presuppositions proper

---

[104] "Essence," 130; "¹WCh," 484.

[105] Troeltsch distinguishes an historical view of causality that conceives of causality in
terms of open-ended connections among events from a natural scientific view of causality
that construes causality in necessary and lawful, and for Troeltsch, reductionistic, terms. See
"Essence," 133–34; "¹WCh," 486.

[106] Explaining how the criticism of historical phenomena is carried out in a "purely historical"
definition of the essence, Troeltsch writes: "It is a criticism of historical formations in terms
of the ideal which lies within their main driving force. It is what is commonly called an
immanent criticism. To this extent it is in fact conceived purely historically; for the historical
is measured by the historical, the individual formation is measured against the spirit of the
whole conceived intuitively and imaginatively" ("Essence," 142; "¹WCh," 534).

to the philosophy of history. They are only wrong when they fail to recognize the inner connection between what he is doing and the basic characteristics and concepts of the historical method in general.[107]

This shows clearly that a philosophical or normative element is intrinsic to Troeltsch's notion of historical inquiry and even to a "purely historical" method. While its normative judgments will not appeal to miracle or church authority, this method will nevertheless express a normative position. Thus, Troeltsch's purely historical approach encompasses both empirical-historical and philosophical-historical tasks in a way that uses the tools of modern historical sciences.

Locating the Essence: Origins or Development?

In reflecting on a purely historical approach to the definition of the essence of Christianity, Troeltsch struggles with the question of where such an approach turns in Christian history for an indication of its normative essence. In other words, is the identity of Christianity most clearly expressed in its origins, in its subsequent development, or somewhere else? I treat both of these questions in greater detail in the next two chapters in which I analyze Troeltsch's conception of Christianity as offered in the *Social Teachings*. Here it will suffice to outline briefly the way in which Troeltsch grapples with these questions in the 1903 essence essay. As he articulates his view of Christianity's origins and development, Troeltsch seeks once again to conceptualize Christianity in a way that recognizes the complexity and internal diversity of all historical phenomena and affirms its value and significance in the past, present, and future.

Troeltsch's position on the importance of the original period for a conception of Christianity's essence is split between two basic convictions: first, that the origins must in some way be privileged; and second, that the origins cannot really be privileged if one takes historical questions and methods seriously. Troeltsch bases his first conviction, he says, on a purely historical view, according to which the originating period of an historical phenomenon is recognized to be its purest and most potent one and, therefore, worthy of an elevated and foundational status in the conceptualization of that phenomenon. Accordingly, Troeltsch views "the historical proclamation and

---

[107] "Essence," 135; "¹WCh," 487.

personality of Jesus,"[108] with its unique potency and purity, as the foundation of Christianity. Troeltsch labels this a "purely historical" perspective on the "importance of the origins"[109] largely because it is distinct from a dogmatic perspective. The latter perspective views the origins as authoritative because they are the site of the miraculous, supernatural beginning of Christianity, while the former treats the origins as significant for reasons that could stand up to historical scrutiny and an historical worldview.[110] Troeltsch also believes that the origins must have a special place in any conception of Christianity because Jesus is, and must in some way be, a focal point for all forms of Christianity. In Troeltsch's view, Jesus serves as a center or "rallying-point" (*Sammelpunkt*)[111] for later developments, which always relate to the origins afresh. For these reasons, indeed, the origins seem unique in the history of Christianity, and one should regard them as such in any construction of the essence.

On the other hand, however, Troeltsch recognizes the problems of identifying the essence of Christianity with the origins of Christianity. First, one must specify which portion of the origins is normative.[112] Second, one must acknowledge the fact that we have no pure access to the historical

[108] "Essence," 148; "¹WCh," 580.

[109] "Essence," 147; "¹WCh," 579.

[110] Troeltsch held that empirical-historical research would clearly demonstrate the potency of the originating period, event, or personality of a religious tradition—a testimony to the overwhelmingly widespread status of this view in nineteenth-century German historical, sociological, and theological thought. Troeltsch also classified this view of origins as "purely historical," because it testified to the unique value and novelty of historical events or beginnings in a way that a materialistic interpretation of origins could not. Thus, a nonreductive reading of historical events is central to a purely historical perspective. This coheres with what I argued in my section on the nature of purely historical inquiry.

[111] See Ernst Troeltsch, "The Significance of the Historical Existence of Jesus for Faith," in *Writings*, 197; *Die Bedeutung der Geschichtlichkeit Jesu für den Glauben* (Tübingen: Mohr, 1911) 31.

[112] "Essence," 147; "¹WCh," 580. In the second (1913) edition of the essence essay, Troeltsch adds a discussion that intensifies this point even more. He notes that in the origins themselves there is a conflict or tension between the theological perspectives of Jesus and Paul. That is, "in the preaching of Jesus ethical challenge and promise are paramount, while in the preaching of Paul present salvation and the certainty of grace come to the fore. Thus there are already in the two main areas of original Christianity different basic trends, which, even though they may be patent of harmonization, have also had a distinctive influence through the whole history of Christianity. The essence of Christianity has had from the beginning two distinct accents, if not indeed two altogether distinct elements" ("Essence," 149; "²WCh," 416).

Jesus. He is mediated through Scripture (most importantly, for Troeltsch, through Paul) and the early church,[113] and in this mediation there are divergent interpretations of Jesus and "the gospel." Moreover, the historical information about Jesus is ambiguous, and what later Christians would find significant in Jesus' preaching may not be what was significant for him at all.[114] Finally, developments subsequent to the origins exhibit radically different features, values, and interpretations of the gospel, and one must see these, too, as authentic parts of Christianity.[115] These later periods and forms of Christianity are often shaped by their encounters with new circumstances and new cultural contexts and religious movements; they therefore add something to historical Christianity that was not there in original Christianity. Insofar as all these types and manifestations of Christianity have equal claim to the title "Christian," any conception of Christianity must refer to the totality of its historical life and not just to one period. Troeltsch writes:

> The original form [of the essence of Christianity] and the revelations of the essence which emerge in further developments have to be understood together. The essence of Christianity cannot be an unchangeable idea given once for all in the teaching of Jesus.[116]

Taken together, these considerations "severely limit the appraisal of the original time as being above all the authoritative period."[117]

Troeltsch attempts to resolve these complex issues by arguing that the origins be viewed as the "classical period" of Christianity.[118] This does not mean that this classical period solely or absolutely sets the standard for how other periods are to be judged. In fact, in the essence essay, Troeltsch sets up a dynamic interrelation between what he calls the "transcendence" emphasized by the gospel and the "immanence" emphasized by many subsequent forms of Christianity, such as medieval Catholicism and modern

[113] "Essence," 148–49; "¹WCh," 580.

[114] "Essence," 153; "¹WCh," 582. Troeltsch nods to those scholars who argue that Harnack's work on the essence of Christianity presented Jesus' ideas in terms of "the ideals of an ethic applicable to modern circumstances" ("Essence," 125; "¹WCh," 444).

[115] "Essence," 150–51, 153; "¹WCh," 581, 582–83.

[116] "Essence," 151; "¹WCh," 581. In the revised edition, Troeltsch edits the second sentence to read, "If we are to speak of the essence at all, it cannot be an unchangeable idea given once for all in the teaching of Jesus" ("²WCh," 418).

[117] "Essence," 149; "¹WCh," 580.

[118] "Essence," 147; "¹WCh," 579.

ascetic Protestantism.[119] The "transcendence" of the gospel refers to its alleged indifference to the world and its exclusive emphasis on preparation for a kingdom of God that is a new order. The "immanence" of later periods refers to their ability to bring this otherworldly orientation into relation with the structures and thought-forms of the world and particularly of the secular sphere.[120] Thus, while the original period has a central place in any conception of Christianity, it is not the sole referent of the essence but, instead, stands at one place on the continuum of perspectives that constitute this essence.

Troeltsch's discussion of the significance of the origins of Christianity is also a discussion about historical development. In affirming the variety and internal diversity that mark Christianity's origins and history, and in acknowledging the many different conceptions of the essence that emerge throughout its history, Troeltsch hints at a view of historical development as a process involving many forces and contingencies. As in other cases, however, Troeltsch's position on historical development is not entirely clear in the essence essay. It is necessary to discuss briefly the way Troeltsch moves between continuous and discontinuous views of historical development.

On the one hand, Troeltsch wishes to affirm the continuity of Christianity's historical development, not in the Hegelian sense of logical and lawful development, but according to the view that Christianity's essence is "a developing spiritual principle, a 'germinative principle' as Caird calls it, or a historical idea in Ranke's sense."[121] This "driving spiritual force" is able to accommodate the varieties of Christianity and yet hold them together according to a single conception or tendency. Troeltsch suggests that the new additions that are part of Christianity's development were "hinted at" in the origins, even though they could not have been realized without later circumstances and elements.[122] Similarly, Troeltsch states that the essence of Christianity is a continuum, and not, therefore, a singular or simple principle.

---

[119] Troeltsch uses this term to refer to the dominant forms of (sectarian, modern Calvinist) Protestantism that dominate the religious landscape particularly in England and the U.S. He writes, "Calvinism and the sect-group composed of Baptists, Methodists, and Salvationists today constitute a religious unity which also represents a great sociological collective type of Christian thought" (*ST*, 689; *GS* 1:792). He notes that ascetic Protestantism might also be called the "individualistic Protestantism of active-holiness" (*ST*, 690; *GS* 1:793).

[120] "Essence," 154; "'WCh," 583.

[121] "Essence," 151; "'WCh," 581.

[122] "Essence," 150–51; "'WCh," 581.

He describes this continuum as a "spiritual power"[123] and as something coherent that allows for new possibilities and developments. Finally, the notion that one can judge historical traditions according to immanent criticism suggests some degree of continuity or consistency in the historical material that could provide the criterion for judgment.[124]

On the other hand, Troeltsch characterizes Christianity's history as presenting an impressive and nearly unmasterable array of expressions, forms, developments, and ideas. He writes, "The various formations of the Christian spirit display extraordinarily divergent orientations."[125] In describing the path of Christianity's historical development, Troeltsch refers to fortuitous encounters between particular Christian communities and certain intellectual or cultural movements or circumstances, which together produce a new form of Christianity that no germ in the original could have anticipated or suggested.[126]

> Real history contains not only distortions which degrade, exaggerate or counterfeit an idea, but also pure coincidences, a whole variety of phenomena which for their own part arise from quite different contexts, and under given circumstances become involved with the development of an idea which they may influence deeply or with which, for various reasons, they may become firmly enmeshed.[127]

Here, Troeltsch questions the assumption that historical development itself could demonstrate the continuity of Christianity or provide the criterion for determining its essence. He points out that "reality nowhere displays the essence. . . . It displays instead great, divided churches, in none of which the essence can be perceived to be realized, and which do not even realize the essence all together."[128] The challenge of defining the essence, therefore, is to find a way to account for this wide variety of plural and often unrelated phenomena that make up Christianity.

Troeltsch sees clearly the profound implications of how one defines and classifies origins and development. That is, both determine how much variety will be tolerated and where authority will be located in one's conception of

---

[123] "Essence," 153; "¹WCh," 582.
[124] "Essence," 142; "¹WCh," 534.
[125] "Essence," 153; "¹WCh," 583.
[126] "Essence," 142, 155; "¹WCh," 534, 584.
[127] "Essence," 142; "¹WCh," 534.
[128] "Essence," 141; "¹WCh," 534.

Christianity. Acknowledging and allowing for plurality, variation, and even discontinuity in Christianity are critical for a sufficiently complex construction of its historical reality. At the same time, demonstrating the value and meaning of Christianity depends, in part, on a clear indication of its authoritative, or at least representative, expressions or tendencies. As he develops and adjusts his conception of Christianity in his subsequent works on Christian history, Troeltsch continues his attempt to work out acceptable and serviceable understandings of Christianity's origins and development—understandings that can do justice to Christianity's complex constitution while maintaining a strong sense of its meaning for the present and future.

A New View of Authority: Affirming Christianity in the Modern World

The question of religious authority is one of the most important and central themes of Troeltsch's essence essay. Troeltsch argues that the project of seeking an essence of Christianity suggests a new view of and attitude toward traditional sources of authority. Traditional Catholic and Protestant theologies, he states, would have found this project impossible. The former, based on ecclesiastical authority, would have sought to identify, instead, "the faith of the church," while the latter would have inquired after "the revelation of the Bible" as the normative statement about Christianity.[129] To ask about the essence of Christianity is to confess that one no longer recognizes the absolute authority of church or Scripture. It places one in a position of accountability, rather, to a range of sources, the chief of which is perhaps "modern historical thinking."

> The person for whom the dogmas of the church have collapsed, and for whom the presuppositions of modern history are a matter of course, will find in such an approach the only way in which we can clarify our religious conviction and become certain of our Christianness.[130]

Thus, the adoption of an "essence program" is equivalent, in Troeltsch's view, to a rejection of traditional sources of authority and a quest for new ones.[131] One can now criticize tradition; its "normative authority [has been]

---

[129] "Essence," 128; "¹WCh," 483.
[130] "Essence," 136; "¹WCh," 488.
[131] Troeltsch makes it quite clear that the quest for an essence of Christianity belongs

reduced."[132] This raises a question: If old conceptions of authority no longer have validity for determining Christianity's normativeness, then on what basis can one demonstrate or affirm its meaning and value for modern life?

Troeltsch clarifies that the quest for an essence of Christianity is not simply a rejection of Christianity and a statement of allegiance to modern sciences. On the contrary, it is an attempt to reconcile the two and to defend modern Christian faith against the excesses of both. According to Troeltsch, the dogmatic defender of traditional Christianity and the "radical modern opponent" of Christianity have more in common than one would think. Both limit Christianity to its traditional, miraculous conceptions of church and Scripture. The dogmatist wants to defend the supernatural authority of the church and its doctrines and even seeks to use historical methods (though dubiously) to attempt to demonstrate that Christianity is fundamentally about these miraculous and authoritative claims.[133] The radical opponent also equates Christianity with these supernatural claims and argues that, insofar as these claims are not sustainable in a modern world, Christianity is incompatible with modern sensibilities. This radical position refuses to acknowledge modern forms of Christianity or Christian faith that are not based on miracle as genuinely Christian. In this, the radical has much in common with the dogmatist. This is precisely Troeltsch's problem with Eduard von Hartmann.[134]

---

uniquely to those who have accepted a modern historical worldview and *not* to those who hang on to a dogmatic or supernatural view of the normativeness of the Bible and doctrine. Against those dogmatists who attempt to pursue a construction of the essence of Christianity, Troeltsch writes, "this use of the word 'essence' is only misleading; it appears to accept the modern historical way of thought, and to pick out genuine characteristics of the real phenomena; but by making these into an authoritative norm because of their basis in a supernatural communication, it makes the whole work of historical abstraction redundant. . . . Anything which contradicts the doctrines fixed in this way as authoritative truth thus naturally no longer comes under the term Christianity and also cannot be used in the formulation of the latter. This is a use of the word 'essence' which twists it into its opposite" ("Essence," 136; "¹WCh," 487–88).

[132] "Essence," 132; "¹WCh," 485.

[133] Troeltsch attacks traditional church historians and dogmatic theologians who (as part of their rhetorical devices against modern historiography) claim to follow an historical method while using it in a devious way to support their unscrutinized claims about the authority of dogma ("Essence," 136; "¹WCh," 487–88).

[134] "Essence," 135; "¹WCh," 487 (in the 1913 edition, Troeltsch adds David Friedrich Strauss's name to Hartmann's and characterizes them both as "radical opponents" of Christianity; see "Essence," 135; "²WCh," 399). At the end of the 1903 edition of the essence

Troeltsch allows that, depending on one's personal attitude toward Christianity, an inquiry into the essence of Christianity may lead to a negative result. One who doubts Christianity's future will likely end up with a pessimistic view of its continued viability in the modern world. Troeltsch appears to say that this is part of the risk of such an endeavor. Yet, he also seems quite confident that a positive valuation of Christianity will produce a view of the essence of Christianity that has much to offer present and future religious communities. Troeltsch's definition of the essence as an ideal concept implies that the quest for an essence of Christianity is closely linked to the effort to affirm Christianity and to demonstrate that it can indeed have a present and future in the modern world. This is what Troeltsch admires about Harnack's book on the essence of Christianity. He writes:

> This is also the reason for the great success of Harnack's book. It addresses itself to modern man with the historical presuppositions which he takes for granted, and shows him on the basis of these presuppositions the coherent spirit of Christianity so that this can work on his conscience, imagination and feelings.[135]

Troeltsch's view of the quest for an essence of Christianity is closely linked, therefore, to an effort to reconceive *and renew* Christianity according to new sources of authority and new focal points.

This new and nondogmatic approach to defining and affirming the essence of Christianity departs from traditional definitions of normative Christianity in several ways. First, although the New Testament is important as a source of Jesus' ideas and of the affirmations of early Christians, it is not the main source for a conceptualization of normative Christianity, nor is it given any miraculous or supernatural status. Second, the church figures as an important institution but not as a supernatural dispenser or guarantor of revelation. Thus, the church's development proceeds according to normal historical processes.[136] Third, Christian tradition and history are no longer centered mainly on doctrine, but are broadened to recognize and

---

essay, Troeltsch includes a long paragraph directed against Hartmann ("¹WCh," 682–83). In his revised 1913 edition of the essay, Troeltsch rewrites and extends this paragraph into a full-blown critique ("Essence," 171–76; "²WCh," 441–46).

[135] "Essence," 136; "¹WCh," 488.

[136] In other places Troeltsch argues that a modern scientific view of history does not rule out the possibility of divine guidance or participation in the course of events. See *ST*, 915–16 n. 388; *GS* 1:714 n. 388.

include extra-ecclesial movements and phenomena as part of the material to be considered and conceptualized. Finally, although an effort to define Christianity's essence may indeed acknowledge its uniqueness and value, such an effort also analyzes Christianity in the context of larger historical and religious developments.

If one no longer relies on traditional sources of authority to support one's claims about Christianity's normativity, how is the abiding meaning and value of Christianity affirmed in an essence of Christianity approach? In his efforts to address this issue toward the end of his essay, Troeltsch's notion of the essence as an ideal concept, or a construct of ethics, becomes highly important. Although Troeltsch offers no clear answer to the question, he states that the normativity or value of Christianity for the present and future will be grounded in the conscientious and imaginative act of the historian/theologian,[137] who moves from a careful consideration of the main features of Christianity's past and seeks to provide a vision of how these features or ideas will continue anew into the future. Troeltsch states, "It is always a question of submitting to that which has already been acquired and of newly creating the value for the future from within a personal appropriation of what has been acquired."[138] Christianity's normativity will come from a "creative use of the intellectual heritage," evaluated in its own terms and in conversation with present and future concerns.[139]

Conclusion: The Essence of Christianity and Troeltsch's Emerging Theory of Christianity

A central claim of this chapter is that Troeltsch's 1903 essence essay contains the elements of an emerging theory of Christianity—a theory seeking to do justice to both the historical complexity and the contemporary value of Christianity as a tradition. As the next three chapters will show, this nascent theory also deeply shapes and informs Troeltsch's work in *The Social Teachings of the Christian Churches and Groups*. In concluding this chapter, therefore, I shall outline the features of this emerging conception

---

[137] In the introduction to this study, I emphasize that Troeltsch as an historian was guided by strong normative and theological concerns and questions. Similarly, Troeltsch has a broad view of the theologian's task. For Troeltsch, historical investigation and understanding are central to the task of theological inquiry and construction.

[138] "Essence," 166; "WCh," 680.

[139] "Essence," 161; "WCh," 653.

of Christianity as it is left at the end of the 1903 essence essay and will be taken up in the *Social Teachings*.

Troeltsch pursues a conception of Christianity that is located at the intersection of historical and normative tasks in the study of history. He holds that any theory of Christianity must be rooted in empirical-historical research and the complicated data it yields. Such empirical-historical rooting can do justice to the complex, pluriform structure of historical entities (*Größe*), such as Christianity, and clearly differs from what Troeltsch would call a dogmatic approach to conceptualizing Christianity. Troeltsch characterizes the dogmatic approach as evading a fully rigorous historical treatment of Christian history. Furthermore, the empirical-historical moment in Troeltsch's method guarantees a measure of objectivity to the conception of Christianity being pursued.

At the same time, Troeltsch seeks a conceptualization of Christianity that is not merely an objective reconstruction of past historical facts. Such a conceptualization must also demonstrate Christianity's continuing value and vitality, as well as its potential contribution to modern life. Therefore, Troeltsch is wary of separating empirical from philosophical (or normative) treatments of Christianity. In Troeltsch's view, empirical-historical work has its own integrity, but even so, it ought not be completely removed from questions about the present and future. Similarly, a philosophical-historical or normative construction of Christianity would lack credibility and grounding in the realities of historical life without a solid rootedness in empirical history. Thus, Troeltsch attempts to keep the empirical and philosophical moments of essence-construction in conversation and mutual relation. I suggest that Troeltsch associates this connection between empirical and normative historical pursuits with a "purely historical" method and worldview. Such a worldview affirms the uniqueness and value of historical phenomena, the complexity of historical development, and the importance of discerning and affirming the principles that guide or inform the development and course of historical complexes such as Christianity.

This dual commitment to empirical-historical integrity and philosophical-normative assessment of Christianity's value and meaning also informs Troeltsch's understanding of Christianity's origins and development. As I have begun to show, Troeltsch is well aware of the problems of assigning the origins a normative or unique place in any conception of an historical complex, but he insists, nevertheless, that they must be privileged in some way in order to gesture toward a continuity of meaning throughout Christianity's history. Similarly, Troeltsch seeks a conception of historical development that can establish continuity and coherence among Christianity's major forms and affirmations, while also making room for radical discontinuities and changes in Christianity's history.

Finally, Troeltsch's efforts in his 1903 essence essay to offer a many-sided understanding of the nature of the concept of an essence of Christianity suggest that he already has doubts about its fruitfulness as a tool for conceptualizing Christianity. He goes to great lengths to stretch the notion of an essence of Christianity so that it can accommodate a wide variety of historical formations and do so objectively, but also with a view to affirming Christianity's value for the future.

Equipped with his rich but tension-filled conceptualization of Christianity as articulated in the 1903 essence essay, Troeltsch pursues over the next ten years a variety of historical projects in and through which he seeks to clarify how he might best portray the identity of Christianity. In the next three chapters, I explore the ways in which Troeltsch continues to pursue and refine his 1903 conception of Christianity in between the lines of his major historical work, *The Social Teachings of the Christian Churches and Groups.*

CHAPTER TWO

Christian Origins and the Identity of Christianity

The next three chapters focus on Troeltsch's "favorite book,"[1] *The Social Teachings of the Christian Churches and Groups*. In this work Troeltsch traced the history of Christianity's social doctrines and relation to culture from its beginnings through the nineteenth century. Troeltsch's method in the *Social Teachings* was a significant departure from previous efforts in the area of church history. Instead of a history of doctrine oriented toward the authority of the institutional church, Troeltsch wrote an historically-oriented sociology, or what has been called a *Religionsgeschichte des Christentums*.[2]

The impetus for the book came originally from a request Troeltsch received to review Martin von Nathusius's book, *The Contribution of the Church to the Social Question*,[3] for the *Archiv für Sozialwissenschaft und Sozialpolitik*. Looking back on this invitation, Troeltsch would later explain that his dismay at the ignorance concerning Christianity's relation to sociological factors led him to write not a book review, but "a book of nearly one thousand pages."[4]

---

[1] Letter to Paul Siebeck, 18 January 1914, in Drescher, *Ernst Troeltsch*, 222, 407–8 n. 284.

[2] Graf and many others have noted that Troeltsch sought to transform traditional church history into a *Religionsgeschichte des Christentums* (history of the Christian religion). He held that the dominant form of church history was too closely tied to a legitimation of the institutional church, with its focus on the history of doctrine and its tendency to label as "heretical" most forms of extra-ecclesial piety (such as the piety of the sects). See Graf, "Ernst Troeltsch: Kulturgeschichte,"145–47. See also Ulrich Köpf, "Kirchengeschichte oder Religionsgeschichte des Christentums? Gedanken über Gegenstand und Aufgabe der Kirchengeschichte um 1900," in *Der deutsche Protestantismus um 1900* (ed. Graf and Hans Martin Müller; Gütersloh: Gütersloher Verlagshaus, 1996) esp. 53–58.

[3] *Die Mitarbeit der Kirche an der Lösung der sozialen Frage* (3d ed.; Leipzig: Hinrichs, 1904).

[4] Troeltsch, "My Books" (1922), in *Religion in History*, 372; "Meine Bücher," in *GS* 4:11.

The *Social Teachings* appeared over the course of a four-year period (1908–1912)—the first half in gradual installments in the *Archiv* from 1908–1910, and the completed entire work as the first volume of Troeltsch's *Gesammelte Schriften* in 1912.

Troeltsch's work on the *Social Teachings* took place during the time of his engagement with members of the Eranos Circle and with Max Weber in particular. As he wrote the *Social Teachings*, Troeltsch became preoccupied with questions such as, "To what extent are the appearance, the development, the modification, and the modern impasse of Christianity sociologically conditioned, and to what extent is Christianity itself an actively formative sociological principle?"[5] To understand the current condition of Christianity in its modern context, Troeltsch turned to history, exploring the various ways Christianity had organized itself internally and positioned itself in relation to society.

The *Social Teachings* emphasizes the internal diversity and historical complexity of Christianity, on the one hand, and is oriented toward questions about Christianity's possible meaning and place in the modern world, on the other. It perhaps should not be surprising, then, that Troeltsch once referred to the *Social Teachings* as a systematic presentation of "the various definitions of the essence of Christianity at various times."[6] Indeed, the *Social Teachings* is arguably one of the most important works for understanding Troeltsch's view of the issues, problems, and concerns that attend the question of Christianity's essence, yet the term "essence" (*Wesen*) rarely appears in the text.[7] Instead, Troeltsch charts the developments and tensions that mark

---

[5] "My Books," in *Religion in History*, 372; "Meine Bücher," in *GS* 4:11.

[6] Troeltsch states this in a footnote to his essay, "The Dogmatics of the History-of-Religions School." In the note, he calls attention to his essay on the essence of Christianity, and then states, "My historical writings in general have been devoted to the task of indicating this synthesis or setting forth the definitions of the essence of Christianity at different times. I call special attention to *Die Soziallehren der christlichen Kirchen und Gruppen* ("The Dogmatics," in *Religion in History*, 108 n. 3; this note also appears in the first American edition of this essay: "The Dogmatics of the 'Religionsgeschichtliche Schule'," *American Journal of Theology* 17 [1913] 13 n. 2). Troeltsch did not include this footnote in the German edition of this essay, which was printed in the second volume of his *Gesammelte Schriften*. Instead, he shortened most of the footnotes to include only bibliographical references and no comments. For more information on the publication and editions of this essay, see note 1 of my Introduction, above.

[7] "*Wesen*" appears in only scant and scattered places, usually not in a phrase such as "essence of Christianity." In fact, not once in the *Social Teachings* does Troeltsch use the term "essence of Christianity" to make a constructive claim about Christianity's characteristic

Christianity's history, thus demonstrating and exploring historically what he had asserted philosophically in his essay on the essence of Christianity: namely, that Christianity is a diversity of developments and forms rather than a single phenomenon.

Despite Troeltsch's own acknowledgment of the connection between the *Social Teachings* and the essence essay, no study has focused sufficiently on how the *Social Teachings* reflects and affects his perspective on the concept of an essence of Christianity.[8] Furthermore, while a number of recent studies have illumined the place of sociological methods and categories in the *Social Teachings*,[9] the task remains to analyze the implicit theory of historical and normative Christianity that is presented in this work.

In chapters 2, 3, and 4 of this study, I clarify the model of Christianity that underlies and informs Troeltsch's historical narrative in the *Social Teachings*. All three chapters explore the ways in which Troeltsch seeks to conceptualize Christianity as an internally diverse yet loosely unified historical phenomenon with resources for shaping the future. By examining how Troeltsch grapples with historiographical categories such as origins (chapter 2), development (chapter 3), and ideal type (chapter 4), we will then be in a position to see how

---

ideas, features, or nature. On the contrary, one of the few times the term appears in this text is in association with those Protestants who use it (illegitimately, in Troeltsch's view) to suggest that medieval Catholicism was contrary to the essence of Christianity. See *ST*, 207; *GS* 1:186.

[8] John Clayton ("Can Theology Be Both Cultural and Christian? Enrst Troeltsch and the Possibility of a Mediating Theology," in *Science, Faith, and Revelation* [ed. Bob E. Patterson; Nashville, Tenn.: Broadman, 1979] 82–111) notes very briefly that the results of Troeltsch's study of the history and development of Christianity in the *Social Teachings* "confirmed and reinforced" Troeltsch's claims in the essence of Christianity essay (101). That is, Troeltsch's *Social Teachings* demonstrates that Christianity is pluriform, changing in every period and context, and presenting no single "essence." Thus, Clayton states, "There is much sense in regarding the *Soziallehren* as the execution of much of the program proposed in 'Was heißt "Wesen des Christentums"?'" (110 n. 155). Berthold Lannert offers a brief discussion of several important connections between Troeltsch's treatment of *Urchristentum* in the *Social Teachings* on the one hand and his views expressed in the essence of Christianity essay on the other. "Die Bedeutung der religionsgeschichtlichen Forschungen zur Geschichte des Urchristentums," *Ernst Troeltschs Soziallehren* (ed. Graf and Rendtorff) 80–103.

[9] See Friedemann Voigt, *"Die Tragödie des Reiches Gottes?" Ernst Troeltsch als Leser Georg Simmels* (vol. 10 of Troeltsch-Studien; Gütersloh: Gütersloher Verlagshaus, 1998); and Arie Molendijk, *Zwischen Theologie und Soziologie. Ernst Troeltschs Typen der christlichen Gemeinschaftsbildung. Kirche, Sekte, Mystik* (vol. 9 of Troeltsch-Studien; Gütersloh: Gütersloher Verlagshaus, 1996).

Troeltsch's composition of the *Social Teachings* leads him to complexify and all but abandon the idea of an essence of Christianity later in his career. The task of the current chapter will be to examine Troeltsch's treatment of earliest Christianity (*Urchristentum*) in the *Social Teachings*. Is the whole of "authentic" Christianity contained in its origins? Is the earliest period valued as Christianity's highest or purest form, and therefore as the standard against which all other forms are to be judged? If not, then what is Troeltsch's operative view of the place of the origins in Christianity's historical development? Sorting out Troeltsch's view of early Christianity is not an easy task. Indeed, as I have shown in the previous chapter, already in 1903 (in the first edition of the essence essay), Troeltsch struggled with the question of what place the original period ought to have in an account of Christianity as a whole. In the second edition of the essence of Christianity essay in 1913, the year after Troeltsch finished the *Social Teachings*, these complexities surrounding earliest Christianity are emphasized and elaborated even more.[10]

In the *Social Teachings* Troeltsch makes no simplistic appeal to earliest Christianity or to the preaching of Jesus as the most authentic or legitimate form of Christianity. He locates certain sources of continuity in the earliest period and tends to link later developments in Christianity to a germ (*Keim*) that was present from the beginning. Troeltsch also claims that the concerns and foci of the earliest Christians were "purely religious," a classification that might suggest a spiritualized, apolitical view of Christian origins, and not a historicized one.[11] At the same time, Troeltsch does not limit early Christianity to the first-century communities around Jesus or Paul, but includes early Catholicism in this period as well.[12] This enables him to emphasize the

---

[10] In ch. 5, I detail the changes Troeltsch makes to the 1903 essay when he revises it for its inclusion in the second volume of his *Gesammelte Schriften* in 1913.

[11] Richard Horsley, for example, discusses the problems with apolitical readings of Christian origins in his work with Jonathan Draper. Horsley also traces the legacy of modern individualistic readings of Jesus' message to Harnack and Troeltsch. See Richard Horsley and Jonathan Draper, *Whoever Hears You Hears Me: Prophets, Performance, and Tradition in Q* (Harrisburg, Pa.: Trinity, 1999) 15–28, esp. 21–28.

[12] Troeltsch includes in the "original" period of Christianity "the period of the Gospel" (the time during which Jesus was alive), the Pauline community, and early Catholicism. While the gospel (the ideas contained in Jesus' preaching) contains many of the main ideas that will shape subsequent forms of Christianity, both Paul and early Catholicism contribute elements that will also be constitutive for Christianity's historical development. Troeltsch's grouping of all three forms of Christianity into the first period of Christian history, which

diversity of earliest Christianity. Furthermore, Troeltsch attributes great value to later developments in Christianity that, in his mind, have no obvious relation to the origins. For example, according to Troeltsch, the fusion of Stoic natural law and early Christian theology and ethics enables Christianity to become an effective social force in the world—something that it could not have done on its own.

In order to identify the status and interpretation Troeltsch gives to Christian origins and thereby to illuminate their place in his conception of Christianity, I take up the following topics in this chapter. First, I analyze Troeltsch's characterization of early Christianity's historical context. I explore the ways in which he attempts to situate the origins of Christianity in this context while also separating them from it. Second, I consider whether Troeltsch regards the features of early Christianity as determinative (in a causal sense) for Christianity's subsequent historical development. Finally, I ask what kind of normative significance Troeltsch assigns to Christianity's origins.

By conducting this three-tiered analysis, I argue that Troeltsch insists on a complex reading of the origins of Christianity that neither holds them up as exclusively normative nor discounts their formative influence for Christian history. Instead, Troeltsch seeks to construct Christian identity in conversation with Christian origins but not in subservience to the earliest period. It is also important to recognize that at stake for Troeltsch in discussions of the origin of Christianity are questions about the status of religion in an increasingly modernized and secularized society, and the possible contribution of Christianity to his present-day culture.

The Relation of Earliest Christianity to Its Historical Context: Christian Origins as "Purely Religious"

One way to assess Troeltsch's view of Christianity's origins is to explore how he relates them to their historical context. Does Christianity emerge as something wholly new, or is its emergence somehow contingent upon previous and contemporaneous religious, cultural, and social forces? What was the

---

he calls "the old church" (*die alte Kirche*), enables him to portray the origins of Christianity as continuous, pluriform, and in some ways even discontinuous. Occasionally he speaks of Jesus, Paul, and early Catholicism as constituting a unity called "early Christianity." In other cases, he presents them as sources of divergent theological and sociological ideas that shape Christianity in different ways.

nature and quality of the community around Jesus, and does its character imply anything normative about Christian identity? Troeltsch's historical account of Christian origins is fraught with ambiguities and tensions. On the one hand, he locates the emergence of Christianity in the context of larger religious developments of late antiquity.[13] Christianity originates during a period of renewed religious interest and the decline of what Troeltsch calls "popular religions."[14] It begins as a small community with a rigorous ethic of preparation for the kingdom of God and indifference to the world,[15] and eventually becomes "the receptacle for the new ideas which grew out of this [late antique] religious development."[16] As one religious movement among many with similar tendencies, earliest Christianity shares features with other religious and philosophical movements of the time, such as Stoicism,[17] which

---

[13] *ST*, 43; *GS* 1:25. Lannert argues that Troeltsch's treatment of earliest Christianity in the *Social Teachings* must be seen in relation to the intensive and groundbreaking research pursued by members of the history of religions school in the first decade prior to the book's composition. Lannert notes that the turn toward "*Urchristentum*" and away from the New Testament canon as the proper object of study in constructing a history of the beginnings of Christianity was an innovation and signature of the history of religions school. See Lannert, "Die Bedeutung," 81–82.

[14] *ST*, 43; *GS* 1:26.

[15] Johann Hinrich Claussen makes the interesting point that Troeltsch, as a philosopher of culture, actually uses the notion of Jesus' "world-indifference" not to support a disengagement with culture but to do the opposite—to recommend a critical engagement with culture and to guard against the absolutization of any one perspective on social organization. *Die Jesus-Deutung von Ernst Troeltsch im Kontext der liberalen Theologie* (Tübingen: Mohr, 1997) 103–17, 228, 248.

[16] *ST*, 44; *GS* 1:26.

[17] Stegemann rightly states that Troeltsch gives an insufficient account of Jesus' Jewishness. See Wolfgang Stegemann, "Zur Deutung des Urchristentums in den 'Soziallehren'," in *Ernst Troeltschs Soziallehren* (ed. Graf and Rendtorff) 51–79. In the *Social Teachings*, Troeltsch considers the Jewish "background" of Jesus' thought, stating that "the Gospel ethic should be interpreted throughout in the light of its religious motive, which Jesus inherited from Judaism [*aus dem Hebraismus zukam*]" (*ST*, 181 n. 53; *GS* 1:106 n. 53). Troeltsch also alludes to certain questions that he then neglects to answer, such as the degree to which Jesus' preaching was "novel" in relation to its Jewish context, and the extent to which Jesus' view of morality was continuous with Jewish notions of law (*ST*, 52, 53, 58; *GS* 1:35, 36, 44). The issue of Jesus' uniqueness in relation to his environment as well as his relationship to Jewish law are significant ongoing topics in current historical-Jesus research. See, for example, Paula Fredriksen, *Jesus of Nazareth, King of the Jews: A Jewish Life and the Emergence of Christianity* (New York: Knopf, 1999). For more on the depiction of Jesus' Jewishness in nineteenth-century German scholarship, see Susannah Heschel, *Abraham Geiger and the Jewish Jesus* (Chicago: University of Chicago Press, 1998).

for Troeltsch represents "a complete analogy with the sociological thought of Christianity."[18]

On the other hand, Troeltsch is not certain how closely the origin and development of earliest Christianity ought to be linked to the social conditions of the time. He is unwilling to conclude that earliest Christianity was determined *only* by "external" forces and historical contingencies. He writes, "Indeed, it is absolutely certain that the great religious crisis which marked the close of the ancient world was a result of vast social crises."[19] As he enumerates these crises, however, Troeltsch is careful not to give them too much power, noting that "the influence of these social and historical developments [on the shape and message of earliest Christianity] was only indirect."[20]

Troeltsch's Language of "Purely Religious" (rein religiös)

This tension concerning the nature and extent of earliest Christianity's relation to its social setting is echoed in one of the most startling claims Troeltsch makes in his account of the origin of Christianity, namely, that it was a "purely religious" movement. Troeltsch begins his treatment of early Christianity with the following statement:

> In order to understand the general tendency [*Grundrichtung*] of Christianity as a whole, in its relation to social problems, it is of the utmost importance to recognize that the preaching of Jesus and the creation of the new religious community [*Gemeinde*] were not due in any sense to the impulse of a social movement.[21]

Instead, Troeltsch argues that Jesus' preaching and the community that formed in response to it had a "purely religious" (*rein religiös*) character and concern.[22] Uninvolved in (because largely unaffected by) the major economic,

---

[18] *ST*, 65; *GS* 1:53.

[19] *ST*, 47; *GS* 1:30–31.

[20] *ST*, 48; *GS* 1:31. By suggesting that social factors have an "indirect" causal effect on religious developments, Troeltsch is expressing, as Clayton emphasizes, a notion of the "relative independence" or "limited autonomy" of religion. Clayton rightly points out that while Troeltsch affirmed the reciprocal relationship between religion and culture, he "never . . . relinquished the view that religion is in some sense a relatively autonomous factor in society and culture" ("Can Theology Be Both Cultural and Christian?," 92).

[21] *ST*, 39; *GS* 1:15. I have altered Wyon's English translation here.

[22] *ST*, 39; *GS* 1:15.

social, and political events of the day, and not focused on the social situation of its members, the earliest Christian community (according to Troeltsch) was centered on the gospel ethic as found in the fundamental ideas of Jesus' preaching. Jesus' message, according to Troeltsch, was rooted in "a definite idea of God" and of God's relation to humanity, such that, "to Jesus the whole meaning of life is religious."[23] All is directed toward the preparation for the imminent coming of the kingdom and the judgment of God that would accompany it. Although Troeltsch views the kingdom of God as "the rule of God on earth, to be followed, later on, by the end of the world and the judgment,"[24] it is less a developed social conception or societal vision than a simple ethical urgency. God's moral command and absolute authority call the individual to an intense obedience and "purity of intention" in all religious and moral actions.[25] Indeed, all the early Christian literature, according to Troeltsch, was directed toward religious (and not political) questions, such as "the salvation of the soul, monotheism, life after death, purity of worship, the right kind of congregational organization, the application of Christian ideals to daily life, and the need for severe self-discipline in the interest of personal holiness."[26] Consequently, the members of Jesus' community were urgently, obediently, and conscientiously focused on preparation for the imminent coming of the kingdom, to the exclusion of all else. Theirs was a *religious* movement.

At first glance, it is somewhat surprising that the scholar who intended to replace the traditional "idea-oriented" or "doctrinal" histories of Christianity with a work that would situate the development of Christian teachings more fully in the context of social, political, economic, and intellectual forces would employ such seemingly problematic terminology as "purely" or "essentially religious." It is reasonable to ask whether Troeltsch, in using this language, was attempting (covertly) to establish earliest Christianity as normative by suggesting that it was "unique" or unaffected by social conditions or causes. Before engaging in a full analysis of the reasons Troeltsch used this kind of argumentation, therefore, it is helpful first to clarify what Troeltsch meant by both "purely" and "religious."

---

[23] *ST*, 50; *GS* 1:34.
[24] *ST*, 51; *GS* 1:35.
[25] *ST*, 52; *GS* 1:35.
[26] *ST*, 39; *GS* 1:16.

The term "purely religious" sounds particularly odd to English speakers, who might associate the adverb "purely" (*rein*) with "purity" or the quality of being "unmediated." In that case, Troeltsch seems to suggest that Christianity had some kind of miraculous origin, not at all explicable within its surrounding or preceding historical context, but simply deposited in time through an act of divine revelation and intervention. Such a claim, of course, would be contrary to what Troeltsch argues in many places. For Troeltsch, it is unacceptable to protect certain points in history from the normal causal processes assigned to all other parts of history. Although "*rein*" indeed commonly means "pure" (as in pure or clear water), it also means "fully," "plainly," "distinctively," or "clearly." Troeltsch uses the adverb in this latter sense throughout the *Social Teachings*. For example, he refers not simply to "purely religious" phenomena (such as earliest Christianity's ethical orientation), but also to events, processes, ideas, or movements that are any of the following: "purely personal,"[27] "purely secular,"[28] "purely economic,"[29] "purely spiritual,"[30] "purely political,"[31] and "purely rationalistic."[32] In each case, Troeltsch uses the term "*rein*" to indicate *the proper way to classify or understand something* and not necessarily to suggest that this something is somehow ahistorical or unmediated by other factors.

But what does Troeltsch mean by "religious" in the phrase "purely religious"? I address this question more fully below, but a preliminary suggestion can be offered at this point. Troeltsch appears to use the term "religious" in a way that relies on definitions typical in much of nineteenth-century German Protestant thought. In this context, the term signifies something centered on the inner life or personality and oriented toward "higher" or supramundane values, feelings, and concerns.[33] We can glean this meaning from several of Troeltsch's descriptions of the "ideal of the Gospel," which is consistently described as "purely religious." In general, Troeltsch describes this "ideal of the Gospel" as "the supernatural values of the love

---

[27] *ST*, 993; *GS* 1:967.

[28] *ST*, 646; *GS* 1:717.

[29] *ST*, 991; *GS* 1:965.

[30] *ST*, 492; *GS* 1:469.

[31] *ST*, 810; *GS* 1:953.

[32] *ST*, 631; *GS* 1:691.

[33] Troeltsch states that "a religious doctrine like that of Christian monotheism . . . takes religion out of the sphere of existing conditions and the existing order and turns it purely into an ethical religion of redemption" (*ST*, 85; *GS* 1:76).

of God and of the brethren."[34] He associates this with several qualities: the valuing of inner personality, the tendency to gather in small communities characterized by intimacy, a lack of interest in practical matters of the larger social and political world, and a close relationship between the individual and God. Troeltsch summarizes these qualities with two basic traits. First, the "religious" in "purely religious" stands for a primary orientation toward and concern with uncompromising divine commands and values (such as love of God and neighbor) that are elevated above any "practical" concerns. Second, this "religious" orientation implies a hostility toward the world,[35] not in the sense of a hatred for creation or an ascetic mode of self-denial, but in the sense of an apathy toward practical concern for the organization of the larger society,[36] and a total devotion to that which is seen as a holy preparation for some future order to be established by God.[37]

Although these explanations begin to clarify what Troeltsch meant by "purely religious," they must be supplemented by the following observations. Both the meaning of "purely religious" and Troeltsch's aim in using such a characterization to describe Christianity's origins must be understood in the context of debates on historical method that marked Troeltsch's day and in relation to the larger argument of the *Social Teachings*. Further, Troeltsch's appeal to purely religious phenomena can be illuminated by a consideration

---

[34] *ST*, 202; *GS* 1:181.

[35] *ST*, 202; *GS* 1:181–82.

[36] Troeltsch often defines the "secularization" (*Verweltlichung*) of the church as the act of establishing its organization and structure since, in his view, a "purely religious" community would have no formal, practical, or graduated constitution. Accordingly, he states that "during the time of Jesus' life on earth there was no sign of a visible community" (*ST*, 62; *GS* 1:49); later, referring to the development of a hierarchical church structure in early Catholicism, he comments that "this is the real secularization of the church" (*ST*, 94; *GS* 1:87).

[37] A quotation from Troeltsch's text further explicates the two characteristics that he appears to associate with the "religious" element of that which he calls "purely religious." He writes: "The Gospel gave rise to two tendencies, which led . . . in the direction of . . . a decided otherworldliness. . . . The first of the influences which led in this direction was the central position assigned to love to God and man as the supreme end in life, both in ethics and religion, to which all else is subordinate, and alongside of which the institutions of this world—with the possible exception of the family—only receive scant attention. . . . The second influence was the rigorism of the ethic of love and of intention, which renounces law and violence, and which tries, whenever it is at all possible, to achieve everything through personal influence and by an inner victory over evil" (*ST*, 238; *GS* 1:228; see also *ST*, 161; *GS* 1:175; and *ST*, 307; *GS* 1:331).

of Troeltsch's definition of religion, which was always concerned with the question of its significance for culture (*Kulturbedeutung*).[38]

"Purely Religious" or "Purely Social"? Troeltsch's Dispute with Marxist Historians

Troeltsch's emphasis on the "purely religious" character of earliest Christianity is directed against certain Marxist historians who argued for a political and economic interpretation of the emergence of Christianity, calling it a "purely social" movement.[39] In particular, Troeltsch takes on the interpretations of Karl Kautsky,[40] Albert Kalthoff, and Robert von Pöhlmann, who argue that Christianity originated as a proletarian class movement with a communistic conception of community. This earliest community is then overturned by the entry of the upper classes into Christianity in the second and third centuries and by the creation of the Catholic church.[41]

Troeltsch's argument against such a position is twofold. First, he disagrees with its general reconstruction of the historical situation of early Christianity. In Troeltsch's view, the earliest Christian community was not organized around a particular social question or criticism of the existing order. Precisely because of their position as lower class town-dwellers, the earliest Christians were not affected by many of the major "socio-historical events" of the imperial period, and they actually experienced a "gradual improvement in the

---

[38] Graf argues that Troeltsch's theory of religion had as its most fundamental concern the question of the special cultural meaning and role of religion in the crisis situation of modernity, that is, in the context of modern developments that threatened individual freedom and subjectivity, such as capitalism and bureaucracy. The task of a theory of religion then becomes the definition and demonstration of religion as a site and source of individual freedom in the modern world. See "Religion und Individualität," 220.

[39] *ST*, 165 n. 10; *GS* 1:17 n. 10.

[40] Constance Benson's claim in *God & Caesar: Troeltsch's 'Social Teaching' as Legitimation* (New Brunswick, N.J.: Transaction, 1999) that Kautsky's work is the *primary* impetus for Troeltsch's writing of the *Social Teachings* in its entirety is highly implausible. While Troeltsch's arguments about the "purely religious" nature of earliest Christianity surely need to be seen as responses to Kautsky's work, it is an exaggeration to classify the entire *Social Teachings*, with its more than 500 footnotes (only a very small number of which refer to Kautsky) and its obvious engagement with issues, debates, and conversations beyond those treated by Kautsky, as primarily a response to one person. Surely Troeltsch's *Social Teachings* was an engagement with political questions of his day, and an implicit contribution to the debate about the "social question," as Benson states. Yet, this does not mean that it was primarily concerned with refuting Kautsky.

[41] Troeltsch details these positions in notes 10 through 14 (*ST*, 165–70; *GS* 1:17–24).

conditions which took place in urban life."[42] In addition, the general religious trend in late antiquity was not, according to Troeltsch, toward social criticism or activism, but rather toward the "inner life" and a general interest in the personal, ethical, and religious spheres.[43]

Second, and more importantly, Troeltsch objects to the conception of causality that results from the Marxist interpretations of historians like Kautsky. Although Troeltsch respects the validity and contribution of Marxist insights concerning the study of history,[44] he resists what he sees as the reductive tendencies of certain Marxist accounts of causation. Concerning Kautsky's methodological assumptions about the relation between the church and "the social," Troeltsch writes:

> There is . . . no question [in Kautsky's work] of a religious-sociological development issuing from a specifically religious motive; the church is simply absorbed into the general course of economic and social development, within which at the beginning it represents a communistic class movement of the poor, concealing its economic-communistic ideal beneath the veil of its general religious idea of love.[45]

For Troeltsch, a reading like Kautsky's ignores the real power that religious groups, ideas, and institutions can have in history, and instead reduces the religious to something exclusively social.[46] Thus in emphasizing

---

[42] *ST*, 41; *GS* 1:24.

[43] *ST*, 41; *GS* 1:21. Troeltsch also argues, against Kautsky, that not simply Jesus' movement but also other parallel and contemporary religious groups were "purely religious" and not social movements; these parallel movements similarly "did not adopt the policy of preaching a social gospel for a certain class, nor did they advocate an attack on social wrongs" (*ST*, 40; *GS* 1:18–20). In addition, Troeltsch asserts (again, against Kautsky) that the earliest Christians did not belong to a single class (*ST*, 42; *GS* 1:25).

[44] Graf notes that several scholars who reviewed the *Social Teachings* criticized Troeltsch for his "Marxism," by which they meant Troeltsch's "readiness to recognize a relative truth in the differentiations between real and ideal factors and structure and superstructures" (Graf, "Weltanschauungshistoriographie. Rezensionen zur Erstausgabe der *Soziallehren*," in *Ernst Troeltschs Soziallehren* [ed. Graf and Rendtorff] 218).

[45] *ST*, 36 n. 3b; *GS* 1:7 n. 3a.

[46] As Molendijk notes (*Zwischen Theologie und Soziologie*, 19, 21), many of the scholars who were involved in the early twentieth-century debate over the founding of sociology as a discipline (such as Troeltsch, Weber, Jellinek, and Simmel) resisted "a purely reductive interpretation of religion." This should not be read as a rejection of the use of Marxist concepts in the study of history but rather as a rejection of those Marxist interpretations that reduce all events to a single cause.

the independence of religious phenomena, Troeltsch is not denying or overlooking other forces—whether social, political, economic, or cultural—that contributed to Christianity's structure and form,[47] but rather defending a view of causality and development that acknowledges the influence of a variety of social forces, including religious ones. For Troeltsch, Marxist interpretations like Kautsky's put forth a dubiously monocausal view of historical development.[48]

In arguing for the "purely religious" nature of early Christianity over against those calling it "purely social," therefore, Troeltsch wishes to preserve a religious "origin" for Christianity and thereby to avoid either a reductionistic account of it as arising only from social causes or an historical presentation of it as primarily concerned with social problems. If early Christianity is a purely social movement, as certain Marxist historiographers insisted, then religion must ultimately be an illusion, a by-product of social realities, forces, and agendas. Without its own ability to serve as an origin or stimulus to development, religion cannot be a lasting and valuable aspect of culture. However, once one *recognizes* the religious orientation and origin of Christianity and, indeed, of the religious developments of late antiquity generally, then "it is quite permissible to study the connection between the sociological problem and these religious ideals."[49] By referring to an indirect conditioning or effect of social forces on religious phenomena, Troeltsch objects to a view of causation or influence as automatic or all-powerful and promotes a more open-ended mode of interaction between social forces and religious ideas.[50]

---

[47] Ibid., 19.

[48] As Graf explains, "Troeltsch's critique is aimed at the monistic principle according to which history is moved through one metahistorically invariant power of development. He himself starts from the view that historical reality is shaped by a plurality of forces" ("Ernst Troeltsch: Kulturgeschichte," 138). Graf is explaining Troeltsch's objections to Paul Barth's Marxist historical method (as Troeltsch articulated them in an 1898 review of Barth's book, *Die Philosophie der Geschichte als Soziologie,* in *Theologische Literaturzeitung* 23 [1898] 398–401), but these objections characterize Troeltsch's critique of certain kinds of Marxist methodologies generally.

[49] *ST*, 50; *GS* 1:34.

[50] In his essay, "Religion, Wirtschaft und Gesellschaft," Troeltsch states that the relation between social and religious forces in any development must be judged "from case to case" and not simply credited to the singular influence of either social or religious factors (*GS* 4:32).

For Troeltsch, the reality and integrity of religion can be preserved only by demonstrating that certain phenomena are, at root, religious, as opposed to economic, social, or political. In the *Social Teachings*, Troeltsch employs the notion of "naïve religion" to bolster his portrait of earliest Christianity as "purely religious."[51] Troeltsch classifies the early Christian movement as one emerging out of the "lower classes," with their capacity for creative, "primitive" energy, and their "simplicity of feeling" that is united with a "non-reflective habit of mind."[52] The earliest Christian movement was characterized by its "naïve vital religious content," and was energized by a "naïve revelation."[53] In fact, Christianity in its origins is an example of "the popular character and outlook of all naïve religion."[54] Those who joined Jesus' movement "came from religious groups of this humble type,"[55] and even Paul was a "contemplative," a "creative, mystical soul" whose "whole outlook was entirely independent of the spirit of purely scientific inquiry, balanced criticism, and the higher world culture of the epoch."[56] For Troeltsch, demonstrating the naïve religiosity of the earliest Christians substantiates his claim that Christianity, at its origins, was a distinctively religious movement. This move then serves to protect the autonomy of religion in general.[57]

[51] In "Religion and the Science of Religion," in *Writings*, 82–183; "Wesen der Religion und der Religionswissenschaft," in *GS* 2:452–99, Troeltsch sketches a program for the science of religion that begins with an exploration and cataloging of the most basic expressions or cases of "religiosity as a datum," that is, expressions of what Troeltsch calls "naïve religion." Such expressions appear where religious experience (for whatever reasons) has not been reflected on by means of a scientific sensibility or consciousness (*Writings*, 89; *GS* 2:463). These "direct" expressions of intense and all-consuming religious experience are generally found, according to Troeltsch, among "primitive" peoples studied by archaeologists and anthropologists, as well as among "one-sided or exclusively religious personalities, sects, and groups" (*Writings*, 90–91; *GS* 2:464–65). Such many and varied manifestations of naïve religion enable the scholar to "grasp the characteristic and essential features of this sphere of culture" (*Writings*, 92; *GS* 2:467).

[52] *ST*, 44; *GS* 1:27.

[53] *ST*, 45, 44; *GS* 1:27.

[54] *ST*, 45; *GS* 1:27.

[55] *ST*, 45; *GS* 1:28.

[56] *ST*, 45; *GS* 1:29.

[57] The autonomy (*Selbstständigkeit*) of religion is a central theme of Troeltsch's writings on the nature and science of religion, including his essay, "Religion and the Science of Religion." There he defends the autonomy of religion against what he sees as the distorting and destructive effects of positivistic views of religion. According to Troeltsch, positivistic approaches view religion as a creation of the "primitive" human psyche, a prescientific (and therefore ultimately erroneous) way of ordering and explaining the world (*Writings*, 84; *GS*

If we consider a central concern that drives Troeltsch's work in the *Social Teachings*—that is, to point to the potential of religion to contribute to modern society—we understand more clearly what is at stake in Troeltsch's defense of the "purely religious" origin and autonomy of Christianity. In order to assert that religion continues to have an important role in the modern world, Troeltsch must show it to be a substantive, existent phenomenon with its own productive power. Thus for Troeltsch the independence of religion, and in this case, the ability of religion to serve as the primary cause of earliest Christianity, is linked to its possible role in shaping culture. We get a glimpse of this in the following statement:

> Only those who see in all spiritual movements merely the influence of social movements, and especially those who imagine that all religion is merely the reflection of social conditions in transcendental terms, will see in them a direct cause of the religious crisis. In reality, however, all impartial religious research reveals the fact that, to some extent at least, religious thought is independent; it has its own inner dialectic and its own power of development; it is therefore precisely during these periods of a total bankruptcy of human hope and effort that it is able to step in and fill the vacant space with its own ideas and its own sentiment.[58]

According to Troeltsch's characterization, the period of earliest Christianity was one such instance in which religion was able to play a significant role in revitalizing a particular dimension of human life that was otherwise stagnant. In the quotation above we glimpse, perhaps, a further (implicit) suggestion that, in the context of the threatening conditions of modern capitalism and secularization, religion might once again be able to exert a substantive and positive influence. Unlike Max Weber, who was more pessimistic about the

---

2:458). Taking a strictly empirical and naturalistic approach to classifying phenomena and organizing experience, positivism "recognizes only assured facts and the ordered connections between them" (*Writings*, 82; *GS* 2:455). Religion, then, "must be explained in terms of some function of which it was itself not conscious," and therefore has no integrity and no future (*Writings*, 107, 84–85; *GS* 2:484, 458–59). Troeltsch states that "the way must be held open for religion to be fully apprehended. It must be possible to analyze it in its own terms. It must be examined at least provisionally as a completely independent phenomenon, which it claims itself after all to be" (*Writings*, 85; *GS* 2:458). Positivism, according to Troeltsch, decides ahead of time what the nature of religion is, and is therefore inadequate as an approach to religious inquiry. Troeltsch favors a "critical idealist" view of religion, which recognizes religion's independence, creativity, and diversity.

[58] *ST*, 48; *GS* 1:31.

potential of religious ideas and organizations to contribute and to serve as a corrective to modern capitalistic society and the bureaucratic state, Troeltsch maintained a belief in religion's potential for positive influence.[59] Thus, Troeltsch's historical investigation sought to identify these positive religious forces and to demonstrate that religion, and specifically Christianity, had been an effectual force in the past and perhaps could be again.

"Purely Religious" as a Specific Kind of Social Community

Troeltsch also characterizes Christianity's origins as "purely religious" for purposes that are central to several of his tasks and arguments in the *Social Teachings*. First, Troeltsch wishes to be able to distinguish between religiously based and nonreligiously based sociological communities, and to demonstrate that each will lead to fundamentally different structures guided by fundamentally different values and ideas.[60] This is key to Troeltsch's larger aim in the *Social Teachings*—to determine what social doctrines have marked Christianity in the past, how effective these have been in addressing social problems, and what kind of contribution Christianity might make to the social situation of Troeltsch's day. Troeltsch himself makes reference to this central concern in the conclusion to the *Social Teachings*. Reflecting retrospectively on the results of his survey, he states, "The first thing we learn is, that the religious life . . . needs an independent organization, in order to distinguish it from other organizations of a natural kind."[61] If an organization founded upon religious ideals and traditions produces no distinctive kind of community or attitude toward the world, then there would be no question, in Troeltsch's mind, of a Christian contribution to society or of an "independent Christian social model."[62] The independence of religion

---

[59] See Graf, "Friendship between Experts," 225. See also Ruddies, "Ernst Troeltsch und Friedrich Naumann," 259.

[60] See, for example, *ST*, 27, 30, 31; *GS* 1:6, 9, 10.

[61] *ST*, 1006; *GS* 1:980.

[62] Voigt, *"Die Tragödie,"* 184. Voigt states that, for Troeltsch, "an analysis of Christian sociality must differentiate analytically the general sociological events, to which the Christian community [*Gemeinschaft*] is also subjected, from the special content, in this case, the social ideal of the Christian community. The point of this differentiation is to test whether and in what way the Christian social ideal leads to forms of socialization [*Vergemeinschaftungsformen*] which have their own character, so that they can be differentiated from forms of socialization of other (nonreligious) life circles" (183). Without such a distinctiveness, religious communities would be just one kind, or one expression, of a more basic social phenomenon. They would be a particular form of a more fundamental (sociological) content (185).

would be sacrificed. Troeltsch wants to affirm the potentially positive role that religion could play in modern society. Therefore, his historical investigation into the distinctiveness of religiously based social organizations attempts to contribute to this contemporary question.

Troeltsch argues that religiously based sociological systems have unique features that can illuminate their history and their relation to other social forces. Primary among these features is their difficulty in establishing a theory of social life and civilization.[63] Because Christianity, according to Troeltsch, is founded on an ideal in which God is the highest authority, it is not easy to determine what a Christian community's relation to other authorities (such as the state) ought to be, and how much certain religious values ought to be compromised in relation to other so-called nonreligious forces and institutions. Thus, to explain in part why the earliest church did not achieve the "ideal of a Christian unity of civilization" created in the medieval period, Troeltsch writes:

> After all, it is not so simple to build up a civilization and a society upon the supernatural values of the love of God and of the brethren. The self-denial and renunciation of the world which are connected with the former, and the renunciation of the claim on justice and force which are connected with the latter, are not principles of civilization, but radical and universal religious and ethical ideas, which are only absorbed with difficulty into the aims of the secular structure, and into the protective measures which the struggle for existence has produced.[64]

In fact, Troeltsch says that a purely religious society is difficult to form and inevitably inconsistent in character, since the ideals on which the community is founded must always be brought in relation to the needs and relative contexts of life in the world.[65] Thus, the various ideal types of Christian social formation—the church, sect, and mystical types—are different responses to this difficulty. For Troeltsch, the church is clearly the form of Christianity that is most successful in creating a religious social organization despite

---

[63] See *ST*, 202; *GS* 1:181.

[64] *ST*, 202; *GS* 1:181–82. Later in the text Troeltsch again names these two features of the gospel ethic (the primacy of love to God and neighbor, and the rigor of the ethic of love, which, among other things, "renounces law and violence") as the reasons for Christianity's difficulty in becoming part of the life of the larger world (*ST*, 238; *GS* 1:228).

[65] See, for example, *ST*, 98; *GS* 1:92.

the inherent difficulty of this task. In chapter 4, I discuss in greater detail the pitfalls and contributions of each type for a religiously-based social community.

"Purely Religious" as Lacking a Social Philosophy

Troeltsch's emphasis on the "purely religious" character of early Christianity is also central to one of his most fundamental arguments in the *Social Teachings*, namely, that early Christianity (for various reasons related to its own structure and historical situation) did not have a full-blown, overarching social doctrine, while medieval Christianity did. In this sense, early Christianity was "purely religious" in a way that could not be said of medieval or Calvinist Christianity.[66] Troeltsch states the issue in the following way:

> To what extent was an inward contact with, and penetration of, social life rendered possible, and how far did it lead to an inward uniformity of the collective life? In the ancient world that ideal was never attained; in the Middle Ages and in the daughter churches of the Reformation it was realized, at least in ideal and in theory; in the modern world the discord has again become evident.[67]

According to Troeltsch, early Christianity did not formulate a doctrine of how religious organizations should relate to, dominate, and participate in the larger society as medieval Catholicism and ascetic Protestantism did. Nor did it produce a theory about how the society should be brought into line with a program of social transformation according to Christian ideals as Calvinism in Geneva did. Even when the church was established in late antiquity, the focus remained on the stability and structure of its own organization and not on the transformation of the rest of society according to Christian ideals.

---

[66] This appears to be the sense in which Troeltsch means "purely religious" in the following statement: *"Sobald nun freilich um eine solche Predigt sich eine dauernde Gemeinschaft sammelt, ist es unausbleiblich, daß aus diesem Programm auch eine soziale Ordnung wird, daß die zunächst rein religiös gedachte soziologische Struktur sich in eine soziale Organisation innerhalb des übrigen Lebens umsetzt"* (*GS* 1:49). The English translation does not reflect the language of "purely religious": "We can, of course, foresee that as soon as a message of this kind creates a permanent community a social order will inevitably arise out of this programme, and that the sociological structure, which at first was conceived solely in religious terms [*rein religiös*], will be transformed into a social organization within life as a whole" (*ST*, 62).

[67] *ST*, 34; *GS* 1:14–15.

Troeltsch refers to something rather specific when he distinguishes between forms of Christianity that either have or lack an explicit social doctrine. Troeltsch recognizes only two forms of a Christian social doctrine—that of medieval Christianity and that of ascetic Protestantism. He appears to have especially great admiration for the former.[68] According to Troeltsch, the medieval church had a social doctrine in the sense that it achieved a "uniform Christian civilization" or a "Christian unity of civilization,"[69] which he defines as "the acceptance of relatively favorable actual conditions, and their fusion with the religious and ecclesiastical world into a harmoniously developed whole."[70] This was achieved through the medieval church's belief in "the divinely appointed harmony of nature and grace," which implied a natural and necessary adjustment of social institutions to the ideals and authority of the church.[71] Its social philosophy, therefore, "was indeed an all-embracing sociological system."[72] Although its character and structure are completely different from those of medieval Catholicism, ascetic Protestantism similarly is able to have a significant influence on modern society, and thus also has a social doctrine.[73]

Troeltsch distinguishes a social doctrine that extends to all of society, however, from one that has the capacity to *transform* social life according to Christian ideals. Thus, even though the medieval church organization

[68] As Harry Liebersohn states, "[E]ven though Troeltsch believed that the traditional church type was incompatible with the conditions of modern society, he admired its capacity to embrace all classes, to channel radicalism into constructive courses, and to establish realistic but elevating standards for secular behavior. . . . [A]s a sociologist he called attention to the Catholic Church's record as an exemplary shaper of social stability." *Fate and Utopia in German Sociology, 1870–1923* (Cambridge, Mass.: MIT Press, 1988) 58.

[69] *ST*, 159–60; *GS* 1:172.

[70] *ST*, 306; *GS* 1:330.

[71] *ST*, 303; *GS* 1:325.

[72] Ibid.

[73] See Troeltsch's explanation of how ascetic Protestantism is uniquely suited to modern forms of life, just as medieval Catholicism was uniquely suited to medieval society (*ST*, 691; *GS* 1:794). Despite his admiration for both, Troeltsch argues that neither of these two social philosophies can serve the distinctive needs of his present modern society. Although ascetic Protestantism was initially compatible with modern sensibilities and institutions, Troeltsch argues that the structures of modern society have become more rigid and extreme in ways opposed to their earlier character. Thus Troeltsch's admiration for medieval Catholicism and ascetic Protestantism is not an implicit endorsement of their social forms or doctrines for his present. While Christianity certainly has potential to serve modern society, the peculiar form it takes will have to be newly crafted in the present, and not simply taken from the past. See *ST*, 1012; *GS* 1:984–85.

encompassed the whole of medieval society, its social philosophy "was not a program of actual reform."[74] Troeltsch explains:

> For even now the church did not think in terms of social reform and social politics, or of shaping the connection between the economic-legal substructure and the ethico-spiritual superstructure in harmony with her ideas. . . . In this respect the church . . . was full of the most unpractical idealism. She seemed to think that if the spiritual government of the world were functioning properly, and if faith and love were strong and healthy, then all difficulties would solve themselves.[75]

Instead of infusing social institutions with Christian visions of community and social life, the church simply relied on an understanding of natural law and trusted that secular structures would naturally express a Christian ethic.[76] For Troeltsch, it is Calvinism in Geneva that first carries out the task of not only articulating a social doctrine, but carrying out social reform as well. In Troeltsch's narrative, this is the first time "a social transformation in harmony with Christian ideals" is initiated by the church type.[77]

It is central to Troeltsch's construction of Christian history, therefore, that the early church is distinguished from the medieval church in its lack of a social doctrine, and that the pursuit of social reform remains foreign to both. In emphasizing that early Christianity was "purely religious," Troeltsch sketches out his conception of the differences among the various forms of Christianity and hints at the challenges facing Christianity in his own time.

"Purely Religious": Concluding Reflections on Its Meanings

In describing earliest Christianity as "purely religious," Troeltsch is not simply making a normative claim about what Christianity ought to be in all periods. Nor is Troeltsch arguing that "true" or "authentic" Christianity has a social view (or lack thereof) similar to that of the earliest communities. Nor is Troeltsch making a covert claim about Christianity's superiority or uniqueness. On the contrary, one might just as easily suggest that because he

---

[74] *ST*, 303; *GS* 1:325.
[75] *ST*, 246; *GS* 1:240. I have changed Wyon's translation here.
[76] *ST*, 270; *GS* 1: 273.
[77] *ST*, 622; *GS* 1:677. According to Troeltsch, the sect type tends to articulate a demand for the transformation of society by means of its rigorous commitment to Christian ideals of the Sermon on the Mount, but it lacks the social organization, influence, and engagement in social (secular) institutions to carry out such programs.

views earliest Christianity as *lacking* the means for any significant societal influence, it is therefore a deficient model for thinking about Christianity's possible role in modern society.

The foregoing analysis shows that Wolfgang Stegemann's comment that Troeltsch "works implicitly with an absolute beginning of Christianity" is an overstatement.[78] In fact, Troeltsch distances himself from what he considers a certain Protestant view of the origins of Christianity, in which the original period must be absolutely new or unique in order to be significant. In a letter to Friedrich von Hügel, Troeltsch expresses his dissatisfaction with this Protestant view, while aligning himself with what he calls a more "liberal Catholic" view:

> [The liberal Catholic interpretation of Christianity] is a religious-historical point of view, according to which Christianity is the assembly point [*Sammelpunkt*] for late antique religion, and it takes hold and spiritually penetrates only from a new or deeper center. . . . Protestants, including even Harnack, cling too tightly to an abstract truth, which must have been contained already in the original, and which—if not supernaturally communicated—must at least be radically new in order to be classified as revelation.[79]

While Troeltsch surely makes many of the problematic claims about earliest Christianity and the preaching of Jesus that were typical of his circle of scholars, he by no means insists upon an absolutely unhistorical beginning of Christianity.[80] Nor does he use some allegedly ahistorical interpretation of early Christianity in order to argue for its supposed normativity.

We have seen that, in his account of earliest Christianity as purely religious, Troeltsch wishes to defend a complex historical portrait of Christian origins (focusing on, for example, its relation to social and historical factors, as well as its distinction from other forms of Christianity) and to leave the door open for

---

[78] Stegemann, "Zur Deutung," 63. Stegemann supports this claim by arguing that Troeltsch focused only on Jesus' ideas and message, and not on his social or historical context.

[79] Letter to Friedrich von Hügel, 10 March 1903, in Ernst Troeltsch, *Briefe an Friedrich von Hügel*, 63–64.

[80] Stegemann's claim ("Zur Deutung," 64) that Troeltsch "remains dependent on a finally ahistorical interpretation of the rise of Christianity" is thus incorrect. It is more accurate to suggest that Troeltsch attributes an apolitical quality to the earliest period. Furthermore, neither an ahistorical nor an apolitical origin of Christianity would necessarily make it normative for Troeltsch. That is, Troeltsch does not associate ahistorical beginnings (if they even exist) with intrinsic normativity.

an exploration of its possible contributions to modern life. Although Troeltsch neither needs nor desires to make a heavy-handed normative appeal to the origins of Christianity as representing the essence of Christianity, he does wish to tell a story in which something about the beginning of Christianity is significant and unique. For Troeltsch, earliest Christianity establishes certain possibilities and contours that shape the subsequent historical development up to and including his own present cultural and religious context. It is to these features of earliest Christianity that we now turn.

The Origins as the Site and Source of Lasting Elements of Christianity

Troeltsch objects to a conception of Christianity in which everything important is contained in its origins, which, for his time, often meant the ideas of the gospel as preached by Jesus. In the 1903 edition of the essence of Christianity essay, Troeltsch writes, "Thus it must be unavoidably concluded that the recognition of the essence [of Christianity] cannot be exclusively based on the original time and on the preaching of Jesus."[81] For Troeltsch, the "identity" of Christianity must be constructed out of a consideration of the whole of Christian history, taking into account both earlier and later expressions and historical forms. The origins of Christianity nevertheless provide certain core elements of Christianity that will be present throughout its history, albeit in radically revised forms and in combination with a variety of contrasting social conditions and circumstances.

In the earliest community, the ideas of Jesus' preaching "determine the form of the sociological structure," which is characterized by two ideas: individualism (the affirmation of the value and sanctity of the individual) and universalism (the affirmation of the value of community or fellowship). According to Troeltsch, the individualism of the gospel is a *radical* (or extreme) individualism in which the intimate and immediate relation of the individual to God is affirmed and is the basis of a focused and rigorous devotion to God's commands as articulated in the ethic of the gospel. Universalism expresses the fellowship that exists among all who are related to God. Troeltsch argues that universalism is implied in individualism insofar as all those who are children of God (as emphasized by individualism) will find their ultimate union in God (an expression of universalism). For Troeltsch,

---

[81] "Essence," 151; "'WCh," 581.

these two sociological ideas are present in all other forms of Christianity in a variety of ways. Sometimes one is prioritized and the other almost invisible; other times the two combine in a unique way to form a new kind of community.

Individualism and universalism, and the way they are related in the idea of the kingdom of God, are the sources of many other features and dynamics that mark all forms of Christianity.[82] They are related to what Troeltsch calls the radicalism and conservatism that arise in Christianity. Radicalism—which springs from individualism—represents an uncompromising commitment to the law of God as expressed in Jesus' preaching. Conservatism—which springs from universalism—signals a more Pauline emphasis on the formation of the community into a body of Christ, in which each person has a place and role. Individualism and universalism also correspond to the sect- and church-types, respectively. Mysticism, which in Troeltsch's schema is a distinctively modern form of Christian spirituality, is traced along with the sect-type back to early Christian individualism. In early Catholicism, universalism gains the upper hand in the creation of an authoritarian and hierarchical church based on a conception of universal truth, while individualism is expressed only in the monasteries and in the ability of each individual to receive a share in salvation through submission to the structures of the church. Calvinism's combination of the two gives a more central place to individualism through its unique emphasis on personality, while maintaining a strong position for universalism through its understanding of fellowship as created by God's predestinating will.

Troeltsch connects several other themes of Jesus' preaching to later developments in the history of Christianity. Jesus' "heroism" and "moral rigor" have a faint relation to the asceticism that arises in early and medieval Catholicism. Similarly, the "love communism" that characterizes Jesus' community is carried on in monastic and other reform movements in Christian history. Modern sects draw upon the apocalyptic orientation of Jesus' community and the moral ideals expressed in the Sermon on the

---

[82] Troeltsch was not the first to use the terms "individualism" and "universalism" to describe the earliest form of Christianity. They are employed in Harnack's 1902 work, *The Mission and Expansion of Christianity* (ed. and trans. James Moffat; Gloucester, Mass.: Smith, 1972), which Troeltsch used as a source for his own historical narrative in the *Social Teachings*; they were also important categories for Georg Simmel, who used them to describe the uniqueness of the Christian idea of the kingdom of God as a perfect balance of individualism and universalism.

Mount. Finally, Jesus' views on the family are the beginning of a central place for this institution throughout Christian history, solidified by Paul's articulation of a model of the family conforming to a particular social type, namely, patriarchalism.[83]

Thus, Troeltsch demonstrates the formative influence of the original period for the rest of Christian history by identifying individualism and universalism as fundamental ingredients of all Christian communities or institutions.[84] He insists, however, that the way these two elements take shape in any period has to do with unpredictable religious, social, political, and economic circumstances. So while Jesus' ideas and even Pauline doctrines are formative for the rest of Christian history, they do not determine or produce subsequent forms. These arise through unforeseeable forces and conditions that mark each period of Christianity.

Status and Normative Significance of Christian Origins

Now that we have examined Troeltsch's view of early Christianity's distinctive quality (as purely religious) and constitution (as a combination of individualism and universalism), it is helpful to revisit what place the origins have in Troeltsch's theory of Christianity. Both in the essence essay and in the *Social Teachings*, Troeltsch makes several statements that suggest that he generally does not view earliest Christianity as the normative form of Christianity against which all later forms are to be judged, or to which all other forms must correspond. He rejects arguments built on an appeal to origins. Yet, two observations must be made. First, Troeltsch indeed places special value on early Christianity and highlights its formative influence in Christian history. Second, Troeltsch occasionally associates the "true Christian ethic" with that of the earliest period, thus seemingly contradicting his arguments against such a practice. If Troeltsch does not make a simplistic appeal to the origins as the normative form of Christianity, how can one account for the

---

[83] I discuss Troeltsch's understanding of and attitude toward patriarchalism in greater depth in chs. 3 and 4.

[84] Claussen illuminates the significance of these categories (individualism and universalism) for Troeltsch's stance as a philosopher of culture. That is, Troeltsch uses the twofold ethic of Jesus to maintain that, in any social ethic, there should be a balance between the individual and the community. This enables him to criticize religious or ethical stances that overemphasize one to the detriment of the other. See Claussen, *Die Jesus-Deutung*, ch. 2 and pages 184–219, 290.

intermittent though indisputable places in Troeltsch's text where he appeals to a "true Christian ethic" or true "Christian idea" that is traced to or equated with Jesus or Paul?[85] I will examine this conundrum in more detail.

In the essay on the essence of Christianity, Troeltsch views the origins of Christianity as its "classical period." It follows implicitly from my discussion so far that Troeltsch gives this same classical status to Christianity's origins in the *Social Teachings*.[86] That is, for Troeltsch, earliest Christianity, including first and foremost "the Gospel" and Paul but also early Catholicism,[87] is "classical" for the rest of Christianity in several ways: 1) it provides the main ingredients that will be present in some form in later Christianity;[88] 2) it is a period in which Troeltsch believes Christianity was uniquely vivid and devoted to gospel ideas (this applies especially to the community around Jesus);[89] and 3) it is a focal point that later Christian churches and groups will repeatedly reinterpret and revisit, each attaching their own understandings to the earliest message(s).[90] By designating the earliest period as the "classical period" of Christian history, Troeltsch clearly gives this period a special place

[85] For example, in his discussion of Calvinism's creation of a Christian society, Troeltsch explains that "the real ideals of the Gospel" (which, we are to assume, were unconcerned with the social order) needed to be adapted, so that Calvinism could adjust and orient itself to "the practical conditions of life" (*ST*, 623; *GS* 1:677).

[86] I have made this argument in my "Conceptualizing Christianity: Troeltsch on Christian Origins in *Die Soziallehren*," in *Mitteilungen der Ernst-Troeltsch-Gesellschaft* XIII (2000) 35–47, esp. 43.

[87] According to Lannert, it was Troeltsch's innovation to include *Frühkatholizismus* in the same period as "the Gospel" and "Paul." That is, all three together form earliest Christianity. Here Troeltsch resists the typical characterization wherein there is a dramatic split between the gospel of Jesus and the development of early Catholicism, which was treated as a separate period by historians such as Baur, Ritschl, and Harnack. Instead, Troeltsch's more sociological approach to the history of early Christianity enables him to assert a continuity between Jesus, Paul, and early Catholicism. See Lannert, "Die Bedeutung," 98–99.

[88] It is crucial to note that Troeltsch does not limit the "ingredients" of Christianity to those provided by the earliest periods. Instead, he includes in the fundamental elements of Christianity ideas and developments that enter Christianity *after* the time of Jesus and Paul, such as the Stoic idea of natural law, or the Calvinist notion of calling.

[89] Troeltsch relies on the assumption, common in his time, that it is part of the essence of religions to originate among "simple" and "naïve" people, who can provide the emotional devotion and energy that is important for the longevity of a religious tradition. See *ST*, 44–45; *GS* 1:26–27.

[90] In "What Does 'Essence of Christianity' Mean?" Troeltsch states that "it is admittedly true that while Jesus maintains the central position each age interprets him really quite differently and puts its own ideas under his protection" ("Essence," 147; "²WCh," 413).

and significance in a theory of Christianity. In doing so, however, he in no way equates true Christianity unequivocally with Christian origins.

Nevertheless, there are some cases in which Troeltsch uses certain features of earliest Christianity as standards for true Christian thought. For example, when a form of Christianity develops a social doctrine that engages the secular world in a comprehensive way, Troeltsch often contrasts this development with basic "Christian ideas," which he associates with uncompromising ethical ideals[91] and lack of interest in secular structures and concerns. Thus, Troeltsch notes that the Christian unity of civilization achieved by the medieval church could not have been established directly by Christian ideas.[92] It also required certain social conditions that could enable the church to dominate society and an alliance with thought forms that could make the absolute ideals of the gospel relative, thereby making a compromise possible. Troeltsch refers to "the fiction of a Christian natural law,"[93] suggesting that "true Christian thought" could never be equated with the world-engaging and compromising orientation of a theory of natural law. Similarly, Troeltsch notes that the medieval church relativized "the radical principles of the true Christian ethic."[94]

Troeltsch also occasionally associates what he sees as a Pauline view of equality and inequality with the "true Christian ethic," and he contrasts this with later views in Christianity. He describes the "aristocratic" view of inequality,[95] wherein God is seen to have established social inequalities and divided people into "ruling peoples and slave peoples," as a theory that does not correspond to "the Christian point of view" (*die christliche Idee*).[96] On the other hand, Troeltsch rejects egalitarian conceptions of equality by saying that they "have not been developed out of the dialectic of purely Christian

---

[91] Given that the sects are characterized by their maintenance of an uncompromising commitment to the law of God as expressed in the Sermon on the Mount and the Decalogue, it is not surprising that Troeltsch states that "very often in the so-called 'sects' it is precisely the essential elements of the Gospel which are fully expressed" (*ST*, 334; *GS* 1:367).

[92] *ST*, 207; *GS* 1:185–86.

[93] *ST*, 160; *GS* 1:173

[94] *ST*, 271; *GS* 1:275. Later in the *Social Teachings*, Troeltsch states that Tolstoi's ideas are "a reminder of the essential fundamental features of the Gospel, which had been obscured by the doctrine of relative natural law" (*ST*, 729; *GS* 1:847–48).

[95] Troeltsch claims that Aristotelianism introduced an "aristocratic" conception of inequality into Christian social thought and that Thomas Aquinas appropriated it in his vision of social order.

[96] *ST*, 298; *GS* 1:316.

thought."[97] Here Troeltsch associates the *true* Christian view of equality and inequality with that held by Paul and uses this view as a standard for "purely Christian thought."

Troeltsch's occasional tendency to associate "true Christian ideas" with the earliest period should be interpreted in conversation with other positive and negative assessments he makes in the *Social Teachings*. First, it is *not* clear that, in contrasting later forms of Christianity with the "true ideals of the Gospel" as expressed by Jesus, Troeltsch is thereby criticizing the later modification. This is supported by the fact that Troeltsch shows great admiration for both medieval Catholicism and Calvinism in Geneva. He clearly views them as legitimate forms of Christianity even though he notes that they could have arisen only by modifying the "true ideals of the Gospel." Second, however, it cannot be denied that Troeltsch occasionally uses Christian origins as a normative measure for later movements, as, for example, when he criticizes and attempts to rule out of bounds what he sees as either aristocratic or revolutionary democratic conceptions of inequality and equality.[98] In these cases, however, we ought to remember that, even as he wrote history, Troeltsch was engaged in cultural diagnosis and debate. Here we can perhaps overhear Troeltsch's critique of competing political visions of modern German society.

The conclusion to be made is a complex and ambiguous one. In general, Troeltsch does not have a conception of Christianity wherein consistent and exclusive normative status is assigned to the earliest period. Instead, he often affirms later developments that diverge significantly from the character of "original" Christianity, and he argues against attempts to view everything in terms of "the Gospel." Yet, Troeltsch acknowledges certain features of Christianity that existed from the beginning and that constitute permanent tensions in its development. Finally, in rare cases, Troeltsch uses the ideas of earliest Christianity as indicators for true Christian thought. In these cases he seems less interested in pointing to the intrinsic authority of earliest Christianity and more interested in reflecting on social and political questions of his day.

Beyond its status as the "classical" period of Christian history, Troeltsch gives no clear or consistent normative position to the gospel ideas and the

---

[97] *ST*, 370–71; *GS* 1:411.

[98] In the next chapter, I discuss the indirect but nonetheless normative assessment of different views of equality and inequality that takes place in the *Social Teachings*.

community around Jesus. Although the "original period" provides essential
elements of Christianity, it does not determine how later forms will develop.
Moreover, the gospel community does not necessarily represent what is most
valuable in Christianity, as I have shown in my discussion of Troeltsch's
admiration for medieval Catholicism and ascetic Protestantism on the one
hand, and his assessment of the relatively ineffectual social doctrines of
earliest Christianity on the other. Troeltsch, therefore, does not measure later
developments against Christian origins. At the beginning of his chapter on
medieval Catholicism, Troeltsch states explicitly that he wishes to avoid a
practice, common among many of his Protestant colleagues, of justifying
certain forms of Christianity (for example, Lutheranism) as more continuous
with the gospel than other forms. He writes:

> Above all, we must be on guard against a tendency of the theologians
> . . . to discover everywhere either deformations of or derivations from
> the Gospel, or to discern everywhere foreshadowings of and preparations
> for the Reformation solution of the problem.[99]

Troeltsch follows this statement with an appeal to Ranke's suggestion that
"every historical epoch has its own direct significance in the sight of God,"
and he proceeds to argue for the relative and unique value of each period
of Christianity:

> Medieval religion and its social doctrines are neither a perversion of the
> "essence of Christianity," nor a phase of development serving other ends
> of Christian thought, but an expression of the religious consciousness
> corresponding to the general social structure, with its own advantages
> and truths, and its own faulty and terrible side. Medieval religion, and
> its corresponding form of social philosophy, should be understood
> first of all as they are in themselves; we ought only to consider their
> connection with tradition in so far as they drew from it, for their own
> need, the necessary historical nourishment and stimulus.[100]

---

[99] *ST*, 206–7; *GS* 1:186. Against what he sees as a typical Protestant view (as represented,
he notes, by Harnack) that Catholicism is a perversion of the essence of Christianity as found
in the gospel, Troeltsch writes to his friend Friedrich von Hügel: "I have never doubted that
Catholicism has its roots in the Gospel and that it necessarily (i.e., causally understood)
emerges out of the development of the Gospel" (Letter to Friedrich von Hügel, 10 March
1903, in Troeltsch, *Briefe an Friedrich von Hügel*, 65).

[100] *ST*, 207; *GS* 1:186.

Troeltsch thus objects to a conception of Christianity founded on and judged by a single and simplistic criterion and, instead, insists on more sympathetic and rigorous attention to each historical development in its own right.

Conclusion

What are the major conclusions one can make from this analysis of the interpretation and status Troeltsch gives to Christianity's origins? That is, what is the place of the earliest period in Troeltsch's larger conception of Christianity, and what does this reveal about Troeltsch's conception of historical development and normative Christianity? My analysis shows that Troeltsch views the origins of Christianity as the source of many but not all of the most important ingredients and tensions that will shape the rest of Christian history. These origins can serve as a common point of reference to which all subsequent forms of Christianity turn as they negotiate their own religious and sociological orientation.[101] While Troeltsch assigns a questionable purity and uniqueness to this period, he neither relies upon an absolute beginning of Christianity nor completely divorces earliest Christianity from social influences or forces. Finally, while Troeltsch looks to the original period as the "classical period" to be reinterpreted and engaged by every subsequent form of Christianity, he does not locate normative Christianity in its origins. On the contrary, Troeltsch seems to believe that Christianity must move beyond and add to the earliest form of Christianity in order to be an effective force in society.

This analysis of Troeltsch's view of Christian origins demonstrates the complex issues that Troeltsch is grappling with in his conception of Christianity as a tradition. Troeltsch resists a simplistic appeal to the origins as the "true" or normative expression of Christianity's fundamental meaning or identity. At the same time, Troeltsch wishes to maintain some level of

---

[101] The earliest period is not the only point to which later forms of Christianity will turn. Other periods can also provide important elements of tradition that will then shape subsequent periods. An example of this is the concept of natural law as it is worked out in the medieval church. Troeltsch states that modern approaches to Christian ethics have more in common with medieval views of natural law than with insights of the original period. He writes, "Thus the problem presented by the Middle Ages is one of great historical significance; it is also of importance for all modern historical social doctrines, which, in general, have a closer connection with mediaeval ideas than with those of the Primitive Church" (*ST*, 203; *GS* 1:182).

continuity across the various forms of Christianity, and thus he identifies fundamental elements that emerge in early Christianity and shape subsequent developments. Furthermore, Troeltsch is concerned about how his depiction of Christianity's origins and development will influence debates about the role of Christianity in society in his own time. In order to gain a more comprehensive understanding of Troeltsch's view of the relation between the origins of Christianity and later periods in Christian history, I now turn to an analysis of Troeltsch's conception of historical development. This enables me to indicate in further detail how Troeltsch allows for both continuity and change in his conception of Christianity.

CHAPTER THREE

Charting Continuity and Change: Troeltsch's Conception of Historical Development in the *Social Teachings*

In "The Cultural Significance of Calvinism"[1]—an essay written during the middle of his work on the *Social Teachings*—Troeltsch offers a remarkably illuminating and transparent account of the goals driving his historical research. Defending himself against the attack of Kiel historian Felix Rachfahl, who had lumped Troeltsch's work in the same category as Max Weber's and had criticized both on numerous counts,[2] Troeltsch explains the difference between his scholarly project and Weber's. Where Weber's analyses of Calvinism are of a strictly economic-historical nature,[3] Troeltsch's studies of Protestantism are historical investigations of an essentially religious nature.[4] His task, he says, is to give an account of the religious elements of Protestantism and to place Protestantism in its broad cultural-historical environment, showing its positive and negative effects in the realm of culture.[5] "At issue for me," states Troeltsch, "is an understanding of Protestantism in the great overall circumference of its relations, and not an economic-historical

---

[1] Troeltsch, "Die Kulturbedeutung des Calvinismus" (1910), *KGA* 8:143–81.

[2] For a detailed account of the exchanges between Weber, Troeltsch, and Rachfahl on the issue of Calvinism's relationship to capitalism, see Rendtorff and Pautler, "Einleitung" to *KGA* 8:31–46.

[3] Troeltsch, "Die Kulturbedeutung," 148.

[4] Ibid., 150.

[5] Ibid., 150. By "positive and negative," Troeltsch does not suggest some kind of normative assessment of Calvinism's influence historically. Rather, his intention is to explore the ways in which Calvinism contributed to the rise of the modern world through both direct and indirect influence.

problem."[6] For Troeltsch, this means viewing Protestantism in relation to a range of causal forces and cultural spheres, and exploring its dependence on, as well as its contribution to, social conditions and cultural developments. In his historical writings it is typical for Troeltsch to express his desire to offer a double-sided picture of Protestantism's relationship to modern culture. And indeed this is exactly how Troeltsch describes his aims concerning Protestantism in his reply to Rachfahl. He wants, on the one hand, to provide a corrective to the widespread scholarly overestimation of early Protestantism's influence on the creation of the modern world,[7] and to show instead Protestantism's profound dependence on cultural conditions and its marked contrast to the modern world. But he also wishes, on the other hand, to emphasize Protestantism's undeniable contributions to modern culture. Troeltsch defends himself against Rachfahl's charge that he overemphasizes the significance of religious motives for the development of the spirit of capitalism. "I have never asserted a completely unlimited effect of religious causality,"[8] writes Troeltsch. At the same time, Troeltsch insists that religion be recognized as a genuine "player" and causal force in the realm of culture.[9] He criticizes Rachfahl's "insurmountable mistrust of the practical effectiveness of religious teachings,"[10] and accuses Rachfahl of "historical materialism"[11] insofar as Rachfahl "holds religious ideas as unimportant for historical relations."[12]

Troeltsch's efforts to emphasize both the dependence and the autonomy of religion in relation to other cultural forces express not only his conception of historical causality—a conception that will be analyzed below—but also his complex portrait of Protestantism. Troeltsch put it well in his essay on the relation of Protestantism to the rise of the modern world:

> There can, of course, be no question of modern civilization's having been produced simply and solely by Protestantism. All that comes into question is the latter's share therein. But even this share is nothing simple and homogenous. It differs in different departments

---

[6] Ibid., 150–51.
[7] Ibid., 150, 161.
[8] Ibid., 165.
[9] Ibid., 180.
[10] Ibid., 153.
[11] Ibid., 161.
[12] Ibid., 159.

of civilization, and in them all is something more or less complex and elusive.[13]

For Troeltsch, Protestantism itself is an amalgam of diverse social and theological tendencies. Indeed, this conviction comes through strongly in his essay on the cultural meaning of Calvinism. Rachfahl's tendency to speak of Protestantism in general terms, and to fail to differentiate among diverse forms of Protestantism, is deeply irritating to Troeltsch. Thus, Troeltsch endeavors to emphasize the differences among the various forms of early and modern Protestantism, and to trace their diverse legacies in relation to the modern world.

Troeltsch's historical writings, then, are marked by two interrelated questions: How can the history of Christianity be told so that it 1) places Christian historical development in a web of multiple causal forces, including social, economic, political, cultural, and religious ones, and 2) plumbs Christianity's diverse and distinctive resources in search of a positive contribution to the crises of modernity? Both of these questions are integral to Troeltsch's conception of historical development in the *Social Teachings*. For Troeltsch, the question of historical development is not simply a factual one — though it surely is that — but is also an ethical one insofar as it compels the historian to explore diverse historical trajectories and traditions with an eye to their possible continuing contribution to contemporary life.

In this chapter, I examine the model of historical development that shapes Troeltsch's historical narrative in the *Social Teachings*. In what follows, I analyze the ways in which Troeltsch accounts for continuity and change in Christianity's social forms and doctrines. Following upon this discussion, I explore how Troeltsch envisions the relationship between social factors and religious developments. I show that as Troeltsch crafts his complex conception of historical development, he simultaneously brings Christianity's history into conversation with developments in modern society. Thus, Troeltsch's conception of Christianity's historical development expresses the twofold character of his theory of Christianity as a complex historical phenomenon with resources for modern life.

---

[13] *PP*, 41; *BP* in *KGA* 8:233.

Pluralistic Causality

Just as there is no single view of Christian origins articulated in the *Social Teachings*, so is there no obvious conception of causality at work either explicitly or implicitly in Troeltsch's historical narrative. Troeltsch gives no consistent answer to the question of what causes historical growth and change, and he presents no singular overarching conception of causality under which all events are explained and organized. Instead, he cites numerous sources for any given development in the history of Christianity, remaining open to the power of religious ideas, theological and philosophical traditions, social conditions, political arrangements, and economic developments to influence Christian social forms and doctrines.

In fact, this insistence upon a "pluralistic causality," that is, the interaction of a multiplicity of causal forces, *is* the operative theory of causality in the *Social Teachings* and in many of Troeltsch's other works on the history of Christianity and Protestantism. Troeltsch states as much at the outset of his treatment of medieval Catholicism:

> We are dealing, it is true, with the history of the social philosophy of the Church, with a doctrine, with an idea. But history of this kind does not, on that account, need to be treated purely as a process of dialectic. However largely original ideas may have their own dialectical consequence and development, still the fundamental ideas in the great fruitful systems of life are not simple and uniform; rather, to a great extent, they themselves are already the result of a complex. On the other hand, in the unending and involved interplay of various forces, as Eduard Meyer so aptly puts it, everywhere we have to take into account the element of accident and surprise, i.e., the clash of independent causal sequences, which have no inner connection with each other. Both these elements are strongly marked in the history which we are studying in this book.[14]

For Troeltsch, the history of Christian social doctrines and forms of organization is indeed about the history of ideas, including their influence in history and their development over time. Yet, the basic ideas that shape Christian social teachings themselves are products of diverse processes and traditions. Troeltsch implies that not only ideas and their histories, but also a host of

---

[14] *ST*, 206; *GS* 1:185.

other unpredictable causal forces are at work in the historical development of Christianity.

These views are consistent with what Troeltsch expresses elsewhere, most notably in his entry on historiography in the *Encyclopaedia of Religion and Ethics*,[15] first published in 1913. In this article, Troeltsch states that a primary task of history as a "pure theoretical science" is to generate conceptions of causality and to derive historical knowledge from these causal conceptions.[16] In the modern period this has become a particularly complicated and difficult task, since the "web of causality" has been "enormously enlarged and at the same time disintegrated."[17] That is, the modern historical and scientific consciousness has brought with it an awareness of the complexity of causal interactions among social, religious, political, and economic ideas, forces, and structures, while previous philosophical and religious conceptions of causality (whether natural, or based upon appeals to divine revelation and abrupt intervention) have lost their authority. Thus, he argues, an adequate conception of historical causality must be able to account for a multiplicity of forces and must be based upon theories and methods that are acceptable to modern ways of thinking.

Troeltsch's conception of historical causation as it can be distilled from the historical narrative crafted in the *Social Teachings* is informed by his commitment to the following affirmations about historical development: 1) no phenomenon should be reduced to one causal origin; 2) development ought to be construed as proceeding in both predictable and unpredictable ways; 3) development is influenced by contingencies or historical accidents; and

---

[15] "Historiography," *Encyclopaedia of Religion and Ethics*, 716–23.

[16] He writes, "Such purely objective causal explanation, based upon the widest possible experience and the most methodical application of experience, constitutes the distinctive character of history as a pure theoretical science" (ibid., 720 col. 1). Troeltsch distinguishes between historical study that is guided by "distinctively theoretical and scientific interests" and that which is grounded in other interests or attitudes, such as aesthetic or moral. Troeltsch is aware that all knowledge (including scientific-historical knowledge) is affected in some way by the interests and attitudes of the inquirer. Nevertheless, he wishes to distinguish as much as possible those kinds of scholarly pursuits that aim to be "scientific," "theoretical," and as "objective" or "empirical" as possible, on the one hand, from those that have a more overt constructive interest or commitment, on the other. See ibid., 718 cols. 1 and 2.

[17] Ibid., 717 col. 2. Troeltsch states something similar at the close of the *Social Teachings*. Speaking of the importance of new insights into the role of economic and social influences in the development of religious ideas, he states, "As in all other spheres of life, so also in that of the history of religion, the conception of the causal connection is considerably widened and altered by giving fresh attention to this cooperating element" (*ST*, 1002; *GS* 1:975–76).

4) new forces can be introduced into or arise within an historical trajectory. Let us discuss each of these in turn.

Troeltsch's model of pluralistic causality partially rests on what can be called an antireductionist view of causation. No singular causal force necessarily determines or takes precedence over any other factor in the causal mix. Indeed, according to Troeltsch, this is part of what distinguishes historical from natural causation. The latter, he argues, traces all events to a "changeless, all-pervading, and, in all particular cases, identical law of reciprocity." The former is influenced by and founded upon many forces, including nonquantitative factors such as psychological motivation.[18]

In the *Social Teachings*, Troeltsch expresses this antireductionist view of causality in two ways. First, as I have shown in chapter 2, Troeltsch bases his critique of Marxist historians largely on their refusal to recognize religion as a legitimate force in social and historical development. He describes their view of causality as marked by a "doctrinaire fanaticism" that wishes to reduce every historical event to one cause or origin, that is, an economic one.[19] Second, just as he opposes a view of causality centered only on economic influences, so does he resist a conception of Christianity's development as shaped only by religious influences. Indeed, despite his effort to protect the "independence" of religious phenomena, Troeltsch recognizes and draws attention to the importance of economic and social factors for Christianity's development. Against efforts to remove Christianity from the web of causal connections that characterizes history or to see all religious developments as arising from some "law" or "necessity," he writes, "Causality knows no hierarchy; no degree of greater or lesser importance, and so it is no depreciation of previous theories (as many people suppose) if this newly discovered [economic and social] causality is granted just as much right to exist as those which were previously in a position of honour."[20] For Troeltsch, acknowledging the role of social and political forces in shaping Christianity's history in no way threatens the integrity of Christianity, but rather makes possible a more thorough and illuminating understanding of it.

The various forces that Troeltsch includes in his conception of development produce both predictable and unpredictable outcomes. Some processes work

---

[18] "Historiography," 719 col. 2. Troeltsch continues to hold this position even in his late works. See *GS* 3:48–49, 55–56.

[19] *ST*, 466; *GS* 1:432.

[20] *ST*, 1003; *GS* 1:976.

themselves out in a way "akin to logical evolution."[21] Troeltsch describes the development of the idea of papal authority and a papal-centered hierarchy, for example, as "the dogma which completes the sociological tendency [in Christianity] toward unity, as it was bound to develop and become complete once the process had begun by which the church and the Christian priesthood were conceived as the body of Christ."[22] Troeltsch recognizes a clear and logical progression from the Pauline idea of centering and unifying the community around the mystical Christ, to the formalization of this unity in the establishment of bishops who alone control and administer the sacraments, to the organization of these bishops under a common and central authority. It is a move that begins with an urge toward community and union, and completes itself in the full establishment of an institution whose unity and authority stretch over everything. "In this we see absolutely clearly the completion of the sociological idea of the church."[23]

Other logical developments see their effects not immediately but after a long period of delay. The tendency in Christianity toward the sociological form of the sect was latent in the basic ideals of earliest Christianity but was not "activated" until a much later historical, social, and religious situation. Speaking of the church as the "conservative" tendency in Christianity and the sect as the "radical" tendency, Troeltsch notes that while both were there from the beginning, "in the central period of the Middle Ages, however, this second tendency broke forth afresh with extraordinary power."[24] The emergence of the sect "adds a new feature to the presentation of these doctrines, a feature which had been latent from the very beginning, but which only now emerges clearly."[25] Thus, whether produced immediately or later, some developments in Christianity's history are more or less predictable.

Troeltsch also describes historical development, however, in a way that often emphasizes the unpredictable or surprising outcomes of certain tendencies and forces. Medieval Catholicism was built on a unique theory

[21] "Historiography," 720 col. 2.

[22] *ST*, 228; *GS* 1:211.

[23] *ST*, 227; *GS* 1:211.

[24] *ST*, 330; *GS* 1:359.

[25] *ST*, 330; *GS* 1:361. Another example is the delayed effect of the fusion of Christian and Stoic thought in the third century. Centuries later this ancient fusion "now produces fresh forms of life" (*ST*, 259; *GS* 1:254). Again, in the early modern period the rationalistic elements first introduced into Christianity by Stoicism become active and help contribute to the destruction of the medieval synthesis.

combining organic and patriarchal thought. While the elements of this theory made possible the church's unity of civilization, their later development would produce surprising results. He writes:

> The various underlying tendencies connected with this [organic and patriarchal] theory, however, later on in the process of historical development have led away from Catholic doctrine in a very different direction, to emancipation and secularization, to modern developments of individual elements. The constituent parts which represented the ideas of the organism, of individualism, and of natural law were joined with the nascent liberalism, while the patriarchal and positivist ideas were linked up with the purely realistic absolutist doctrine of sovereignty, whether in the form of the Machiavellian tyranny, or as we see it in the religious guise in the doctrine of Divine Right.[26]

Thus, the elements that make up a particular theory develop in unpredictable ways, especially when combined with new ideas or when transformed through a new historical situation.

The unpredictability of historical development is closely related to the issue of contingency. Troeltsch often attributes contingencies, or historical accidents, to the intersection of disparate causal lines (*Kausalreihen*) that come together in particular historical settings and create new and unforeseeable results.[27] Troeltsch refers to the connection between capitalism and Calvinism, for example, as an "historical accident" insofar as neither alone would have produced the phenomenon they together helped create, that is, bourgeois capitalism with a spiritual support. Troeltsch says the same about Catholicism and medieval feudalism.[28] As Troeltsch explains, "The Christian ethic only attained a great actual importance for world-history when it was supported by an 'accident' of this kind. In itself alone, when it did not receive

---

[26] *ST*, 293; *GS* 1:310.

[27] Troeltsch defines contingency as "the convergence of a series of mutually independent causes. . . . In virtue of this contingency, processes of development are commingled, furthered, amplified, obstructed, and sometimes even completely arrested; though, of course, the syntheses thus fortuitously brought about may occasionally give rise to new and fruitful developments" ("Historiography," 720 col. 2, and 721 col. 1).

[28] Troeltsch writes of Calvinism and capitalism, "The conjunction of these two elements itself is an historical accident, as I have said already in describing the similarly comparatively close affinity between the mediaeval system and the Catholic ethic" (*ST*, 915 n. 388; *GS* 1:714 n. 388).

this support, it simply remained in the realm of theory."[29] Highlighting the contingency of Christianity's historical development, Troeltsch notes that other forms of Christianity might also have been capable of great historical influence had an "accidental" and compatible social system been available at the same time and place.[30]

By "accident" Troeltsch does not mean anything dismissive or pejorative. He is simply acknowledging the interdependence of religious and social developments. In fact, Troeltsch even suggests that the divine might be present in accidents and contingencies. "If I speak here of an 'accident,' this is naturally meant logically, i.e., that here there is no immanent development, not that these things have happened *sine Deo*."[31] This is an important comment. It reveals the error of assuming that Troeltsch kept the religious and social separate and shows instead that Troeltsch suspected that God is somehow present in the whole historical process.

In Troeltsch's conception of historical development, processes converge to create new phenomena and forces that are introduced into the complex or amalgam that is Christianity's history. He writes, "In the historical process, moreover, there ever emerges the fact of the new, which is no mere transformation of existent forces, but an element of essentially fresh content, due to a convergence of historical causes."[32] Thus, Troeltsch tells of the entrance of wholly new elements into Christianity—elements which were not there in the beginning, were not a part of Jesus' or Paul's preaching nor a part of some founding revelation at the base of Christianity. These elements would not have emerged by means of Christian ideas or developments alone. Troeltsch, therefore, conceptualizes Christianity as syncretic and allows for genuine novelty in the development of an historical phenomenon. Something which was not present at the origin, therefore, can come to be a prominent and authoritative feature of Christianity in a later period.

---

[29] *ST*, 915–16 n. 388; *GS* 1:714 n. 388.

[30] By reserving an important place for contingency in his conception of historical development, Troeltsch shows that he does not view development simply as straightforward progress, but also insists on the possibility of regression and "exhaustion . . . as well as advance" ("Historiography," 720 col. 2). This is further demonstrated by the fact that he acknowledges that some expressions of Christianity do not develop at all. He points out, for example, that the "aggressive type" of sect with its apocalyptic vision and its acceptance of violence as a legitimate form of social action "burnt itself out [*ist erschöpft*] in the seventeenth century" (*ST*, 802; *GS* 1:942).

[31] *ST*, 916 n. 388; *GS* 1:714 n. 388.

[32] "Historiography," 719 col. 2.

Troeltsch frequently uses the word *Verschmelzung* (fusion) to refer to the syncretization of Stoicism and Christianity in the period of the early church. Originally, Stoicism is distinct from Christianity, a parallel movement in late antiquity. In the third century, Christian scholars begin to appropriate certain religious and philosophical elements of Stoicism—namely, those ideas connected with the Stoic doctrine of natural law—that enable Christianity to solve problems and tensions it could not have dealt with by means of its own resources. Stoicism thus gives the early Christian ethic, which Troeltsch describes as "clumsy both in its terminology and its conceptions," a "theoretical foundation and a terminology."[33] The Stoic doctrine of natural law, along with its view of humans as common possessors of divine reason, provides a solution to the problem of the relation between the church and the state.

This appropriation of Stoic natural-law thinking transforms Christianity decisively, not only in the period of early Catholicism, but also for many centuries to come. As Klaus Tanner notes, Troeltsch holds that the early church's doctrine of a Christian natural law, based largely upon an appropriation of Stoic thought, "sets free two opposing impulses," one which compromises with and accepts the world as it is in its fallen condition and another which is driven by a revolutionary element which does not compromise but instead demands change in accordance with the law of God.[34] The former is at work in the construction of a "uniform Christian civilization" in the Middle Ages,[35] while the latter is at work in the early modern movements that lead to the destruction of church domination in the seventeenth century. Were it not for Stoic elements of Christianity, such developments may have never occurred.[36] Here, then, something that was not original to Christianity nevertheless decisively shaped its history.

---

[33] *ST*, 143; *GS* 1:144.

[34] Klaus Tanner, "Das 'Kulturdogma' der Kirche. Ernst Troeltschs Naturrechtsdeutung," in *Ernst Troeltschs Soziallehren* (ed. Graf and Rendtorff) 127. Tanner also notes that the actualization of one of these impulses depends not simply upon the "ideal factors of historical development," but more upon "the sociological forms in which Christian ideas are transmitted" (ibid.).

[35] *ST*, 159; *GS* 1:172.

[36] As Tanner states, "With the help of natural-law thinking, Christianity first developed culture-forming and reforming impulses" ("Das 'Kulturdogma,'" 125).

Continuity: Seeds of Possibility and Development

In the previous chapter, I showed how Troeltsch establishes continuity in Christian history and among diverse forms of Christianity by holding up individualism and universalism as fundamental elements of every Christian social organization and community. Thus his affirmation that a multiplicity of complex and contingent forces contributes to Christianity's historical development does not rule out the continuity or coherence of Christian tradition and history. In his historical narrative, Troeltsch often uses the term *Keim* ("seed," "germ") to demonstrate the continuity—however marked or slight—between two historically distant forms of Christianity. He also uses it to link a later development with some feature or possibility within earliest Christianity.[37]

Troeltsch links the organizational structure of society and church in the Middle Ages to previous forms of Christianity, dating back to its origins. On the one hand, Troeltsch states that the "ladder-like organization of society" that marks medieval Christianity is unprecedented and could never have occurred in earlier periods of Christian history. It was inextricably linked to feudalism and was based on certain religious and social understandings that were in stark tension with those of earlier forms of Christianity. Yet Troeltsch is able to find a germ, or seed (*Keim*), of this medieval church organization in certain aspects of early Catholicism, Paulinism, and the gospel. The medieval unity of civilization, which emerges out of the context of feudalism and the power that was afforded church leaders through their roles in the territorial churches

---

[37] Georg Iggers (*The German Conception of History*, 184) underestimates the degree of continuity that remains in Troeltsch's conception of historical development even after he has left his Idealist tendencies behind and has moved again to a more Rankean perspective. Iggers argues that in the *Social Teachings* Troeltsch presents the different forms of Christian social organization as "isolated static facts" and does not "trace their dynamic relationship." Instead, "history appears as the recurrence of change, among different types of institutions and ideas, instead of development. Troeltsch no longer speaks of growth, but now refers to Ranke's concept of the immediacy of all epochs to God." Iggers is referring in part to Troeltsch's change from his position in *The Absoluteness of Christianity and the History of Religions*, which maintains a more idealist unifying schema under which all religious developments were ordered and related, to his presentation of historical development in the *Social Teachings*, which Iggers rightly describes as more skeptical about the possible convergence of all diverse historical forms and religions into one unified process. Iggers overlooks the significant continuity and interrelation between different forms of Christianity in the *Social Teachings* and also overestimates the degree to which Troeltsch has fully adopted a Rankean perspective.

(*Landeskirchen*), is built in part on the early Catholic (*frühkatholisch*) idea
of the absolute authority of the priesthood (and eventually of the pope) and
the absolute truth possessed by the church. Early Catholicism develops the
notion of a sacramental church and a conception of the priesthood in which
only priests are able to administer the sacraments. This produces a hierarchical
sacerdotal system—a system of theocratic authority—that "contained the
germ [*Keim*] of a ladder-like organization of the whole of society."[38] This
germ is not developed until the later social situation provides the propitious
context and conditions for its actualization.

Similarly, the hierarchical system of early Catholicism itself has its germ
in Pauline patriarchalism, in which differences in ability and strength are
made "ethically fruitful" by assigning each person a role in a larger patriarchal
sociological system. Those who are strong "serve" and "take care of" the
weak, while the weak serve and obey the strong. The basic idea of Christian
patriarchalism, which Troeltsch identifies as a new sociological type, is "the
willing acceptance of given inequalities, and of making them fruitful for the
ethical values of personal relationships. . . . All action is the service of God
and is a responsible office, authority as well as obedience." This is the germ
of the early Catholic formation of a "compact social system, with its various
grades of authority and subordination."[39]

Stretching the link back further into the past, Pauline patriarchalism has
its germ in the "basic idea of the worth of personality [read *individualism*]
and of the unconditional fellowship of love [read *universalism*]" that are the
sociological characteristics of the gospel.[40] Thus, although the medieval view
of the church—its structure, its authority—is far from the ideas and ideals
that marked the earliest community around the gospel, Troeltsch is able to
identify a "germ" of medieval Catholicism in earliest Christianity. He traces
the movement of this germ through its development in Pauline patriarchalism,
early Catholic sacerdotalism, and theocratic authority, and finally into the
overarching medieval system of organization.

By finding "germs" of later developments in earlier aspects of Christianity,
Troeltsch is not suggesting some kind of determinism in his model of

---

[38] *ST*, 99; *GS* 1:93.

[39] *ST*, 78; *GS* 1:68. Already in his explication of the Pauline conception of patriarchalism
Troeltsch foreshadows its ultimate course: "[Patriarchalism] only attained its full development
certainly in the Middle Ages, and then acquired its specific character with which we shall
deal later on" (*ST*, 78; *GS* 1:67).

[40] *ST*, 76; *GS* 1:66.

continuity. In other words, a germ does not inevitably or lawfully lead to or produce a later manifestation. What a germ or seed will become depends in large part on the social and political contexts in which a religious organization is located. In fact, alongside his affirmation of the continuity between the ideas of the gospel and medieval Catholicism, Troeltsch points out how foreign the medieval unity of civilization and the hierarchical structure of the medieval church were to the basic ideas of the gospel: "The Gospel, which was a completely non-sacramental and purely ethical Gospel, has thus assimilated a complex of ideas which was also alien to its basis in Judaism."[41] Again Troeltsch challenges those who assume that the early church contained the ideal of a "striving after a unity of Christian civilization," stating that "[t]he whole of our inquiry up to this point . . . proves that this assumption is unwarranted."[42] Moreover, the gospel's same basic religious ideas of the value of personality and the universal fellowship of love, that is, of individualism and universalism, are developed and articulated in a variety of contrasting forms of Christianity, including the theocracy of the medieval period, monasticism, Lutheranism, Calvinism, and radical sects. Thus, a particular seed or germ does not develop into only one form of Christianity, but rather when combined with particular social and religious situations, it can be present in different forms and in quite contrasting religious and sociological structures. Therefore, in identifying the germ in early Christianity that could lead to medieval Catholicism, Troeltsch simply finds a coherence between earlier and later phenomena, and is not sketching a linear course of inevitable development. Nevertheless, while traditions develop in unpredictable and unforeseen ways based on their interaction with social and other forces and circumstances, what ultimately arises can be connected with elements or tendencies that were present in earlier forms of Christianity. By pointing to sources of continuity in Christian history, therefore, Troeltsch defends the

---

[41] *ST*, 95; *GS* 1:89.

[42] *ST*, 202; *GS* 1:181. In a footnote to this discussion of the distance between the ideals of the early and medieval churches, Troeltsch writes, "My treatment of the subject will show, above all, that this Catholic unity of civilization, regarded from the historical or from the systematic point of view, is not the obvious 'flowering' of the Christian idea" (*ST*, 199 n. 80; *GS* 1:182 n. 80). To refute appeals to simple continuity between two different forms of Christianity, Troeltsch emphasizes the distance between medieval and earliest Christianity. Yet Troeltsch asserts a continuity between the gospel and Catholicism when he argues against those who suggest that Catholicism was contrary to the "essence" of Christianity, while the Reformation was a continuation of the essence. Here Troeltsch attempts to refute arguments that would try to hold up one form of Christianity as more normative than another.

coherence of its identity over time, while also testifying to the role that ideas continue to play in influencing historical development.

The Interaction (*Wechselwirkung*) of Religious and Social Phenomena

The analysis in the two previous sections suggests that Troeltsch's conception of historical development shows a dual commitment to taking seriously the continuity and integrity of Christianity as a *religious* historical phenomenon, while simultaneously insisting that Christianity be located in the complex web of social-historical processes and causal interactions. At times this dual commitment is difficult to maintain.

Troeltsch's treatment in the *Social Teachings* of the connection between Calvinism and modern democracy demonstrates the complex relation he is trying to maintain between religious and social factors in his conception of historical development. Troeltsch's basic argument about the relation between Calvinism and democracy is that although Calvin's Geneva was not a democratic society, it nevertheless produced "an impulse in the direction of democracy."[43] The elements of Calvinism that cohered well with democratic ideals were as follows: 1) Calvinism protected the welfare of the individual, primarily in the form of the right to revolt against oppressive and unjust rulers; 2) Calvinism taught that the structures and decisions of the state should conform to reason; 3) through the sermon, Calvinism appealed to the voice and interest of the masses; 4) Calvinism held that when all political authorities are lacking or corrupt, the law should come from the will of the people; and 5) Calvin's view of natural law had a stronger rational element than did previous versions in Christianity.

Troeltsch emphasizes that these features and ideas of Calvinism were not themselves directly democratic in the modern sense of the word. Democracy, according to Troeltsch, is characterized primarily by its foundation in a rationalistic conception of equality, wherein society is constructed so as to support and defend the equality of all persons by virtue of their common possession of reason. Calvinism's democratic tendencies derive not from an abstract or rationalistic conception of society or human nature, but from Christian interpretations of natural law, Old Testament law, and New Testament ideals. Troeltsch explains, for example, that the emergence of

---

[43] *ST*, 628; *GS* 1:684.

a social contract idea in Calvinism is different from the notion of a social contract in its "later purely rationalistic realization, which it experienced in the classical modern natural law of the Enlightenment, set free from theology."[44] The Calvinistic version derives from previous notions of natural law in Christianity, such as the "Aristotelian-organic theory" developed in medieval Catholicism. Troeltsch further qualifies this by adding:

> At the same time this social contract according to natural law is interpreted essentially in light of the Old Testament Scriptures, in which it is regarded as a covenant between God on the one hand and the ruler and the people on the other; it is thus something quite different from the primitive social contract of classical natural law. The ideas of natural law and of a covenant are applied in a thoroughly theological manner, since they represent an original archetypal ingredient contained in the Bible and in every governmental relationship whose aim is not so much that of making possible a rational construction of the state as that of the exercise of a moral and religious control of the dominant historic powers.[45]

In the Calvinistic conception of society, therefore, the primary concern is not a rationalistic construction of the state nor a rationalistic defense of equality.[46]

At the same time, however, Troeltsch cannot deny nor does he wish to deny that Calvinism contributed to the rise of modern democracy. Calvinism's primary contribution to democracy was to serve as a "spiritual backbone"[47] and additional "impetus"[48] for democracy's principles and ideas. Through its religious ideas, Calvinism helped "prepare the way" for the rise of democratic theories that otherwise might not have emerged with such power.[49] Further, the

[44] *ST*, 631; *GS* 1:691.

[45] *ST*, 632; *GS* 1:692.

[46] Troeltsch states that "by the very fact of its fundamentally religious and metaphysical individualism, by its retention of the idea of the essential inequality in human life, and by its conservative feeling for law and order, it [Calvinism] has escaped the most dangerous results of democracy: mere majority rule and abstract equality" (*ST*, 640–41; *GS* 1:703).

[47] *ST*, 640; *GS* 1:702.

[48] *ST*, 671; *GS* 1:757.

[49] Troeltsch argues that, in order to rise to prominence, certain democratic theories that had entered Christianity around the third century through its fusion with Stoicism needed to sever their connection with Christian thought so they could be formulated and developed in a different way. Thus Calvinism "prepared the way" for this split by developing doctrines that had strong democratic tendencies. See *ST*, 640–41; *GS* 1:702.

inward affinity between Calvinism's ideas and democratic structures helped sustain these structures when they arose. This is especially the case when the free church system arises. Because the free church system emphasized strong individualistic and sect elements—ultimately to the extent that it not only broke away from the church type but actually helped destroy the medieval and early Protestant idea of a church control of civilization[50]—it also promoted the rearrangement of society according to a democratic separation of church and state.[51]

Troeltsch discusses not only what we might call the indirect influence of Calvinism on societal changes, but also the impact of social conditions on the development of Calvinist thought itself. Thus the question is not simply, "Did Calvinism contribute to a certain social form?" but also "Did a certain social form (or setting) contribute to the shape of Calvinism?" Here again Troeltsch's answer is a cautious "yes and no." Troeltsch states that "from the very beginning the Genevan situation helped to determine Calvin's political, social, and economic ideal." This "led to that adaptation to conditions which only revealed its full significance at a much later period."[52] This last comment is an allusion to the development of modern and democratic religious systems that emerge out of the history of Calvinism, namely the free church system and ascetic Protestantism in general. Thus, the social setting helps shape not only Calvin's ideas, but also helps account for the development of these ideas in new directions at a later period. When the free church system arises, it is in large part a result of the reciprocal influence of newly revised and developed religious ideals and the principles and social conditions of a democratic society.

The tension that Troeltsch is trying to maintain among religious ideas, social conditions, and secular ideas is illustrated in his dual position that: 1) when Calvinism and modern society are united, it is largely because Calvinist ideas have adjusted to social conditions and not because Calvinism could have achieved this rapprochement on its own; but 2) precisely because this adaptation to modern society indeed occured, it "must have been based inwardly on the spirit of Calvinism."[53] Something about the nature of Calvinism itself must have made it particularly open to, if not singularly

[50] *ST*, 656; *GS* 1:733.
[51] *ST*, 656–57; *GS* 1:734.
[52] *ST*, 625; *GS* 1:681.
[53] Ibid.

productive of, this kind of development. Speaking of the relation between Calvinism and French and American democracy, Troeltsch argues that although Calvinism helped "prepare the way" for both forms of democracy, "this preparatory process developed against the actual intention of Calvinism." Nevertheless, "there is certainly a facility of Calvinism for adapting itself to democracy."[54]

Troeltsch's treatment of the relation between Calvinism and democracy illustrates some of his normative concerns about the quality of modern democratic and capitalist institutions and trends in his own time. While Troeltsch is eager to acknowledge a reciprocal influence between religious and social developments, he also wishes to maintain some limited autonomy for Christianity, its social forms and social ideals.[55] This is not only to preserve Christianity's integrity but also to separate it normatively—when he wishes to do so—from certain developments in modern society. Specifically, although Troeltsch is eager to underscore the connection between and compatibility of Christian views of the person and the modern appreciation for the freedom of the individual personality, he also wishes to distinguish modern Christianity from the values of modern capitalism and rationalistic individualism. Thus by acknowledging continuities and discontinuities between Calvinism and modern democracy, Troeltsch is able to affirm the connections between Christianity and modern society while leaving room for a Christian critique of certain modern institutions. In the next section, I explore in more detail the normative elements in Troeltsch's construction of Christianity's historical development.

The Boundaries of Christian Social Philosophy

Although Troeltsch wishes to construe Christianity's historical development in a way that places it squarely in the flux of historical changes and relationships, and therefore expects that Christianity will take many forms, he also places limits on Christianity's possible development. Christianity may indeed be transformed through its reciprocal relation to other historical forces, but there are boundaries beyond which a particular development becomes "non-

---

[54] *ST*, 640; *GS* 1:703.

[55] Troeltsch emphasizes Calvinism's limited autonomy when he explains that "Calvinism has become that form of Christianity which has an inward affinity with the modern democratic movement, and can enter into contact with it without injuring its religious ideas" (Ibid.).

Christian." Indeed, as Troeltsch crafts his account of Christianity's historical development, normative considerations are also at stake. Troeltsch constructs historical Christianity in dialogue with what he perceives as the strengths and weaknesses of various forms and aspects of modernity. The boundaries Troeltsch establishes for Christianity's development can be identified by tracing the way in which he crafts Christianity's historical development in relation to Stoic ideas. Through his depiction of the affinities and contrasts between Christianity and Stoicism, and through his portrait of their overlapping but distinct historical trajectories, both Troeltsch's complex picture of historical development and his normative concerns about modern German society are revealed. I have shown the way in which Troeltsch's account of the fusion of Christianity and Stoicism in the third century C.E. signals the important place he reserves for novelty in his conception of historical development. My discussion here will show that as he crafts his narrative of Christianity's historical development, Troeltsch uses the category of Stoicism to place limits on Christianity's development and to bolster the critique of modern rationalism that is implicit in the *Social Teachings*.

The Compatibility of Stoicism and Early Christianity

In the early sections of the *Social Teachings*, Troeltsch emphasizes both the affinities between Stoicism and Christianity[56] and the ways in which Stoic concepts supplement and improve upon Christian social doctrine. In the context of late antiquity, for example, the Stoics articulated ideas that were "very similar" to those contained in Jesus' preaching.[57] For Troeltsch, the distinctiveness of the gospel ethic[58] was its dual value of the individual

---

[56] Troeltsch also lists several ways in which Stoicism is different from earliest Christianity. Stoicism is an "upper class" faith, "bound up with all the existing institutions," and lacking any message of "world renewal"; Christianity, on the other hand, in its earliest stage, is "a movement of the lower classes," remote from social institutions, and proclaiming a "new type of community" (*ST*, 67–68; *GS* 1:54–55). Nevertheless, the general impression in the early sections of the *Social Teachings* is that the two are quite similar.

[57] *ST*, 64; *GS* 1:52.

[58] Troeltsch calls the ethic of Jesus' community "the Gospel ethic" and equates this with "the fundamental idea underlying the preaching of Jesus" (*ST*, 51; *GS* 1:34). Despite his efforts to problematize reconstructions of earliest Christianity and claims about the historical Jesus, Troeltsch (in his section on Jesus' movement in the *Social Teachings*) nevertheless basically follows Harnack's interpretation of "the Gospel," or "Jesus' preaching," as fundamentally about "the fatherhood of God and the brotherhood of man." Yet Lannert points out that Troeltsch vacillates between a view like Harnack's and a more history-of-religions

and the community, or its "individualism" (the emphasis on the "individual soul" and its relation to God) and its "universalism" (the call to fellowship or community). The Stoic conception of the universal law of nature leads to a similar dual emphasis on the "religious and ethical personality" (read *individualism*) and the urge toward ethical unity and participation in a social system (read *universalism*). Thus at this point in Troeltsch's historical narrative, Stoicism "forms a complete analogy with the sociological thought of Christianity."[59]

In early Catholicism, Stoicism provides the theoretical foundation that enables the church to resolve its relation to the "secular" world, and that later becomes instrumental in the medieval church's achievement of a unity of civilization.[60] Until this point in its history, the church had only been able to focus on and conceptualize its inner order, but it had not worked out an understanding of its relation to orders or systems "beyond" the church. Troeltsch describes the church's (and early Christianity's) view of the state until this time as caught in a dualistic tendency of accepting the existing order on the one hand and yet opposing it on the other—but with no theory to explain or resolve this dualism. The Stoic doctrine of natural law enables the church to understand laws of the state as part of the natural law that is from God. This means that the church can accept and compromise with the secular order. At the same time, Christians are able to avoid a deification of the state by seeing the laws of the existing order as tarnished by the fall; these can then be contrasted with the true natural law that ruled before the fall, in the original state, and their harshness and distance from the true law of God can be explained.

Natural law is divided, therefore, into what Troeltsch calls a relative natural law, corresponding to sinful conditions, and an absolute and uncorrupted

---

interpretation (emphasizing the apocalyptic orientation of Jesus' message) along the lines of Johannes Weiss. See Berthold Lannert, "Die Bedeutung," 92–93.

[59] *ST*, 65; *GS* 1:53. Elsewhere, Troeltsch states, "Stoicism and Christianity in their origins were analogous in many respects." See "Stoic-Christian Natural Law and Modern Secular Natural Law," in *Religion in History*, 329; "Das stoisch-christliche Naturrecht und das moderne profane Naturrecht," in *GS* 4:176.

[60] Troeltsch states that "the fiction of a Christian natural law . . . will be the means through which it will become possible to speak of a Christian unity of civilization at all" (*ST*, 160; *GS* 1:173). Troeltsch also alludes to the importance of early Christianity's appropriation of Stoicism for the medieval unity of civilization in several other places, including *ST*, 257–58, *GS* 1:252–54; and *ST*, 268–70, *GS* 1:271–73.

natural law of the original state prior to sin.[61] The relative natural law is both "a result of sin and a remedy against sin."[62] That is, with the concept of a relative natural law, the laws of the state can be explained as the result of sin, while human obedience to them can be encouraged and demanded by holding them up as a remedy against further sin. Here, then, the church compromises with the secular order. The absolute natural law remains, however, as the untarnished and uncompromising ideal, corresponding to the original state of humans before sin. This absolute natural law can be used to criticize secular laws, and it can also be held up as an ideal lived out only in the monasteries and priesthood.

Thus Troeltsch presents the history of early Christianity in a way that emphasizes Stoicism's compatibility with Christianity.[63] This underscores Stoicism's value as a resource for the development of reforming and communal impulses in Christianity.[64]

Foreshadowing the Dialogue with Modernity: Latent Tensions between Stoicism and Christianity

In his treatment of early Christianity, Troeltsch alludes to the "rationalism" of Stoicism's view of the human person and its accompanying vision for society.

> In this Natural Law, however, there still remains the root idea of Stoic rationalism—that is, that God is related to the universe as the soul is to the body, and the rational equality of all beings endowed with reason; from this root rationalistic reactions will arise, until, in the seventeenth century, when they have developed their full power, they will destroy the ecclesiastical civilization itself.[65]

In Troeltsch's view, Stoics held that the original state of human nature before corruption is "characterized mainly by freedom, equality, and absence of force."[66] It follows that the ideal for human society is to live in absolute

---

[61] *ST*, 154; *GS* 1:164.

[62] *ST*, 153; *GS* 1:164.

[63] Troeltsch states that "at this point the doctrine of the church was so closely related to that of the Stoics that we may almost infer that there was some direct connection between the two" (*ST*, 154; *GS* 1:165).

[64] See Tanner, "Das 'Kulturdogma,' " 125.

[65] *ST*, 161; *GS* 1:174.

[66] *ST*, 152–53; *GS* 1:162.

equality and freedom. As Troeltsch writes, Stoicism's "rationalist ideal . . . infers or deduces, at least for the primitive state [*Urstand*], the principle of abstract equality from the possession of reason by all."[67] This view of the person, and the corresponding view of society, is not compatible with that of an absolute ecclesiastical authority that rules over church and society and places human beings in a hierarchical system of organization. For this reason, as Troeltsch states, this rationalistic view ultimately will help bring about the destruction of the medieval unity of civilization.

This fact alone does not trouble Troeltsch. Despite his admiration for medieval Catholicism he does not bemoan the destruction of ecclesiastical civilization.[68] Indeed, in his allusions to "Stoic rationalism" in the early sections of the *Social Teachings*, Troeltsch signals a tension between Stoic and Christian conceptions of the human person and the social order. Unlike Christian social doctrine, Stoic rationalism promotes complete social equality, often producing radical democratic or revolutionary movements and ideas.

Troeltsch obviously prefers what he calls the Christian view of equality and inequality,[69] as well as the social forms this view entails. Christian social philosophy promotes spiritual but not social or secular equality. The Christian view of equality has a *religious* basis, that is, one founded on an understanding of the relation between humans and God, and is, therefore, limited to the religious sphere.[70] All humans are created and loved by God, and are thus equal in God's sight. This equality, however, does not necessarily extend to the secular world.[71] Although for Troeltsch this view of equality and inequality was implicit in the gospel itself, it is first articulated by Paul and is built into his unique sociological theory of love-patriarchalism (*Liebes-*

---

[67] *ST*, 76; *GS* 1:65.

[68] Harry Liebersohn rightly states that "even though Troeltsch believed that the traditional church type was incompatible with the conditions of modern society, he admired its capacity to embrace all classes, to channel radicalism into constructive courses, and to establish realistic but elevating standards for secular behavior. . . . [A]s a sociologist he called attention to the Catholic Church's record as an exemplary shaper of social stability" (*Fate and Utopia in German Sociology*, 58).

[69] Troeltsch states that there is a "peculiar conception of equality and inequality which belongs to the Christian religious-sociological idea" (*ST*, 71; *GS* 1:60).

[70] *ST*, 72; *GS* 1:60.

[71] Troeltsch is not here advocating what he would call an "aristocratic" notion of natural inequality, which he also sees as "un-Christian." On the other hand, Troeltsch is opposed to "a doctrinaire equalitarianism" that "outrages the patent facts of life" (*ST*, 1005; *GS* 1:978).

Patriarchalismus).[72] In this vision of a hierarchical but loving community, "natural" differences between people are respected (that is, maintained) and "overcome" not through a doctrine of natural equality but through a system of mutual service, wherein the weak serve the strong, and the strong serve the weak through protection and guidance.[73] While this basic view of equality and inequality and its attendant vision of social relationships will be revised and adjusted in many ways throughout Christian history, it nevertheless remains the basic principle and norm of all Christian social philosophies.[74]

With this articulation of Christian patriarchalism, we learn that Stoicism, despite its similarity to Christian thought, is also quite foreign to it in certain respects. As I have indicated above, Troeltsch sometimes refers to this opposition in the language of two forms of individualism. Christianity's metaphysical or religious individualism values the individual and the personality but does not intrinsically imply a doctrine of social equality. Stoicism's "rationalistic individualism" ultimately demands social equality and democratic structures, and it uses revolutionary tactics to attain them if necessary. Troeltsch is not antidemocratic,[75] but he expresses great ambivalence, nevertheless, toward certain dimensions of modern democracy by commenting on the "dangerous results" of defining society according to the ideas of "mere majority rule and abstract equality."[76] Furthermore, Troeltsch associates "rationalism" not only with radical democracy and conceptions of equality, but also with the capitalism and bureaucracy of modern society.[77]

[72] *ST*, 71; *GS* 1:60.

[73] Troeltsch describes this patriarchalism as a new sociological type centered on "the basic idea of the willing acceptance of given inequalities, and of making them fruitful for the ethical values of personal relationships. . . . All action is the service of God and is responsible office, authority as well as obedience" (*ST*, 78; *GS* 1:68).

[74] Toward the beginning of the *Social Teachings*, Troeltsch states that "Christianity will always instinctively fight shy of all ideas of equality, in spite of its close relationship with them" (*ST*, 76; *GS* 1:65).

[75] It is well known that Troeltsch became more appreciative of democracy after World War I. Yet, even in his 1904 essay "Political Ethics and Christianity," Troeltsch recognized a strong connection between democracy and Christian ideals. See *Religion in History*, 173–209; *Politische Ethik und Christentum* (Göttingen: Vandenhoeck & Ruprecht, 1904).

[76] *ST*, 641; *GS* 1:703.

[77] Troeltsch discusses these connections between rationalism, rationalistic individualism, and the modern conceptions of the state, economics, and technology in his 1907 essay "The Essence of the Modern Spirit." In each case, Troeltsch suggests that, while these modern phenomena are based on a theory of abstract rationalism and individualism, they ultimately destroy or disregard the individual. He states, "Capitalism presupposes political and legal

He views these latter forces as founded upon a rationalism that ultimately destroys true individualism, or respect for the individual personality. Troeltsch wishes to separate Christianity's social doctrine from these "rationalistic" dimensions of the modern world. Thus, at the outset of his historical narrative, Troeltsch sets up a subtle opposition between Christian and Stoic thought that will later become a central component in Troeltsch's critique of certain dimensions of modernity.

In this early period of Christianity's history, however, the tension between Stoic and Christian thought is present but produces no significant conflict. In fact, early Christian notions of the freedom and value of the individual prove to be quite compatible with the Stoic view of the original state, so that Troeltsch regularly refers to "the Stoic-Christian absolute natural law" throughout his history of Christianity. In early Catholicism, this conception of an absolute natural law helps preserve the individualism of the gospel. Early Catholicism was focused on the social organization of the church and, therefore, emphasized universalism and suppressed individualism, both of which were native to the gospel ethic. The theory of a relative natural law reinforced this emphasis on universalism (or the social organization) insofar as it helped craft a vision of hierarchy and a variegated social structure, compromising with the secular order and social arrangements. This then contributed to the neglect of the gospel's ideal of individualism. Troeltsch notes that this ideal, however, "lived on in the idea of the Primitive State and of the absolute Natural Law, which kept continually before the minds of men the ideal of freedom, of union with God, of equality, and of love to God and in God."[78]

Yet, this "ideal of the Primitive State" and its view of equality "has been drawn from the Stoics, and . . . is conceived in an abstract and rationalistic way."[79] If left unchecked, it will produce social and political forms that are incompatible with Christianity. But because at this point in history this Stoic-Christian "doctrine of the Primitive State" combined not only "Stoic-

---

individualism, the freedom of the individual to choose and change his domicile, his right freely to dispose of his person. . . . But it is the fate of capitalism constantly to undo its own prerequisites. It recognizes the individual only as the entrepreneur or the hired hand. . . . Capitalism's main effect . . . is an abstract, depersonalizing rationalism" ("The Essence of the Modern Spirit," in *Religion in History*, 248–49; "Das Wesen des modernen Geistes," in *GS* 4:310–11).

[78] *ST*, 162; *GS* 1:175.
[79] Ibid.

rationalistic ideas" but also religious elements, "for a long time the influence of this Stoic admixture was not too dangerous."[80]

Nevertheless, the fusion of Christianity and Stoicism in late antiquity has made Stoic rationalistic ideas part of the stock of resources and tendencies that can influence Christianity's historical development.[81] By alluding to the tension between Christian and Stoic conceptions of the self and the ideal social order, Troeltsch foreshadows the development of two distinct trajectories that will ultimately split apart in the modern period.

The Gradual Split of Stoic "Rationalism" and Christian Social Philosophy

Because he has assigned Stoic ideas a place in Christianity's history, Troeltsch is able to explain why Christian movements or ideas occasionally arise that partake of a particular rationalistic view of equality or that tend toward social revolution. A radical Christian movement promoting equality and revolution can be accounted for without attributing its ideas mainly to Christian sources or tendencies. As he sets up this periodic and progressive "awakening" of the Stoic rationalistic elements in Christianity, Troeltsch begins to show why Stoic and Christian ideas eventually split apart in the modern period.

Indeed, as he crafts Christianity's historical development and nudges it in certain directions, Troeltsch ultimately attributes the emergence of all radical democratic and revolutionary movements and doctrines within Christianity to the Stoic rationalism that entered Christianity early in its history. The democratic and revolutionary elements of medieval Catholic organic thought derive, for example, from the linking of the "individualistic law of nature" derived from Stoicism and the "Christian world of thought."[82]

---

[80] Ibid. Troeltsch states outright that this opposition between the Stoic rationalistic equality of the original state and the Christian religious conception of the person was "an anticipation of the opposing tendencies which were destined to break away from each other at a later time" (*ST*, 162; *GS* 1:175–76).

[81] Troeltsch mentions, for example, that Stoic convictions concerning the democratic origin of imperial authority "introduced into the ecclesiastical literature of Natural Law sporadic elements of the democratic, 'social contract' idea, as the basis of the power of the state, at first, however, without any practical significance." At this point, he states, "there was no kind of inward connection between this democratic idea of Natural Law and the entirely inward and purely religious permanent Christian idea of personality" (*ST*, 155; *GS* 1:167–68). This connection occurs only much later with the emergence of radical Calvinistic movements that take up elements of a modern rationalistic natural law.

[82] *ST*, 289; *GS* 1:305.

The radical sects of the late medieval period take up "characteristic features of the divine law and of the natural law in the sense of the absolute Stoic-Christian-social doctrine."[83] The violent and revolutionary tendencies in the Hussite movement leave "the main ideas of Wyclif and of Huss . . . far behind" and instead adopt "the rationalistic-Stoic-Christian doctrine of equality."[84] Troeltsch elaborates:

> Further, it is significant that in this Christian radicalism the peculiarly Christian ideas of love, and the purely religious individualism which includes secular inequality, are partly mingled with, and partly separated from, equalitarian individualism and its communistic-democratic result; it is evident that the latter is not an essentially [*eigentlich*] Christian idea, but a rationalist idea which arose out of Stoicism.[85]

Although Troeltsch acknowledges the element of ancient radical Christian thought that is compatible with Stoic rationalistic individualism and equality, he ultimately separates the two and attributes them to distinct traditions. This can be seen again in Troeltsch's treatment of radical Calvinism. Johannes Althusius, who takes "the first step toward a rational construction of the State" and thus away from a church-dominated model to a modern one, is also influenced primarily by Stoic tendencies.[86] Troeltsch states that although Althusius's thought is "still in line with the general thought of Calvinism . . . the main trend of his thought was influenced by the humanistic ideas of Stoicism, by the theory of pure natural law. . . . [H]e constructs his theory of society from the point of view of the freedom and equality of individuals."[87]

At this point in Troeltsch's historical narrative—that is, when he begins to introduce the emergence of new, more radical forms of Calvinism that will ultimately help bring about a number of changes in modern society and modern Christianity—it becomes increasingly important for Troeltsch to be able to separate basically "Christian" from basically "Stoic" tendencies. In order to maintain some kind of distinction between "modern Christian" and "modern secular" visions of society, Troeltsch makes a sharper division

---

[83] *ST*, 356; *GS* 1:391.
[84] *ST*, 364–65; *GS* 1:404–5.
[85] *ST*, 369; *GS* 1:409–10.
[86] *ST*, 634; *GS* 1:696.
[87] *ST*, 635; *GS* 1:696.

between the Stoic and the properly Christian elements in Christianity. In this way he can say the following:

> When society is constructed on a rational basis, and individualism is based upon the equality and freedom of the reason of individuals, then the spirit of Calvinism has disappeared, and we are faced with the fact that the rationalistic ideas of Stoicism have been set free from their fusion with Christian thought, and that this has given rise to a specifically modern individualistic habit of mind.[88]

The spirit of Calvinism has disappeared for Troeltsch because radical forms of Calvinism, despite their modern type of individualism and their increased emphasis on equality, ultimately maintain the basic Christian view of equality and inequality and do not produce revolutionary tendencies. That is to say, radical Calvinism's greater promotion of equality does not change the fact that it is still at bottom a religious or spiritual equality.

Through this long historical development, therefore, the Christian and Stoic ideas once so compatible gradually split apart. What once was a conception of natural law joined with Christian conceptions of the human person becomes "an autonomous rational natural law, which conceived and taught men to realize the purely utilitarian ends of the secular institutions by the light of pure reason alone, without the cooperation of the authority of revelation."[89] Stoic rationalism is carried on in modern natural law and thought forms. Despite its own contribution to the creation of the modern world, Christianity retains a social philosophy that is partly at odds with modern social structures and principles. Concerning ascetic Protestantism, by far the most modern of all of Christianity's types, Troeltsch states: "Its spirit has very largely banished from that which it essentially helped to create. Its creations have passed into other hands, and are being shaped by them according to their own purposes."[90]

Troeltsch's Ambivalence toward Modernity

It would be a mistake, however, to suggest or conclude that Troeltsch is attempting to articulate an antimodern position, or to distinguish everything Christian from everything modern or democratic in his construction of

---

[88] *ST*, 636; *GS* 1:698.
[89] *ST*, 674; GS 1:766.
[90] *ST*, 819; *GS* 1:964.

Christianity's historical development. Indeed, in Troeltsch's view, this is both impossible and undesirable. It is impossible because modern Christian movements, which Troeltsch groups together under the terms Neo-Calvinism and ascetic Protestantism, clearly exhibit, promote, embrace, and help sustain distinctively modern ideas and tendencies. Neo-Calvinism actually does "adjust the relative Natural Law of the fallen State, which, originally, was strongly conservative . . . to the modern classical rationalistic natural law of liberalism."[91] Ascetic Protestantism has been the form of Christianity uniquely suited and related to modernity.[92] And indeed, what Troeltsch in other places calls Christianity's "religious personalism" is a foundation of modern individualism.[93] An antimodern view of Christianity, therefore, is historically indefensible. Moreover, Troeltsch's admiration for ascetic Protestantism as one of the "two great main types of social philosophy which have attained comprehensive historical significance and influence" (the other being medieval Catholicism) indicates that he also regards an antimodern stance as undesirable.[94] For Troeltsch, modern forms of Christianity have both maintained the gospel's individualism (though perhaps neglected its universalism) and have contributed to important elements in modern understandings of freedom and personality. Thus, he recommends not that Christianity turn away from modernity, but rather that it join in the task of building a new structure and foundation for modern society. He writes, "What the new house will look like . . . no one can tell. Christian social

---

[91] *ST*, 673; *GS* 1:762–64. Troeltsch predictably attributes this adjustment not to the traditional Calvinist elements present in these modern forms of Christianity, but to "humanistically inclined jurists, who drew their inspiration from a Stoicism which was freed from Christian influences, and from the Roman Law, and also by modern psychological philosophers, with their habit of deducing everything from experience" (*ST*, 674; *GS* 1:765). Nevertheless, he acknowledges that this conception of natural law "has also been strongly influenced by the Calvinistic and Scholastic conception of the Christian Law of Nature" and, thus, that "it is not difficult to understand how the Calvinism of the free church type, which was democratic and liberal in its practical political experience, adopted these ideas" (*ST*, 674; *GS* 1:766).

[92] In *Die Bedeutung des Protestantismus für die Entstehung der modernen Welt*, Troeltsch writes, "Indeed, the industrial, professional, and business classes in these Calvinistic countries . . . constitute perhaps . . . the most important body of Protestantism at the present day, while the more outward industrial, social, and political forces of modern civilization are also mainly in their hands" (*PP*, 91; *BP*, in KGA 8:301).

[93] *PP*, 30–32; *BP*, 220–23.

[94] *ST*, 1011; *GS* 1:984.

philosophy will bring to the task both its common sense and its metaphysical individualism; but it will have to share the labour with other builders."[95]

Alongside Troeltsch's openness to the possibilities of helping to shape modern society, his deep ambivalence about its tendencies and social forms remains, as does his sense of its occasionally profound opposition to Christianity's social philosophy. This, too, is evident in the way he depicts Christianity's historical development. He expresses this sentiment at the end of the *Social Teachings*, where he comments on the "disintegration" of Christian social doctrine in the context of the vast developments in modern society. He states:

> Above all, the modern bourgeoisie, the Law of Nature, the emancipation of the fourth estate, and, finally, scientific rationalism, have created a new sociological fundamental theory of rationalistic individualism, which is connected, it is true, with the older ideas of Christian individualism, but which in its optimistic and equalitarian spirit is sharply opposed to it.[96]

Troeltsch follows this statement with comments that once again suggest that modernity's rationalistic, or radical, individualism ultimately fails to protect the freedom and personality of the individual.

I have shown that Troeltsch offers an implicit critique of modern rationalism in the historical narrative in the *Social Teachings*. For this task, he employs the category of Stoicism as his primary tool. By continually associating Stoicism with "rationalistic individualism," Troeltsch crafts a genealogy that shows Christian individualism to be distinct from modern rationalistic individualism, which has its roots in Stoicism and not in Christianity. At the end of his essay "The Social Philosophy of Christianity," he writes: "The modern spirit is the staggering culmination of ancient rationalism. It may have absorbed the Christian notion of infinity and the Christian concept of the life of the soul, but it nevertheless forms a complete antithesis to the basic stance of the Christian."[97] In the *Social Teachings*, Troeltsch's use of the term "Stoicism" in his construction of Christianity's historical development helps his reader group together such terms as abstract rationalism, utopianism, utilitarianism,

---

[95] *ST*, 992; *GS* 1:966.

[96] *ST*, 991; *GS* 1:965.

[97] "The Social Philosophy of Christianity," in *Religion in History*, 230; *Die Sozialphilosophie des Christentums* (vol. 17 of Bücherei der Christlichen Welt; Stuttgart: Perthes A.-G., 1922) 29.

democracy, equalitarianism, and rationalistic individualism. For Troeltsch, all of these terms have some connection to a certain aspect of Stoic thought. This association effectively opposes them to Christian perspectives on the individual and society.

In addition, Stoicism becomes an important category against which Troeltsch articulates his own normative view of Christianity's social philosophy. Early in the *Social Teachings*, Troeltsch asserts that it is the nature of Christianity to remain within the limits of conservatism and radicalism. While Christian social doctrine will take many forms throughout its history, it will not reach beyond radicalism to a revolutionary principle. Similarly, it will reject an extremely conservative relation to political authorities and structures. "A purely and unconditionally conservative doctrine can . . . never be produced by [Christianity]."[98] Troeltsch crafts his presentation of the Christian view of equality and inequality so that it remains within these boundaries. He uses the category of Stoicism to reinforce one of these boundaries by placing Stoic thought just beyond the boundary of radicalism. Unlike Christianity, Stoicism has produced revolutionary movements springing in part from its abstract doctrine of equality. Christianity "only became revolutionary in principle when its ideal (which as will be shown presently had been fused with the Natural Law of the Stoics) broke through the limits which it had prescribed for its conception of Natural Law and assimilated its rationalistic results."[99]

Stoicism, therefore, serves two important functions in Troeltsch's historical narrative in the *Social Teachings*: 1) it serves as a tool whereby Troeltsch expresses his ambivalence about the rationalistic individualism he associates with modernity; and 2) it gestures toward his own view of what ideals Christianity should promote in his own day.

Conclusion

The preceding sections suggest that two main concerns direct Troeltsch's construction of Christianity's historical development: first, Troeltsch wishes to underscore the highly complicated and intertwined dynamics that shape Christianity's history, while maintaining some sense of its continuity and coherence; second, Troeltsch constructs his historical narrative in

[98] *ST*, 86; *GS* 1:77.
[99] *ST*, 87–88; *GS* 1:80.

conversation with his concerns about modernizing forces in German society, suggesting that Christianity can indeed have a role in shaping the future, while carefully keeping Christianity separate from what he sees as ominous features of modernity such as bureaucracy, unlimited capitalism, radical democracy, and extreme forms of rationalism.

My analysis in this chapter also reveals more about Troeltsch's evolving conceptualization of historical and normative Christianity. How does Troeltsch's picture here compare with that offered in the essence essay? On the one hand, the continuities are striking. In the essence essay, it will be recalled, Troeltsch argues that the essence of Christianity is at once a critical, developmental, and ideal concept. That is, in order to give an account of Christianity, one must: 1) criticize its historical formations and select or highlight those that, in the view of the historian, are most important; 2) acknowledge and include in one's construction the whole history or development of Christianity's social forms; and 3) shape that complicated history in conversation with one's ideal for Christianity's future. Troeltsch's presentation of Christianity in the *Social Teachings* includes each of these moments. More important, both the essence essay and the *Social Teachings* resist a simple conception of Christianity, underscoring the variety of its social forms and definitively locating normative Christianity in no one place.

As I shall discuss in more depth in chapter 5, Troeltsch gradually denies the adequacy of the concept of an essence of Christianity as a tool for conceptualizing historical and normative Christianity as he engages in complex historical analysis and reconstruction. Indeed, as I indicated in chapter 1, Troeltsch expresses doubts about the term already in his 1903 essay on the essence of Christianity. By the time of the *Social Teachings*, these doubts are even stronger. Before discussing Troeltsch's eventual assessment of the concept of an essence of Christianity, I explore how another of the central conceptual tools of Troeltsch's *Social Teachings*—the typology of church, sect, and mysticism—is related to his dual effort to offer a complex picture of Christianity's history while addressing contemporary concerns. That is the task of the next chapter.

CHAPTER FOUR

Assessing the Social Possibilities of Christianity: Troeltsch's Use of the Ideal Types

For Troeltsch, as we have seen in the previous chapter, Christianity is a complex historical phenomenon with multiple possibilities for development. It should come as no surprise, then, that Christianity takes on a wide variety of sociological forms. Troeltsch formulates the ideal types of church, sect, and mysticism to represent the dominant and diverse social forms that emerged historically as Christian communities responded to diverse political, economic, and cultural contexts. But the social doctrines and impulses of Christianity are not merely by-products of the tradition's encounter with a range of historical circumstances, according to Troeltsch. On the contrary, he emphasizes that primitive Christianity contained the germ (*Keim*) of all three types.[1] And not one of the types "is a deterioration of the Gospel";[2] in fact, all three are "a logical result of the gospel."[3] Christianity, in other words, has combined diverse and contrasting impulses from the moment of its origin. While the "three main types of the sociological development of Christian thought" were there "from the beginning,"[4] their exact shape and relative success have been partially dependent upon their ability to merge creatively with the social conditions of the world around them. Thus, Christianity's ability to produce strong and creative communal structures is dependent both on its own social impulses and on the conditions of each particular age.

[1] *ST*, 733; *GS* 1:853.
[2] *ST*, 341; *GS* 1:375.
[3] *ST*, 340; *GS* 1:375.
[4] *ST*, 993; *GS* 1:967.

Troeltsch's historical exploration of Christianity's sociological tendencies is tied up with his desire to understand the challenges facing Christian community under the conditions of modernity. "In the modern world," Troeltsch writes, "Christian social doctrines are in an infinitely difficult situation."[5] In previous ages, each ideal type found a way to relate Christian ideals to the surrounding culture. In the present, however, these models of the relation between Christianity and society "have become impossible."[6] The social organizations so far produced by the church, the sect, and mysticism are now incapable of sustaining and nurturing Christian social ideals in a way that is both compatible with modernity and critical of modernity's destructive features. As he analyzes the history of Christian social doctrines and communities, Troeltsch searches for resources in each of Christianity's sociological forms that might be retrieved or emulated in the contemporary quest for a new form of Christianity.

The ideal types are intimately related to Troeltsch's conception of the essence of Christianity as a continuum of varying and sometimes opposing expressions of Christian identity. The three types enable Troeltsch to demonstrate the multiplicity of Christianity's social forms and to explore possible models of Christian social organization for his own day. Thus, the typology of church, sect, and mysticism is central to Troeltsch's efforts to complexify, problematize, and redefine the essence of Christianity.

The Typology of Church, Sect, and Mysticism

Before proceeding to the major demonstrations and arguments of this chapter, it is necessary to define the term "ideal type" and to clarify both how Troeltsch uses it and how Troeltsch describes each one of the types of Christian social formation. Weber employs the term "ideal type" to designate a heuristic device for understanding, categorizing, and comparing objects of investigation. As Weber writes in his essay "'Objectivity' in Social Science and Social Policy," an ideal type does not describe reality but provides an "unambiguous means of expression" for such a description.[7] That is, an ideal type is an abstraction wherein concrete data are conceptualized and formulated into an accentuated, one-sided construct that is then used to compare actual historical realities,

---

[5] *ST*, 381; *GS* 1:424.
[6] *ST*, 1001; *GS* 1:975.
[7] Max Weber, "'Objectivity' in Social Science," 90.

which are always more complex, many-sided, and ambiguous than the type itself. A type is neither an average nor an actual presentation of a particular phenomenon.[8] Instead, writes Weber:

> It is a conceptual construct (*Gedankenbild*) which is neither historical reality nor even the "true" reality. It is even less fitted to serve as a schema under which a real situation or action is to be subsumed as one *instance*. It has the significance of a purely *ideal* limiting concept with which the real situation or action is *compared* and surveyed for the explication of certain of its significant components.[9]

Thus, "ideal" refers not to a positive valuation, but rather to the logical, pure, "controlled" status of a concept that enables comparative analysis of a variety of historical situations and phenomena.[10] Types are "ideal" in large part because they are logical constructions and applications of the social scientist and not direct reflections of reality.

In *The Protestant Ethic and the Spirit of Capitalism* (1904/5), Weber formulates the concepts "church" and "sect" as ideal types of religious organization. In this work, Weber argues that the Baptist sects, along with the Mennonites and the Quakers, represent a new development in Protestantism that differs markedly from traditional Calvinism (itself a church type). Instead of understanding the church as a universal, supernatural institution of the masses, encompassing both the righteous and the unrighteous, the Baptists understand the church as a voluntary society limited to those who are "born-again." "In other words," writes Weber, these groups understand the church "*not* as a church, but as a sect."[11]

Troeltsch appreciates the value of Weber's ideal types as tools for engaging in historical comparison and analysis.[12] In the *Social Teachings*, he draws heavily

---

[8] Ibid.

[9] Ibid., 93.

[10] H. H. Gerth and C. Wright Mills, "Introduction," in *From Max Weber: Essays in Sociology* (ed. and trans. H. H. Gerth and C. Wright Mills; New York: Oxford University Press, 1958) 59–61.

[11] Max Weber, *The Protestant Ethic and the Spirit of Capitalism* (trans. Talcott Parsons; London: Routledge, 1992) 144–45. [Italics mine.] Similarly, in his essay "The Protestant Sects and the Spirit of Capitalism," Weber defines "church" as "a compulsory association for the administration of grace," and "sect" as "a voluntary association of the religiously qualified persons" (*From Max Weber*, 314).

[12] See "Modern Philosophy of History," in *Religion in History*, 312–13; "Moderne Geschichtsphilosophie," in *GS* 2:723.

on Weber's distinction between the church and sect types,[13] developing and modifying both types significantly and distinguishing mysticism as a third additional type. Although each type only emerges fully in a particular historical period,[14] all three can be traced back to the beginnings of Christianity and to the New Testament. The tendency toward each was present in the origins of Christianity, even though later circumstances were required before any one type would appear in full form. In order to analyze Troeltsch's use of this typology, I begin by briefly describing how Troeltsch defines each of the three types of Christian social organization.[15]

For Troeltsch, the church is an institution "endowed with grace and salvation,"[16] which it distributes to the masses. In the church type, salvation is construed as something objective, that is, accomplished by Christ, the founder of the church, and parceled out to others. It is not subjective, or achieved by individuals themselves.[17] As an institution, the church is composed of those born into it. It accepts and dominates the masses as they are, apart from their individual holiness or way of life. As a universal institution, it is based on a conception of universal truth and "long[s] for a universal all-embracing ideal."[18] It seeks to take up the world into itself and, therefore, accepts the world as it is, compromising with secular institutions and incorporating them into its ideal. Finally, the church is a conservative institution in which traditional hierarchies are respected and current social arrangements maintained.

[13] Troeltsch acknowledges his debt to Weber's formulation of the church-sect typology in a footnote: "For the following section I owe some of the most decisive elements in my point of view to the very instructive study of Max Weber" (*ST*, 433 n. 164; *GS* 1:364 n. 164). Here Troeltsch is referring to Weber's essay "Kirchen und Sekten in Nordamerika," which appeared in *Die Christliche Welt* in 1906.

[14] The church type emerges fully in the medieval period, while the sect and mysticism types emerge in their full or final form in the modern period.

[15] In addition to the delineations and discussions of the types that appear in the *Social Teachings*, the following essays also contain succinct and straightforward definitions of the three types: "Epochen und Typen der Sozialphilosophie des Christentums," in *GS* 4:122–56; "Das stoisch-christliche Naturrecht und das moderne profane Naturrecht," in *GS* 4:166–91; and *Die Sozialphilosophie des Christentums*.

[16] *ST*, 993; *GS* 1:967.

[17] According to Troeltsch, the way that salvation is made objective in the church type can vary. In Catholicism, objective salvation is guaranteed by the authority of the priesthood and sacraments. In Lutheranism and Protestantism in general, the Word becomes the source of objective salvation. In Calvinism it is God's electing will that determines salvation.

[18] *ST*, 334; *GS* 1:368.

The sect is a voluntary society composed of those individuals who have devoted themselves to the creation of a strict and holy community modeled on the absolute law of Christ as expressed in the Sermon on the Mount.[19] Salvation is not objective and universally guaranteed but, rather, is sought out through personal piety and ethical activity. It is subjective—that is, earned and appropriated by the individual and not imposed from without as in the church type. Unlike the church, the sect will not compromise with the world but, rather, accepts only those secular institutions that conform to its own view of morality. The sect rejects everything else as the sin of the world. As voluntary societies, sects are small groups of people who have been "born again." They look to Christ not so much as universal Redeemer and founder of the holy institution of the church but, rather, as personal lord, law-giver, and example. Sects demand freedom from the interference of the state but do not necessarily grant their own members freedom of conscience concerning religious matters.[20]

[19] For Troeltsch, the (synoptic) Gospels (and especially the Sermon on the Mount, Matt 5:1–7:27) contain strict laws that express the radical principles of communal fellowship demanded by Jesus. Sects take up this strictness and moral rigor, often stressing "the simple but radical opposition of the Kingdom of God to all secular interests and institutions" (*ST*, 332; *GS* 1:363; see also *ST*, 56; *GS* 1:40; and *ST*, 336, *GS* 1:370). In his efforts to resist and refute the pejorative associations with the term "sect," Troeltsch insists time and again in the *Social Teachings* that the sect type is "rooted in the teaching of Jesus" and thus is as genuinely Christian as the church type. At the same time, Troeltsch indicates that certain sects can be "narrower and more scrupulous than . . . Jesus" (*ST*, 340; *GS* 1:373). In his discussion of the sect type's adherence to an absolute natural law (and rejection of any relative natural law that would compromise with the world), Troeltsch notes that the ethic of the sect type can take many forms. "It can . . . mean the equality and the equal rights of all individuals, and then it leads to democratic and communistic ideas" (*ST*, 344; *GS* 1:378–79). Concerning Troeltsch's and Weber's assessments of the sect type's appropriation of the radicalism of the Sermon on the Mount, see Mark D. Chapman, *Ernst Troeltsch and Liberal Theology,* 167–72. Chapman notes that Troeltsch and Weber viewed the absolute ethic of the sect as a source of motivation to action that was powerful and influential especially in American and British society, but that would ultimately fail as a sustaining ethical perspective. For Troeltsch and Weber, the objective realities of the world required compromise, not just the radicalism of an absolute ethic like that found in the Sermon on the Mount and in the sects.

[20] Troeltsch frequently emphasizes that the particular notion of tolerance in the sects consists in the idea of a peaceful "co-existence of different churches" externally, and "the strictest restraint internally" and *not* in the idea of tolerance advanced, for example, in the rationalistic thought of the Enlightenment ("Die Kulturbedeutung des Calvinismus," in *KGA* 8:177).

Mysticism refers to those for whom religion has become a "purely personal and inward experience."[21] It represents the advent of a radical individualism in the larger society and in Christianity. Thus for Troeltsch, mysticism is a distinctly modern form of Christianity.[22] Although mysticism as an ideal type may have continuities with some features of early and medieval Catholic mysticism and monasticism, it is used by Troeltsch to refer to a religious phenomenon of a different kind, that is, the modern individualistic spirituality of those on the margins of the churches and sects. For them, salvation is conceived in completely subjective terms, occurring through the communion between the individual and God. Although mysticism can exist within and alongside both church and sect, the mystical experience often leads people to form informal and fluid small groups based solely on personal connection and not on religious hierarchy (church) or rigid and energetic conformity to law (sect). Because mysticism[23] underemphasizes worship, dogma, and history,

[21] *ST*, 993; *GS* 1:967.

[22] Caroline Walker Bynum offers an interesting assessment of the continued usefulness of Troeltsch's rather unconventional understanding of mysticism for thinking about the distinctiveness of medieval women mystics. Bynum argues that Troeltsch's category of mysticism effectively captures an "a-institutional" element of medieval women mystics' piety and religious activity. Thus, despite the shortcomings of his conception of mysticism, Bynum argues, it could fruitfully be taken up again and revised by sociologists today. See "The Mysticism and Asceticism of Medieval Women: Some Comments on the Typologies of Max Weber and Ernst Troeltsch," in eadem, *Fragmentation and Redemption: Essays on Gender and the Human Body in Medieval Religion* (New York: Zone, 1991) 53–78. For a recent assessment of Troeltsch's typology in relation to twentieth-century political developments and Protestant movements, see Hartmut Lehmann, "The Suitability of the Tools Provided by Ernst Troeltsch for the Understanding of Twentieth-Century Religion," *Religion, State & Society* 27 (1999) 295–300.

[23] In recent decades, several scholars have turned to Troeltsch's ideal type of mysticism to illuminate the rise and significance of New Age spirituality movements. These scholars argue that insofar as New Age movements focus on the cultivation of individual spirituality, are anti-institutional in their organization, and nondogmatic in their teachings, they conform roughly to Troeltsch's definition of mysticism and spiritual religion. (See Bruce Campbell, "A Typology of Cults," *Sociological Analysis* 39 [1978] 228–40; and Robert Wuthnow, *Experimentation in American Religion: The New Mysticisms and Their Implications for the Churches* [Berkeley: University of California Press, 1978] esp. 78–85.) Wade Clark Roof uses Troeltsch's category of mysticism to analyze a wider range of contemporary religious groups that emphasize inner freedom and personal experience, including not only New Age movements, but also evangelical and charismatic organizations. (See "Modernity, the Religious and the Spiritual," in *Americans and Religions in the Twenty-First Century* [ed. idem; Annals of the American Academy of Political and Social Science 558; Thousand Oaks, Calif.: Sage Publications, 1998] 211–24.) For an example of an expanded typology

it is the weakest form of social organization in Christianity.[24] Its strength is its capacity for tolerance and spiritual depth.[25]

Troeltsch's Adoption of the Types: Historical Background

It is typical to explain Troeltsch's entry into sociological topics and investigations as a direct result of his encounter and friendship with Max Weber. Concerning Troeltsch's appropriation of Weber's typology,[26] for example, Benjamin Reist states that "Weber's contribution to Troeltsch's thought at this point was both formal and substantial. One must add that it was also profound. . . . It is undoubtedly true to say that it was from Weber primarily that Troeltsch gained his insights into the emerging discipline of sociology."[27] In addition to Reist's statement, which is followed by an appreciative, albeit brief, treatment of Troeltsch's presentation of the types

---

that rejects mysticism as a type, see Milton Yinger, *The Scientific Study of Religion* (New York: Macmillan, 1970).

[24] In "Stoic-Christian Natural Law and Modern Secular Natural Law," Troeltsch describes mysticism as consisting in "a radical, non-communal form of individualism. Independent of history, cult, and outward means of communication, the Christian stands here in immediate communion with Christ or with God. . . . Social relations are limited to the natural bond between individual kindred souls, based on similar experiences and a common understanding. No common cultus, no organization needs to issue from it" (*Religion in History*, 327; "Das stoisch-christliche Naturrecht und das moderne profane Naturrecht," in *GS* 4:173).

[25] In a footnote to one of his sections on mysticism in the *Social Teachings*, Troeltsch identifies his own theology with the tendencies of mysticism: "My own theology is certainly 'spiritualist,' but for that reason it seeks to make room for the historical element, and for the ritual and sociological factor which is bound up with it. Naturally I am aware of the difficulties of such an undertaking" (*ST*, 985 n. 504a; *GS* 1:936 n. 504a).

[26] Although Weber was among the first to join the terms "church" and "sect" into a clear and developed typology of religious forms of social organization, the language of "church" and "sect" had been in the air since the mid-nineteenth century, particularly in the field of church history. These categories were used theologically, often to associate "sect" with "heresy." Concurrent with Weber's own work on the sect concept, Gustav Kawerau described the sects in precisely the same way in an entry titled "Sektenwesen in Deutschland" in the *Realenzyklopädie für protestantische Theologie* in 1906. On this point and for a general account of the use of the terms "sect" and "church" in the nineteenth century and around the time Weber and Troeltsch began working with the terms, see Molendijk, *Zwischen Theologie und Soziologie*, 40–42. See also Theodore M. Steeman, "Church, Sect, Mysticism, Denomination: Periodological Aspects of Troeltsch's Types," *Sociological Analysis* 36 (1975) 181–204, esp. 182.

[27] Benjamin A. Reist, *Toward a Theology of Involvement: The Thought of Ernst Troeltsch* (Philadelphia: Westminster, 1996) 107.

in the *Social Teachings*, one can also find more dismissive comments about Troeltsch's independent use of the types and sociological methods in general. H. Stuart Hughes, for example, writes:

> [Troeltsch's] *Social Teaching of the Christian Churches* was a cruder, more incoherent, and infinitely longer version of the same kind of study of the interplay of economic and religious forces on which Weber was simultaneously working. . . . The intellectual categories were mainly borrowed from Weber. But Troeltsch applied them mechanically, almost as though he had not fully understood them. . . . And Weber's typology of social phenomena—his most characteristic legacy to subsequent investigation—in Troeltsch's hands seemed forced and artificial.[28]

Hughes provides no specific argument or textual examples to support this claim beyond a footnote that refers the reader to the final chapter of the *Social Teachings*. Voigt states that such a stereotype "neither does justice to Troeltsch's intellectual independence nor corresponds to the complexity of sociology around the turn of the century."[29]

Voigt and others have shown that Troeltsch's engagement with sociological methods and questions began much earlier than his encounter with Weber, and that his evolving attitude toward sociology reflects the general ambivalence to which the discipline was subjected in the early 1900s. While Troeltsch was intrigued with the possible fruitfulness of a sociological approach to historical analysis,[30] he was also critical of the possible reductive or positivistic orientation of a sociological method. A glance at a handful of Troeltsch's early essays and reviews between 1894 and 1904[31] shows that questions about

[28] H. Stuart Hughes, *Consciousness and Society: The Reorientation of European Social Thought, 1890–1930* (New York: Knopf, 1961) 235.

[29] Friedemann Voigt, *"Die Tragödie,"* 77. Robert J. Rubanowice states that between Weber and Troeltsch "there was a genuine cross-fertilization of ideas and not merely a one-way influence." *Crisis in Consciousness: The Thought of Ernst Troeltsch* (Tallahassee, Fla.: University Presses of Florida, 1982) 45.

[30] Describing his participation in the sociological-historical work of the Eranos Circle, Troeltsch states that, despite sociology's "unstable definitions" and "chaotic methods," he and his colleagues have found the sociological approach to be "of the most fruitful consequence" for the historical and systematic disciplines ("Die Kulturbedeutung des Calvinismus," *KGA* 8:146–47).

[31] Specifically, Troeltsch takes up the question of the legitimacy and value of sociological methods in an essay in 1894 and then again in 1898 in an important review of Paul Barth. In both of these essays, Troeltsch associates sociological approaches either with positivistic conceptions of development or with monocausal views of development. Troeltsch vehemently

the value and importance of sociological methods were topics of interest for Troeltsch prior to his friendship with Weber. Indeed, throughout most of his scholarship from the late 1890s to his final writings, such as *Historicism and Its Problems*, Troeltsch engages sociological analysis as an important contributor to historical projects[32] while also stating his ambivalence about various sociological models of historical development.

This is not to deny the obvious influence Weber had on Troeltsch, who acknowledges the great debt he owed to Weber in his autobiographical essay "My Books."[33] Troeltsch's numerous cultural-historical investigations on the relation of Christianity to the modern world were heavily influenced by Weber's *Protestant Ethic and the Spirit of Capitalism*. Less well known, especially in the United States, however, is that Weber was influenced by Troeltsch's analysis of early Lutheranism as a pre-modern form of Christianity.[34] In addition, Troeltsch actually altered Weber's church-sect typology—not simply by adding a third type but also by sharpening and limiting the definition of the sect type in a way that improved upon some of the problems of Weber's delineation. Troeltsch supplemented Weber's explanation of the difference between the church and sect types by identifying their main theological characteristics.[35] A simplistic attribution of everything sociological in Troeltsch's work (including the types) to Weber misses the

---

opposes both approaches. At the same time, however, Troeltsch hints at the possible fruitfulness of a sociological methodology. In an 1899 review of Söderblom, Troeltsch suggests a use of sociological questions and perspectives that, according to Voigt, is remarkably similar to Troeltsch's approach in the *Social Teachings*. Yet, through 1907, Troeltsch "is more concerned with limiting sociology than taking it up" (Voigt, *"Die Tragödie,"* 94). This history of Troeltsch's engagement with sociology is detailed in Voigt, *"Die Tragödie,"* 85–97.

[32] In his 1916 essay "Zum Begriff und zur Methode der Soziologie," which was a review of Paul Barth's 1915 work *Die Philosophie der Geschichte als Soziologie*, Troeltsch states that he views sociology as an individual discipline (*Einzelwissenschaft*) that "seeks to compare and schematize the forms and conditions of socialization" and, in so doing, is an important *"Hilfswissenschaft"* for history and philosophy of culture (*GS* 4:705–6).

[33] In "My Books," Troeltsch details the point at which he "came under the spell of a very powerful personality, Max Weber," whom Troeltsch credits for impressing upon him the importance of the "Marxist teaching concerning a substructure and a superstructure" ("My Books," in *Religion in History*, 372; "Meine Bücher," in *GS* 4:11).

[34] F. W. Graf and H. Ruddies, "Ernst Troeltsch. Geschichtsphilosophie," 130.

[35] Graf states that in addition to using the typology as a tool for differentiating the various forms of historical Christianity, Troeltsch sought to legitimate the theological applicability of the typology to Christianity as well. See "Weltanschauungshistoriographie," 221.

genuine reciprocity of their relationship and the important differences in their views.[36]

The Types and the Larger Project of the *Social Teachings*

Troeltsch uses many concepts, doctrines, and other tools to show how the ideals of religious communities are related to their specific communal forms. He uses these tools to explore and chart the different ways various forms of Christianity have construed the relation between their own ideals and structures on the one hand, and those of the larger society on the other. Conceptions of natural law, forms of asceticism, views of equality and inequality, conceptions of truth, doctrines of grace and sin, configurations of the relation between the individual and the group, and the ideal types of social organization all enable Troeltsch to sort out different expressions of Christianity and Christian ethics.[37] While the typology is a central organizing and differentiating tool employed in the *Social Teachings*, it is, nevertheless, one of many such tools. To read the *Social Teachings* by focusing primarily on the differences between the types and their corresponding historical forms

---

[36] Troeltsch discusses some of the connections and differences between his and Weber's treatment of ascetic Protestantism in footnote 510 of the *Social Teachings*. There he notes that his presentation of ascetic Protestantism and the conception of the calling "converges with the well-known researches of Max Weber on *Der Geist des Kapitalismus*, etc." But while Weber's research aims at understanding the uniqueness of modern capitalism and its "significance in economic history," Troeltsch remarks that his own study "has a different aim. It only intends to give a clear presentation of the Protestant social ethic for its own sake." Troeltsch notes that he was able to follow Weber's account of ascetic Protestantism because "every time I studied this subject afresh I felt that his argument had proved itself to be a brilliantly acute piece of observation and analysis." Importantly, Troeltsch adds: "For the rest, however, as I would like to take this opportunity to remark, my researches do not start from those of Weber." See *ST*, 986–87 n. 510; *GS* 1:950 n. 510. On the reciprocity that characterized Weber and Troeltsch's intellectual friendship, see F. W. Graf, "Friendship between Experts," 213. He writes, "The potent presence of each man's work in that of the other is an indication and a consequence of their interdisciplinary co-operation in analyzing the historical 'vital force' (*Lebensmacht*) of religion."

[37] Molendijk (*Zwischen Theologie und Soziologie*, 26–27) suggests that there are two main tasks of the *Social Teachings*. The first is to outline the various forms of Christian ethics, for which Troeltsch relies heavily on the notion of natural law. The second is to outline the various forms of Christian organization, which centers on a presentation of the ideal types. The first is more attuned to and reflective of the historical complexity and detail of Christianity, while the second is achieved by broad, ideal-typical strokes.

of Christianity, then, is to miss much of the detail, complexity, and richness of Troeltsch's analysis of Christianity.[38]

The structure and contents of the *Social Teachings*, when considered along with other essays written by Troeltsch between the years 1907 and 1912,[39] indicate clearly that Troeltsch developed the threefold typology while he was writing the *Social Teachings*. Indeed, as mentioned above (see chapter 2), what we now know as the book *The Social Teachings of the Christian Churches and Groups* was published over a period of four years. The first half originally appeared as a series of essays in the *Archiv für Sozialwissenschaft und Sozialpolitik* from 1908 to 1910. Troeltsch researched and wrote the remainder of the book—the sections on Calvinism, the sects, mysticism, and the conclusion—in 1910 and 1911. The entire work was published along

[38] This is especially true since the typology is barely mentioned in the first three hundred pages of the *Social Teachings* and is not even outlined or introduced in the introduction. Furthermore, as recent Troeltsch scholars have shown (and I shall discuss below), it is clear that Troeltsch discovered and developed the threefold typology while writing the *Social Teachings*.

[39] Molendijk's account of the history of Troeltsch's development of the threefold typology (especially the third type, mysticism) is an invaluable resource for understanding the *Social Teachings* and the relation between the church-sect-mysticism typology and Troeltsch's evolving views about the religious situation of his time (see *Zwischen Theologie und Soziologie*, 48–49). The important details here are the following: 1) After first mentioning a "third type" in May 1909 in the *Social Teachings*, Troeltsch then formulates and presents his threefold typology in a developed and clear form in his 1910 presentation at the "Erster Deutsche Soziologentag," titled "Das stoisch-christliche Naturrecht und das moderne profane Naturrecht" (*GS* 4:166–91; "The Stoic-Christian Natural Law and Modern Secular Natural Law," in *Religion in History*, 321–42). After this presentation, Troeltsch consistently uses the threefold typology rather than the twofold version. 2) Troeltsch's formulation of mysticism as a third type is tied up in large part with his discovery that the Spiritualists and Baptists do not belong to the same movement (see *ST*, 729; *GS* 1:848), as he and Weber had originally thought. Troeltsch rejects Weber's classification and determines that the Baptists correspond to the sect type, while the Spiritualists and Quakers correspond to the mysticism type. This distinction is based on Troeltsch's conviction that the Spiritualists hold different views of tolerance and individualism than those associated with the sect. (For these and other details, see Molendijk, 50, 57–60, 66–67). Graf (" 'endlich große Bücher schreiben'. Marginalien zur Werkgeschichte der *Soziallehren*," in *Ernst Troeltschs Soziallehren* [ed. Graf and Rendtorff] 27–48) underscores the extent to which Troeltsch's work on the *Social Teachings* was repeatedly interrupted by other (and smaller) projects, many of which then gradually influenced the shape and argument of the *Social Teachings*. Once the *Social Teachings* was completed, Troeltsch viewed the three types as central to the entire work, even though they only gradually emerge over the course of the volume. (A paragraph Troeltsch composed in 1912 to advertise the book identifies the threefold typology as the organizational principle for the work. See Graf, "endlich," p. 42.)

with the revised *Archiv* essays as the first volume of Troeltsch's collected writings in 1912. Troeltsch does not refer to the types in the introduction to the *Social Teachings*, nor in the chapters on Jesus, Paul, and early Catholicism. He eventually first refers to the types one-quarter of the way into the book in the opening pages of the chapter on medieval Catholicism. There Troeltsch foreshadows in a few short sentences the eventual emergence of a new type, the sect type. No mention is made of a mysticism type at all. In fact, Troeltsch gives his first account of the defining characteristics of the church and sect types long after first alluding to the sect, in the section on "The Absolute Law of God and of Nature, and the Sects," the first half of which appeared in March 1909. There he maintains a dual typology of church and sect. It is only in the publication of the second half of that section in May 1909 that Troeltsch makes his first mention of "a third type."[40]

Thus, two years after he started working on the *Social Teachings*,[41] Troeltsch first began to include references to a threefold typology that includes mysticism. A full articulation of the new third type first appears in the section on "Mysticism and Spiritual Idealism," which itself is the last substantial section of the *Social Teachings* before the conclusion. Indeed, in his writings prior to 1909, Troeltsch either makes no mention of a third type at all, or includes mysticism and spiritual idealism under the sect classification as Weber did. Once he discovers that a third type is needed in order to do justice to the difference between the Baptists and the Spiritualists, Troeltsch increasingly separates the sect from the mysticism type. For Troeltsch, the Spiritualists (and the Quakers) adhere to a form of individualism that emphasizes doctrinal tolerance and personal communion with God in a way not found in the sect type. The Baptists, on the other hand, tend toward a legalistic and strict moral code which is characteristic of the sect type. By the end of the *Social Teachings*, the distinction between the sect and mysticism types is fully developed.

---

[40] Molendijk (*Zwischen Theologie und Soziologie*, 58) makes the very important point that when Troeltsch first published this section in the *Archiv*, he did not give the name "mysticism" to this third type. That name was only added when Troeltsch gathered together the *Archiv* articles and combined them with the rest of his written text to produce the book form of the *Social Teachings* (*GS* 1:1912).

[41] According to Graf ("'endlich große Bücher schreiben'," 30), Troeltsch first mentions that he is working on a book on "the Christian church and its relation to the social problem" in April 1907, in a letter to Friedrich von Hügel. The first published portion of the *Social Teachings* appeared in the *Archiv* in January 1908.

It is a mistake to read the *Social Teachings* as if Troeltsch had the threefold typology beforehand and used it as the primary blueprint or organizing tool for his work. Troeltsch himself states that he did not have such a programmatic plan for the work when he began writing it.[42] Although Troeltsch certainly had at hand the church-sect typology, thanks to Weber's work on Protestantism and capitalism, he does not use church- and sect-type language at all until the end of the section on medieval Catholicism. By the end of his treatment of medieval Catholicism and the beginning of the chapter on Protestantism, however, the church-sect typology is much more central to Troeltsch's project and, by now, as I have noted, Troeltsch has hinted at an independent third type. Indeed, the entire section on early Calvinism, modern Calvinism, neo-Calvinism, the sects, and spiritual religion (mysticism) is nearly incomprehensible without the threefold typology. By the conclusion of the work, the types are the major differentiating terms and are centrally related to the question of how Christianity might best contribute to the shape and quality of modern societ(ies).

Five Uses of the Types

The history of Troeltsch's development of the threefold typology is a complicated one. As I have indicated, Troeltsch did not have a clear conception of the typology prior to his composition of the *Social Teachings* and, therefore, did not apply the typology to his analysis in a simple and straightforward way. It should not be surprising, then, that Troeltsch did not have a single, unambiguous purpose in using his typology. Instead, the typology serves many goals. I shall argue that there are at least five ways Troeltsch uses the typology in the *Social Teachings*. Each of these uses is connected to Troeltsch's concerns and aims as an historian and a theorist of Christianity's "essence."

The Types as Heuristic Devices for Historical Analysis

The first and most obvious way Troeltsch uses the types is in the Weberian sense of a heuristic device for sorting out and comparing the variations and

---

[42] In "My Books," Troeltsch states concerning his composition of the *Social Teachings,* "This time I dropped every programmatic preparation and instead of merely getting ready to, I actually plowed into an indescribably laborious task" ("My Books," in *Religion in History,* 372; "Meine Bücher," in *GS* 4:11).

general tendencies in Christianity's social structure and organization over a long period of time. Here, the types are emphasized as abstractions that do not correspond directly to historical reality. Troeltsch writes: "In actual life, of course, these different types . . . of the Christian fellowship . . . mingle and combine. But this abstract analysis makes the history of dogma much clearer and simpler."[43] Despite their contrasting features, for example, Catholicism, Lutheranism, and early Calvinism can be understood as part of the same general sociological tendency in Christianity: that of the church type.

When Troeltsch is adhering to the more strict ideal-typical use of the types, he presents them as permanent logical possibilities inherent to the concept of Christianity itself. "From the beginning these three forms were foreshadowed, and all down the centuries to the present day, wherever religion is dominant, they still appear alongside of one another."[44] At the same time, and indeed more frequently, Troeltsch connects the types more closely to the history and development of Christianity. In such cases, a particular type is not necessarily a permanent logical type of Christianity but actually stands or falls with the social and historical situation out of which it emerges.[45]

The Types as Weapons against Reductionism

The second use to which the types are put is to support a nonreductive reading of the sociological development of Christianity—a concern that is central to the *Social Teachings*. The types support Troeltsch's desire to refute strictly materialistic readings of Christianity's history and development by showing the ways in which Christian ideas and tendencies lead to and help produce certain communal organizations and social structures. Molendijk rightly states that a central thesis of Troeltsch's *Social Teachings* is that "the Christian idea produces from itself certain social forms."[46] These forms are different combinations of those sociological characteristics that are intrinsic to

---

[43] *ST*, 995; *GS* 1:969.

[44] *ST*, 993; *GS* 1:967.

[45] Indeed, this is the position of Steeman, who argues that the types are tools for periodizing Christianity, and that Troeltsch believes the types are "outdated" historical forms with no future. See Steeman, "Church, Sect, Mysticism, Denomination," 184.

[46] Molendijk, *Zwischen Theologie und Soziologie*, 25. Troeltsch relates each doctrine to a specific communal form, and each communal form to a religious idea of Christianity: "The Christian social doctrines presuppose, first of all, a definite conception of the Christian religious community, in which the religious idea works itself out directly in a sociological form" (*ST*, 203; *GS* 1:183).

Christianity from the beginning, that is, individualism and universalism. The distinction between church and sect, for example, "can be traced right back to Primitive Christianity and the Early Church."[47] Commenting on the church and sect types, Troeltsch writes, "If, then, in reality both types claim, and rightly claim, a relationship with the Primitive Church, it is clear that the final cause for this dualistic development must lie within primitive Christianity itself."[48] In the section on mysticism and spiritual idealism Troeltsch claims that the germs (*Keime*) of each type were present in earliest Christianity.[49]

This emphasis on the origin of each type within early Christianity betrays a teleological dimension to Troeltsch's presentation of Christian history and to the typology itself. Each type is treated as a "force" or "tendency" intrinsic to the teleological life or development of the gospel. The universal or communal tendency of the gospel, for example, once teased out and articulated by Paul, was bound to develop into the church type.[50] In response to this development, however, the individualistic (or sect) tendency of the gospel asserts itself. Speaking of the emergence and dominance of the church type, with its tendency to compromise, Troeltsch indicates that "the Gospel . . . reacted against this materializing and relative tendency" by calling to life its latent sect type.[51] "Only when the objectification of the Church had

---

[47] *ST*, 463; *GS* 1:429. In the first half of the *Social Teachings* (indeed even through the section on Lutheranism, but especially in the section on medieval Catholicism and the reaction of the medieval sects), Troeltsch is still working only with a twofold typology of church and sect. Thus, the church and sect types are repeatedly characterized as two poles that were intrinsic to the gospel: conservatism (church) and radicalism (sect), or compromise (church) and absolute ideals (sect). This twofold typology, which corresponds to a twofold tendency in early Christianity, is expressed in statements such as the following: "The result of the first main section of this book was to bring out the fact that from the very beginning the social doctrines of the Christian Church had a dualistic tendency which caused them to flow in two channels" (*ST*, 329; *GS* 1:359).

[48] *ST*, 333; *GS* 1:364–65.

[49] *ST*, 733; *GS* 1:853.

[50] Troeltsch writes, "The concentration of the hierarchy in the Papacy is the dogma which completes the sociological tendency towards unity, as it was bound to develop and become complete once the process had begun by which the Church and the Christian priesthood were conceived as the Body of Christ" (*ST*, 228; *GS* 1:211). Shortly thereafter he states, "We can see in this also simply the logical result of the sociological idea of a religious community based upon absolute truths and life-values" (*ST*, 230; *GS* 1:215).

[51] *ST*, 380; *GS* 1:423.

been developed to its fullest extent did the sectarian tendency assert itself and react against this excessive objectification."[52]

By treating the types as expressions of different "powers" or "tendencies" inherent in the gospel and implying a particular history of development, Troeltsch is simultaneously refuting reductionism and stretching the strict Weberian meaning of an ideal type. Weber speaks against "the hypostatization of such 'ideas' as real 'forces' and as a 'true' reality which operates behind the passage of events and which works itself out in history."[53] Although Troeltsch acknowledges the fruitfulness of the types in their strictly ideal-typical sense, throughout the *Social Teachings* he links the types much more closely to historical reality than Weber would have, giving them a stronger basis in history and a teleological significance. This corresponds to the general difference between Weber and Troeltsch, the former being more neo-Kantian and therefore maintaining a strict split between human concepts and actual reality, and the latter recognizing the constructed nature of human concepts but wishing to acknowledge the real power of historical forces and the importance of attempting to adjust human concepts to these historical realities as much as possible. Speaking of the classification of medieval sects, for example, Troeltsch states that "it will become plain that this method of interpretation is no artificial scheme pressed into service from the outside, but an interpretation which has arisen out of sympathy with the phenomena."[54]

The Types as Examples of the Connection between the Religious and the Social

Troeltsch's insistence upon a nonreductive reading of Christian history ought not to be misread as a refusal to recognize the intimate relation between the religious and the social. On the contrary, Troeltsch also uses the types to link Christian social doctrines to specific social forms, to show that ideas and contexts are intertwined, and thus to keep the religious and the social together. This is the third use of the typology. There are two ways Troeltsch uses the types to demonstrate a connection between the religious and the social. First,

---

[52] *ST*, 343; *GS* 1:377.
[53] Weber, " 'Objectivity' in Social Science," 94.
[54] *ST*, 349; *GS* 1:383.

Troeltsch holds that the emergence of any given type is tied up with and dependent upon the general social-historical situation.[55] He writes:

> Which of the three types of religious association steps to the fore at any particular moment depends, of course, not merely on a theoretically or psychologically grounded preference for this or that manifestation of the Christian ideal, but also, and pre-eminently, on the compatibility of one prevailing type with the more general tendencies and needs of the times.[56]

The general social situation, then, helps bring about the development or emergence of one or more of the three types. Second, Troeltsch simply makes the observation that certain religious doctrines are intrinsic to certain religious forms of organization, and vice versa. This second claim is demonstrated very clearly in the conclusion to the *Social Teachings*, where Troeltsch details how conceptions of Christ, redemption, or truth vary according to the shape of the religious community that articulates them. For Troeltsch, social doctrines are shaped by the particular form of Christian community in which they are articulated. He writes, "The results of this survey throw light upon the dependence of the whole Christian world of thought and dogma . . . on the idea of fellowship which was dominant at any given time."[57] Thus, certain kinds of Christian communities create certain kinds of social doctrines. The idea of fellowship that characterizes the church type will imply a specific social doctrine. That is, the church type's willingness to compromise with secular society by means of a conception of a relative (as opposed to absolute) natural law flows directly from the idea of fellowship that characterizes the church type, namely, its idea of a universal church encompassing all of creation. Similarly, the sect type's proclamation of a rigorous and radical social ideal that tends to separate it from the larger society flows directly from the sect type's idea of fellowship, which is characterized by an emphasis on the ideals of the gospel and the call to the individual to live according to absolute religious values.

---

[55] Concerning the social theories of the church type in medieval Catholicism, for example, Troeltsch states that "all these theories were not merely the logical outcome of thought; they were the result of conditions which had awakened the impulse to transform and re-create social life" (*ST*, 377; *GS* 1:420).

[56] "The Social Philosophy of Christianity," in *Religion in History*, 225; *Die Sozialphilosophie des Christentums*, 23.

[57] *ST*, 994; *GS* 1:967–68.

This correspondence between types of social community and types of social doctrine becomes important at the end of the *Social Teachings* and stands behind Troeltsch's inability to say what the social doctrine of Christianity in his own time should be. For, indeed, if the church, sect, and mystical types of community are all being weakened by the conditions of modernity, then the kind of religious community which might emerge in the future is unknown. If that is the case, then Christianity's future social doctrines are also unknown insofar as such doctrines are always related to a specific form of community or fellowship.

The Types as Indications of Christianity's Pluralistic Composition

Troeltsch also uses the types to demonstrate that there are different possibilities of development in Christianity, and that Christianity is therefore an internally pluralistic tradition. This fourth use is directly related to the concerns and insights that guide Troeltsch's articulation of the challenges of formulating a singular "essence" of Christianity. Just as Troeltsch resisted a simple, uniform picture of Christianity's nature in his essay on the essence of Christianity, so does he in the *Social Teachings* insist upon a conception of historical (and normative) Christianity that reflects honestly and accurately its complexity and internal diversity, both in the past and in the present. The contrasting types of social organization that are native to Christianity help Troeltsch substantiate his claim about its pluralistic composition.

Affirming the internal diversity of Christianity also helps Troeltsch show that there is not just one answer to the question of how Christianity should relate and respond to social problems and social questions. If no single, once-for-all social doctrine, orientation, or task emerges out of Christianity, then any effort to identify one for the present will always be a new creation, articulated in response to new historical situations and challenges. At the end of his essay "Epochs and Types of the Social Philosophy of Christianity" (1911), where he summarizes the social doctrines of each form of Christianity as spelled out in the *Social Teachings*, he writes:

> Every attempt to enlist Christianity in the mastery and solution of social problems of the present must reckon with this variety, and must observe that all previous social doctrines of Christianity were focused on conditions which are not those of the present, and that these social doctrines cannot simply be applied as a whole to the problems of capitalist society. Whatever contribution the Christian

idea is said to make to the present social philosophy, the problem of the present is always something new.[58]

Troeltsch makes this point not simply to draw attention to the diversity that marks Christian history, but also to underscore the complexity of contemporary questions and problems themselves, and to deny that such problems can be solved simply by appealing or reverting to a particular period of Christian history.

Finally, Troeltsch's interest in affirming the internal diversity of Christianity as a tradition is a by-product of his commitment to a thoroughgoing historical method in Christian history and theology, and more importantly, to a non-authoritarian view of doctrine. That is, Troeltsch seeks a Christianity marked by a toleration of varying understandings of doctrine. His admiration for mysticism has to do in large part with the kind of religious toleration that, in his view, flourishes in mystical and spiritualist circles.

The Types as Tools for Normative Evaluation

While Troeltsch's use of the types is not dictated by a heavy-handed normative intention, it is intimately tied up with his normative concerns about the future of Christianity in the context of modernity. Each type represents an element of Christianity that Troeltsch wants to preserve. The church type attests to the social element of Christianity; the sect type corresponds to the moral, idealistic, and activist dimensions of Christianity; mysticism symbolizes the spiritual depth and freedom of Christian individualism. Thus, Troeltsch uses the types to help sort out various possibilities within Christianity, asking what form Christianity might take in his context, and asking how it might relate or contribute to modern society. Without attempting to legitimate one type over another, Troeltsch explores, therefore, the positive and negative aspects of each type and hints at possible directions for the future. Let us examine one of the subtle ways Troeltsch uses the types to sort out normative questions about the proper shape and quality of Christian community.

---

[58] "Epochen und Typen der Sozialphilosophie des Christentums," in *GS* 4:155–56.

Equality and Inequality in Christian Social Organization[59]

Troeltsch's analyses of the "family and sex ethic" of each historical form of Christianity reveal the normative concerns that underlie his efforts in the *Social Teachings*. Indeed, throughout the *Social Teachings* Troeltsch is intrigued by questions about women's roles in community and society[60] and fascinated with and troubled by different conceptions of equality and inequality that are part of Christianity's history. Troeltsch even notes that a monograph on each topic would be both interesting and useful.[61] As he

[59] Much of the text in this section is taken (with permission) from my article, "Gendered Dimensions of Troeltsch's Typology of Church-Sect-Mysticism," in *Zeitschrift für Neuere Theologiegeschichte/Journal for the History of Modern Theology* 13 (2006) 23–40.

[60] It is not out of the question to suggest that there may be an influence of Marianne Weber on Troeltsch here. Indeed, in his account of Jesus' teachings on marriage and the family in the *Social Teachings,* Troeltsch includes a footnote that refers his readers to Marianne Weber's work, *Ehefrau und Mutter in der Rechtsentwicklung. Eine Einführung* (Tübingen: Mohr, 1907). According to Guenther Roth, this work, which "established Marianne Weber's scholarly reputation," was intended as "an introduction for women and men interested in . . . the practical significance of legal norms for the condition of women . . . [and] contain[ed] a strong attack on patriarchy and a vigorous plea for equality in marriage." Roth—who notes that Marianne Weber was part of a moderate wing of the women's movement—offers a highly illuminating account of Marianne Weber's participation in the intellectual, cultural, and political conversations and activities of Heidelberg. While she (and all women) were excluded from the Eranos Circle, Marianne Weber participated in the Sunday teas that she and Max Weber began hosting for the purpose of intellectual conversation in 1910. See Roth, "Marianne Weber and Her Circle," introduction to the Transaction edition of *Max Weber: A Biography*, by Marianne Weber (trans. and ed. Harry Zohn; New Brunswick, N.J.: Transaction, 1988) xv–lx, esp. xxi, xxv, xxx. In her biography of Max Weber, Marianne Weber (*Max Weber*, 228) comments on Troeltsch's ambivalence about certain democratic ideals, suggesting that "[Troeltsch] did not believe in many things the Webers were striving for—neither in the intellectual and political development of the working classes nor in the intellectual development of women," indicating that such themes were topics of conversation between Troeltsch and the Webers.

[61] Concerning the uniqueness of views on the family, sexuality, women, and marriage found in mysticism, Troeltsch states: "The very fluctuating details connected with this point of view could only be described within the framework of a monograph, but they would present many features of great interest" (*ST*, 801–2; *GS* 1:944). Similarly, concerning the topic of Christianity's view of equality and inequality, and particularly the unique way in which Calvinism comes into closer contact with views of equality that are generally more radical than those found in other forms of Christianity, Troeltsch states: "the history of the problem of equality would be one of the most important contributions which could be made to the understanding of the development of European Society. It is, however, still entirely unwritten" (*ST*, 902 n. 360; *GS* 1:674 n. 360).

describes the views of gender and the family that are characteristic of each of the ideal types of church, sect, and mysticism, Troeltsch carves out a Christian conception of equality and inequality for his own time, while criticizing competing models of social relations and organization.

Early Christianity and the Construction of Christian Patriarchalism

At the outset of the *Social Teachings*, Troeltsch makes a particular view of the family central to Christian values and continues to give it a special if not prominent place throughout the book. Indeed, Troeltsch makes the category of the family central to social organization in general. According to him, the family is "the starting point of all social development" and the "archetype of all social organization since it presents the original picture of these relations of authority and reverence which arise out of the natural organization."[62] Troeltsch argues that although early Christianity (which for Troeltsch includes Jesus' community, Paul's community, and early Catholicism) had virtually no influence on societal norms or social reform, it made a clear contribution to social thought through its conception of the family. Jesus, according to Troeltsch, offers no specific social program, but his "teachings on the family are more intimate and detailed."[63] "Indeed," notes Troeltsch, "the idea of the family may be regarded as one of the most fundamental features of [Jesus'] feeling for human life."[64] Troeltsch bases this claim on his observation that Jesus draws on a Jewish ethical conception of the family, calls God "father," describes his disciples in familial terms, and uses familial images both for the Kingdom of God and in his parables.[65] Insofar as the family is founded on a deep social bond and on a love and respect for each member as a person, it embodies the perfect balance of the two social ideas that (according to Troeltsch) come to characterize Christianity in all its forms: universalism and individualism.[66] Universalism, according to Troeltsch, expresses the

---

[62] *ST*, 544–45; *GS* 1:556.

[63] *ST*, 61; *GS* 1:48.

[64] Ibid.

[65] Ibid.

[66] *ST*, 55–57; *GS* 1:40–44. In general, Troeltsch associates the very quality of family relations with something he sees as essential about Christian values. His admiration of small religious groups modeled on the intimacy of the family can be seen in his favorable depiction of Schleiermacher's view of religious association. See "Schleiermacher und die Kirche," in *Schleiermacher. Der Philosoph des Glaubens* (ed. Max Apel; Berlin: Buchverlag der "Hilfe," 1910) 9–35.

social or communal aspect of Christianity, while individualism refers to Christianity's respect for the value of each individual person. Throughout the *Social Teachings*, Troeltsch tells the history of Christianity as a tale of fluctuation between these two elements of Christian social thought. While all forms of Christianity are combinations of universalism and individualism, the church type generally emphasizes the universal or institutional dimension of Christianity, while the sect types and mysticism "rebel" by accenting the more individualistic dimensions.

According to Troeltsch, the notion of the family was a central if implicit aspect of Jesus' religiosity. It remains for Paul to provide the first explicit articulation of a Christian view of the family. Patriarchalism, a type of social order,[67] becomes the basis of a Pauline conception of communal and family life. In Pauline patriarchalism, social relations are configured according to a model in which inequalities are accepted as natural but are transformed through a cooperative schema in which the weak voluntarily serve the strong through obedience and the strong serve the weak through protection and affirmation.[68] The family is thus a social unit characterized by the father's (gentle) authority and the grateful free subservience of the mother, children, and slaves. Troeltsch calls this type of social order a patriarchalism of love, as opposed to a patriarchalism of authority. While all people partake of a religious equality as children of God, the hidden predestinarian will of God allows for natural inequalities, which are "overcome" through the caring and respectful relations that characterize the social structure. A Christian view of hierarchical family relations makes more humane what would otherwise follow from purely authoritarian social relations.

---

[67] Troeltsch calls patriarchalism a sociological type. He describes it in ways that overlap with Weber's ideal type of patriarchalism as a form of traditional authority. See Max Weber, *Economy and Society* (Berkeley: University of California Press, 1978) 231 and 1009. For a discussion of Weber's conception of patriarchalism as the "pure type of traditional domination" see Reinhard Bendix, *Max Weber: An Intellectual Portrait* (Berkeley: University of California Press, 1977) 330–34.

[68] Troeltsch emphasizes that in Christian individualism, as solidified by Paul, the individual personality is of infinite value, but "equality is definitely limited to the religious sphere" (*ST*, 72; *GS* 1:61). In the Pauline conception of the family, inequalities "are not treated merely in a negative fashion, but they are taken up positively into the sociological basic idea of the worth of personality and of the unconditioned fellowship of love, and they are turned into sources of peculiar ethical value" (*ST*, 76; *GS* 1:66).

Patriarchalism and the Church Type

Paul's patriarchal model becomes the basis for the view of the family in all church types, including early Catholicism, medieval Catholicism, and Lutheranism.[69] Each of these church types emphasizes the importance of the monogamous family as a model of proper social relations and as a way of providing security for women and children. The authority of the father is also central to this conception of the family. In fact, in Lutheranism, Troeltsch says that "masculine domination of a patriarchal kind is taken for granted" because it "belongs to the very essence (*Grundgedanke*) of Lutheranism."[70] In his treatment of medieval Catholicism, Troeltsch states that the emphasis on the father's authority is a remnant of ancient German military organizations. Christianity simply modifies and softens this idea of male domination by articulating values of "love and good will" and by demanding behavior in accordance with a patriarchalism of love. This transforms the quality of relationships and brings people into right relations of willing submission and gentle, responsible authority.[71] Thus the patriarchalism of love acts against the harshness of the patriarchalism of natural authority, which presumably allows the father unlimited power and places no restrictions on his behavior.

Yet Troeltsch implies that this patriarchalism of love in the church type often remains only an ideology that provides a script for talking about Christian social relations and conditions without actually implementing them.[72] An ethic of passive perseverance goes hand-in-hand with this conservative patriarchalism. Since all of social life is modeled on the monogamous patriarchal family in the church type, this passive conservatism comes to characterize the majority of the social doctrines of the church type.

It is clear that Troeltsch is not sympathetic to the level of conservative patriarchalism he sees as prominent, for example, in Lutheranism. As he charts its view of the family as conservative and "masculine," he appears simultaneously to be attacking conservative Lutheranism in his own day.[73] Indeed, in a section on the social theory of Lutheranism, Troeltsch describes

---

[69] Calvinism, which is also a church type, has a slightly different view of the family on account of its incorporation of sect ideals. I shall therefore include it in my discussion of Troeltsch's interpretation of the sect type's view of the family, and not in this section on church types, where it otherwise would belong.

[70] *ST*, 546; *GS* 1:557.

[71] *ST*, 287; *GS* 1:300.

[72] *ST*, 287, 291, 295–96; *GS* 1:300, 308, 312–13.

[73] *ST*, 544; *GS* 1:555.

modern Lutheranism as blending a "masculine hardness and class-conscious ruthlessness," which he contrasts with earlier Lutheranism but views as consistent with Luther's later social thought. He refers specifically to the conservative and authoritarian theories of the "Prussian-German Restoration" in the nineteenth century, when Lutheran social doctrines become, according to Troeltsch, "a weapon in the hands of a ruling class."[74] Troeltsch's portrait of Luther as one who was innovative in his early years and conservative in later years is also a convenient tool in Troeltsch's debates with his conservative Lutheran contemporaries,[75] who fought for a closely linked conservative church and authoritarian state (and who crafted their own historical and theological portraits of Luther and Lutheranism to justify this religious and political vision).[76] By examining the "family and sex ethic" of Lutheranism, Troeltsch is able to sharpen and strengthen his portrait of Lutheranism as an essentially conservative movement. This then lends credence to his decision to classify the Lutheran Reformation as a medieval (and not modern) event,[77] and simultaneously discredits those opponents who would place Luther (and thus a conservative and politically powerful church) at the center of imperial Germany. Troeltsch's claim that early Catholicism, medieval Catholicism, and Lutheranism share conservative (and premodern) social ideals (such as those concerning the family) serves as a provocative rhetorical strategy in his attack on conservative Lutheranism in his own day.

---

[74] Ibid.

[75] Klaus Penzel sees in Troeltsch's critique of Luther's social thought an attack on the legacy of modern German Lutheranism's conservatism, expressed, for example, in its regular acceptance and defense of existing social conditions and institutions. Penzel writes, "It was obvious to [Troeltsch] that Lutheranism was destined to become the backbone of the conservative party in nineteenth-century Prussia-Germany, which, in turn, did its best to keep Lutheran orthodoxy in power." See Penzel, "Ernst Troeltsch on Luther," in *Interpreters of Luther: Essays in Honor of Wilhelm Pauck* (ed. Jaroslav Pelikan; Philadelphia: Fortress, 1968) 296.

[76] Graf points to the tensions between Troeltsch (as a representative of "liberal" "Culture Protestantism") and his opponent in Heidelberg, Ludwig Lemme, a socially conservative Lutheran systematic theologian who construed bourgeois individualism as sinful and who advocated a strong authoritarian state with close ties to the church. See Graf, "Puritanische Sektenfreiheit," 45.

[77] In *Die Bedeutung des Protestantismus für die Entstehung der modernen Welt*, Troeltsch states that "Protestantism [during the Reformation] was, in the first place, simply a modification of Catholicism," and that the modern period only emerges in the late-seventeenth and early-eighteenth centuries (*PP*, 41; *BP*, in *KGA* 8:233).

The Sects and Mysticism: Patriarchalism Modified?

According to Troeltsch, the family and sex ethic of the sect type differs from that of the church type in two ways. Recall that for Troeltsch, the sect type accents Christian individualism (an ethically activating spirituality focused on the relation between the individual and God) while the church type emphasizes Christian universalism (the impulse toward the social and institutional). Thus, the sect's more individualistic orientation allows, first, a greater role for women in certain spheres and activities. This is demonstrated by the fact that some early modern sects have women as preachers and religious leaders. The sect's closer relation to modern rationalistic society means, second, that it tends to view marriage in more instrumental terms, that is, as a way of building up society and creating productive and responsible citizens.[78] Thus (according to Troeltsch) already in Calvinism, a church type with sect elements, the "personality of women is granted a higher degree of independence," and marriage is viewed in terms of its "service to the common good." Sexual passions are restrained so that they can be directed "into other channels."[79] These observations about gender prove immensely helpful in Troeltsch's efforts to clarify and substantiate his view of the differences between Lutheranism and Calvinism. (The former is a church type while the latter is a blend of the church and sect types.) In Neo-Calvinism, the rationalistic element is stronger and the theocratic dimension of early Calvinism has disappeared. This increase in free and rationalistic activity allows for the creation of fellowships and "societies," often organized around issues such as pacifism, antislavery, and women's rights. Troeltsch notes that "the feminist movement has found some support here, long before other denominations dared to broach the subject."[80] In general, therefore, ascetic Protestantism[81] and Neo-Calvinism—both with strong sect elements—view the family in less patriarchal terms than the church type and conceive of the relation between the sexes in a more individualistic way, granting women more independence.[82]

Troeltsch seems to be most fascinated with the view of family and women exhibited in the third type. While in the sect type, "the life of sex is not to

[78] *ST*, 809–10; *GS* 1:951–52.
[79] *ST*, 655; *GS* 1:732–33.
[80] *ST*, 675; *GS* 1:768.
[81] For a definition of ascetic Protestantism, see above, ch. 1, n. 119.
[82] *ST*, 809–10; *GS* 1:951–52.

be used for enjoyment,"[83] in mysticism "eroticism plays a leading part."[84] Mysticism connects the sex and family ethic with its "personal intimate valuation of life," thus spiritualizing familial and sexual relations.[85] This results in the creation of marriage ideals that strongly contrast and oppose the "property view of marriage" espoused by the church type.[86] Mysticism also has an "anti-hierarchical tendency" that is related to its connection with the Protestant doctrine of the priesthood of all believers.[87] Troeltsch's admiration for mysticism as a type of Christian community comes through strongly in the tone he uses to narrate its gender ethic. It is clear that Troeltsch views the quality of association encountered in modern spiritual (or "mystical") communities as capturing something essential and valuable about Christian ideals. This assessment comes through clearly in Troeltsch's essay "Schleiermacher and the Church" (written during the time of his work on the *Social Teachings*), where Troeltsch envisions for modern Christianity a combination of the social cohesion of the church type and the spiritual depth and intimacy of the mysticism type.[88]

Yet despite his seeming appreciation for the more "progressive" views on marriage, women, and the family evident in modern sects and in the spiritual communities of mysticism, Troeltsch is eager to clarify (repeatedly) that these individualistic forms of Christianity still have no notion of equality in the modern rationalistic or democratic sense of the term.[89] Instead, they continue to ascribe to what Troeltsch seems to acknowledge as the basic Christian view of equality and inequality as articulated by Paul and as implied in the gospel: patriarchalism. Thus patriarchalism as a conception of equality and inequality appears to be essential to Christianity itself, and not just to the church type. Troeltsch implies this in the conclusion to the *Social Teachings,* where he includes patriarchalism as one of the "permanent ethical values

---

[83] *ST*, 809; *GS* 1:951.

[84] *ST*, 731; *GS* 1:851.

[85] *ST*, 801; *GS* 1:941.

[86] Ibid.

[87] *ST*, 741–42; *GS* 1:862.

[88] Troeltsch, "Schleiermacher und die Kirche," 30–32. See footnote 122 below.

[89] Concerning ascetic Protestantism's view of the state, Troeltsch explains that "there is a strong sense of the equality of all in the presence of God . . . but which is in no sense an equalitarian view like that of the European democracy" (*ST*, 811; *GS* 1:954). Again, concerning its economic ethic: "here also there is no idea of equality" (*ST*, 813; *GS* 1:956).

contained in the history of Christian social doctrines."[90] Here he states that Christianity offers a unique solution to the problem of equality and inequality, which he details in the same terms as those he had used to describe Pauline patriarchalism.

By focusing on Troeltsch's analyses of the "family and sex ethic" of each ideal type, we are able to discern the ways Troeltsch engages in both descriptive and normative work as he sorts out the various forms of social organization in the history of Christianity. As he refines his portrait of each type, so does he reflect on the strengths and weaknesses of each social impulse in Christianity for pressing societal questions in his own time. Through his own gender analysis Troeltsch expresses his critique of the conservative church model in general and of conservative Lutheranism in particular. The church type's gender ethic exposes its passive acceptance of reigning social arrangements and its general authoritarian tendencies. Troeltsch thereby characterizes the church type as antimodern and seems to align himself with the ideals and forms of association encountered in the sects and mysticism. In so doing, Troeltsch implicitly invalidates conservative Lutheran conceptions of German society (and the place of Christianity within it) in his own time.[91]

It follows, then, that Troeltsch's gender analyses also express his fascination with and general affirmation of the models of religion found in mysticism (and to some extent in the sect type). Both of these types clearly have affinities with the sensibilities of the modern secular world. Thus it would seem that Troeltsch is affirming modern individualism in general. Yet

---

[90] *ST*, 1004; *GS* 1, 978. Troeltsch states, "Only the Christian Ethos solves the problem of equality and inequality, since it neither glorifies force and accident in the sense of a Nietzschian cult of breed, nor outrages the patent facts of life by a doctrinaire equalitarianism. It recognizes differences in social position, power, and capacity, as a condition which has been established by the inscrutable will of God; and then transforms this condition by the inner upbuilding of the personality, and the development of the mutual sense of obligation, into an ethical cosmos. The ethical values of voluntary incorporation and subordination on the one hand, and of care and responsibility for others on the other hand, place each human being in circumstances where natural differences can and should be transmuted into ethical values of mutual recognition, confidence, and care for others" (*ST*, 1005; *GS* 1:978).

[91] Graf makes the important point that notwithstanding his harsh critique of Lutheran social thought and his clear identification of North American sects and spiritual groups (classified under the type of mysticism) as the true sources of modernization in religion, Troeltsch never simply elevates modern Calvinistic sect groups to an unambiguously normative position. Instead, he continues to recognize the ways in which Lutheran forms of piety provide strong impulses toward social cohesion. See Graf, "Puritanische Sektenfreiheit," 64.

such is not the case, as I have shown. While Troeltsch clearly admires the views of equality and gender relations found in the sects and mysticism, he wants to be cautious about embracing modernity's rationalistic individualism too much,[92] and therefore articulates as "essential" to Christianity a conception of equality and inequality that is very similar to the patriarchalism of the church type. Troeltsch's insistence on this patriarchal doctrine of equality and inequality as characteristic of Christianity in all its forms is another indirect expression of his ambivalence toward what he calls "rationalistic" or "utilitarian" conceptions of the person and the community, which he associates with certain aspects of modernity. At these moments, Troeltsch is concerned to distinguish Christian views of society and social relations from certain increasingly predominating modern views. This helps explain why Troeltsch criticizes conservative or authoritarian views of the family and yet does not unambiguously affirm a modern "secular" democratic view of the family, despite his seeming admiration for the nonhierarchical family of mysticism. Thus, as Troeltsch shapes and comments on the types, he does so in ways that reveal his ambivalence about both conservative and radical models of society in his own time.

The Types and the Challenges of Christianity in the Modern World

My analysis of the gendered dimension of each ideal type points to the subtle or indirect ways in which Troeltsch relates the types to normative questions about his own contemporary society and culture. Troeltsch also engages in direct evaluation of each type, focusing on the ability of each type to nurture social cohesion and individual freedom in contemporary religious and cultural

---

[92] This caution comes out clearly in the conclusion to the *Social Teachings*, where Troeltsch discusses briefly the "new sociological fundamental theory of rationalistic individualism, which is connected, it is true, with the older ideas of Christian individualism, but which in its optimistic and equalitarian spirit is sharply opposed to it" (*ST*, 991; *GS* 1:965). Troeltsch sees this "radical individualism" as an "interlude between an old and a new civilization of constraint," noting that a new model of society will be built out of the salvageable elements of the current model along with new additions. Here Troeltsch implies once again that, notwithstanding his ambivalence about certain features of modernity and modern individualism, he nevertheless sees Christianity as a key partner in the task of rebuilding modern society. "Christian social philosophy will bring to the task both its common sense and its metaphysical individualism; but it will have to share the labour with other builders" (*ST*, 992; *GS* 1:966).

life. By examining Troeltsch's assessment of the three types, one can glean insights into Troeltsch's concerns about the capacity of Christianity to respond and contribute to the modern situation.

The strength of the church type, for Troeltsch, is its ability to foster social cohesion and to create strong communal bonds and structures. Thus, he writes, "the churches alone have the power to stir the masses in any real and lasting way."[93] In terms of its capacity to provide a strong organizational structure for religious life, "the church-type," argues Troeltsch, "is obviously superior to the sect-type and mysticism."[94] Sociologically, the church type alone is able to encompass and draw into itself people of all classes and varieties; unlike the sect or the mysticism types, it can take up popular religiosity and accommodate the masses. It provides "a settled form of worship" and not a mere "utopian ideal" of a spiritual religion "without organization."[95] Furthermore, the church type takes on extensive structures of institutional organization and is willing to relate to—and to ally itself with—secular institutions. This allows its influence to extend to all areas of life. In short, the church type corresponds to the ideal of a Christian civilization or a Christian society.

Troeltsch therefore regards the church type as the only form of Christianity so far that has been able to serve as a lasting foundation for social life. He sees the modern situation as one bereft of any significant sources of unity or cohesion. It is structured according to institutions and forces, such as capitalism and rationalistic individualism, that undermine social or collective life. In this context, the church type is held up as the only type that could provide the fragmented modern world with unity and guidance.

The church type, however, also has features that are incompatible with modern perspectives, values, and conditions. According to Troeltsch, the church's authoritarian view of the priesthood and the papacy, as well as its universal conception of religious truth, is no longer defensible or desirable in the modern world. Moreover, the church type ultimately depends on a union of church and state, with the state using compulsion, even in religious matters, to secure unity. The church type is, in short, dependent on a premodern conception of the world. Compared to the sects and forms of spiritual religion,

---

[93] *ST*, 994; *GS* 1:967.
[94] *ST*, 1007; *GS* 1:980.
[95] Ibid.

"the churches are working with ideals of past ages."[96] Thus, Troeltsch states that "the days of the pure church-type within our present civilization are numbered. Ideas which the modern world accepts as natural and obvious do not agree with the views of the church."[97] Many features of the church type are objectionable for theological reasons as well. The church type's pursuit of a universal community and ideal underemphasizes and even destroys the individualism that is also essential to Christianity.[98]

The strength of the sect type, according to Troeltsch, is its maintenance of what Troeltsch sees as the radical ideals of the gospel.[99] It encourages individuals to commit themselves to the creation of a holy community modeled on a strict ideal and vision for religious life and practice. It serves to renew the individualistic energies that are so often suffocated by the church type with its tendencies toward compromise and hierarchical authority and organization.

The value of the sect type can be seen clearly in Calvinism, which is itself a church type, but which nevertheless appropriates sect tendencies that ultimately account for its uniqueness and success as an institution.[100] Calvinism takes up the Anabaptist ideal of a holy community, but instead of turning away from society by forming an exclusive community, Calvinism combines the Anabaptist ideal with the "ecclesiastical spirit of a Christian national and state church."[101] With the sect ideal in hand, Calvinism was able to achieve what no other church type had yet accomplished. It was able to initiate a "social transformation" based on Christian ideals.[102] Traditionally,

[96] *ST*, 381; *GS* 1:425.

[97] *ST*, 1008; *GS* 1:981.

[98] *ST*, 336; *GS* 1:369. Both the sects and mysticism are correctives to the church's neglect of individualism. As a reaction against the church's compromising nature, the sect preserves Christianity's individualism through its radical devotion to uncompromising religious ideals of holiness and moral perfection. Mysticism attunes to individualism through its emphasis on the importance and authority of the relation between the individual and God.

[99] Troeltsch finds this expressed, for example, in the earliest community's indifference to the world and total devotion to the preparation for the coming of the kingdom, and in that same community's focus on the uncompromising and radical ideals of the Sermon on the Mount.

[100] See *ST*, 602, 622–23, 627; *GS* 1:638–39, 676–79, 682–83. At the beginning of his treatment of Calvinism, Troeltsch emphasizes the importance of "that particular point in Calvinism at which, in its main ideas, it came into closer or more permanent touch with the sect type than was the case with Luther" (*ST,* 578; *GS* 1:608).

[101] *ST*, 597; *GS* 1:633.

[102] *ST*, 622; *GS* 1:677.

only the sect type drew on the ideals of the gospel to form a new society; but as the sect type, it had always been unable to extend its influence beyond its narrow borders and into the larger society. The unique integration of sect elements into a church type is what makes Calvinism "the second great Christian definite social ideal of European society."[103] In fact, Calvinism's social influence in Geneva was more comprehensive than even that of Catholicism during the medieval period. As Troeltsch writes, Calvinism "was 'Christian Socialism' in the sense that it molded in a corporate way the whole of life in the state and in society, in the family, and in the economic sphere, in public and in private, in accordance with Christian standards."[104] By combining sect ideals with a church type model, therefore, Calvinism achieves something unique.

Troeltsch sees the energizing power of the sect as essential for Christianity in the modern world. Without the renewing tendencies of the sect, the Protestant churches remain incapable of mobilizing the masses in any meaningful way.[105] But the sect type alone, that is, apart from its role within a church system, is also subject to significant criticism. As he writes the *Social Teachings*, Troeltsch gradually comes to the conclusion that the sect type is ultimately linked to a rigorous dogmatism that does not recognize the validity of the relation between the individual and God but instead demands assent to its strict beliefs and values. The sects "tend toward legalism" and often lack "spontaneity" as well as a "spirit of universalism."[106] The ethic of the sect is "narrower and more scrupulous than that of Jesus."[107] Thus, once Troeltsch discovers the difference between the sects and mysticism (or "spiritual religion"), his sympathy goes toward the latter. Mysticism shares the sect's emphasis on individualism, but with a higher capacity to tolerate a variety of theological perspectives. This is also accomplished without strict biblicism or moralistic restrictions that limit participation in the "external" secular world. Troeltsch comes to believe that mysticism alone is built on a radical individualism. He states that "the only real source of toleration is that individualistic form of spirituality which considers that all external religious forms are merely relative."[108] The sect type demands the kind of political

[103] *ST*, 621; *GS* 1:674.
[104] *ST*, 622; *GS* 1:676.
[105] *ST*, 1009; *GS* 1:982.
[106] *ST*, 337; *GS* 1:371.
[107] *ST*, 340; *GS* 1:373.
[108] *ST*, 673; *GS* 1:761.

tolerance that allows many sects and religious groups to exist beside one another in a single society. But the tolerance of mysticism is also a religious tolerance, allowing for a variety of theological and doctrinal beliefs within a single sect or community.

For Troeltsch, therefore, the strength of mysticism is that it affirms the radical individualism of Christianity, focusing on the quality and value of the relation between the individual and God. This produces the only true religious tolerance in Christianity—that which accepts the validity of each individual's religious experience and convictions and places no authoritative doctrine or rigorous ideal over the individual. Its fundamental sociological theory is a "union of the hearts of all in one common aim, and a complete toleration of all other souls on an equal basis."[109]

Yet, despite Troeltsch's personal affinity with and admiration for mysticism, his criticisms of it are clear. It is a "weakened form of religious life." The conservative ecclesiastical reaction against modern spiritual idealism or mysticism, therefore, was "necessitated by the real nature of Christianity [*Wesen des Christentums*] itself, which is never merely individualistic mysticism, but is always at the same time an ethical driving-power, a recognition of the fact that fellowship is required by the divine will."[110] Because mysticism, or spiritual religion, does not produce stable communal or institutional structures, it will not be able to provide modern society with the cohesion and unity it so desperately needs. Troeltsch's conclusion concerning mysticism is that "[t]his conception of Christianity, which alone meets the needs of the educated classes, assumes the continuance of other and more concrete living forms of Christianity as well; it can never appeal to all."[111]

Troeltsch envisions a form of Christianity that will have the freedom of conscience of mysticism, the individualistic energy of the sect, and the social cohesion of the church. Troeltsch states that the future tasks of Christianity consist "in the mutual interpenetration of the three chief sociological categories, which must be united with a structure which will reconcile them all." These tasks are "of a sociological and organizing kind" and "are more pressing than all doctrinal questions."[112] The fragmented

---

[109] *ST*, 801; *GS* 1:940.
[110] *ST*, 797–98; *GS* 1:937.
[111] *ST*, 799; *GS* 1:938–39.
[112] *ST*, 1009; *GS* : 982.

conditions of modernity are in need of a strong source of social unity. These conditions, however, rightly rule out the compulsory and universal control that is the signature of the church type. Yet, the sect and mystical types alone are incapable of influencing society in any lasting way. At the end of the *Social Teachings*, then, one is left with Troeltsch's rather bleak view that "under these circumstances our inquiry leads to the conclusion that all Christian-Social work is in a problematic condition. . . . [I]t is problematic in particular because the main historic forms of the Christian doctrine of society and of social development are today, for various reasons, impotent in the face of the tasks by which they are confronted."[113] By the end of his historical investigation, Troeltsch's ambivalence about the paralyzing and destructive powers of modernity is once again apparent.[114]

A Spiritual and Sociological "Church"

Despite Troeltsch's seeming despair by the end of the *Social Teachings* concerning Christianity's ability to generate a new form of community that might meet some of the challenges of modern society, there are places in this and others of Troeltsch's contemporaneous works where one can glimpse his proposal for Christian community in a modern context. By examining in more detail Troeltsch's notes on mysticism, and by turning to his essay on Schleiermacher's conception of the church, I shall argue that Troeltsch proposes a new kind of spiritualistic "church" that is characterized by both doctrinal relativism[115] and a firm sociological and historical foundation.

In the preceding discussion of Troeltsch's assessment of the three types, I suggest that Troeltsch sees the church type and mysticism as offering both valuable resources and profound problems for a modern form of Christian community. The church offers a strong sociological basis for community but

---

[113] *ST*, 1012; *GS* 1:985.

[114] Troeltsch writes, "The social problem is vast and complicated. It includes the problem of the capitalist economic period and of the industrial proletariat created by it; and of the growth of militaristic and bureaucratic giant states; of the enormous increase in population, which affects colonial and world policy, of the mechanical technique, which produces enormous masses of material and links up and mobilizes the whole world for purposes of trade, but which also treats men and labour like machines" (*ST*, 1010; *GS* 1:983).

[115] Sarah Coakley (*Christ Without Absolutes,* 112) asserts that Troeltsch espouses a doctrinal relativism that is evident in his works beginning especially in 1913; she sees the second edition of the essence essay as a particularly strong indication of this position.

a dogmatic absolutism that is intolerable in the modern world. Mysticism taps into the depths of modern religious experience and sensibilities but provides no structures for sustained communal life.[116] Together, the strengths and resources of the church type and mysticism point to what Troeltsch sees as the two pressing problems facing Christianity in his day: the "dogmatic-doctrinal" and the "sociological-organizational."[117] On the one hand, in the modern context the traditional dogmas of the church no longer have the same kind of authority as they once did; on the other hand, the major or rising individualistic forms of Christianity in the modern world cannot provide the sociological unity that the medieval churches once did. The question becomes how to create community out of the "chaotic mass of different religious, half-religious, and anti-religious" sensibilities that go along with modern religious individualism.[118] Can the cohesive structures of the old church type be maintained without bringing along their dogmatic absolutism? Troeltsch is obviously sympathetic to the religious and intellectual perspectives that go along with the "modern scientific theology," which he classifies in the *Social Teachings* as part of modern mysticism.[119] This theology's lack of concern for the historical and sociological elements of religion, however, makes it "ecclesiastically impotent."[120] As Troeltsch puts it in his 1910 essay "Schleiermacher und die Kirche," to be effective socially this new religious individualism must either accept old religious organizations or create new ones.[121]

In that same essay, Troeltsch argues that Schleiermacher, beginning with the *Glaubenslehre*, pointed to a new kind of church that combined the new

---

[116] In several places in the *Social Teachings*, Troeltsch suggests that there is an inherent tension, even incompatibility, between toleration, on the one hand, and strong religious organization, on the other. In one of his analyses of mysticism, Troeltsch writes, "The problem of Christian toleration and liberty of conscience in relation to the conditions of the formation of religious fellowship belongs to this group of ideas. There is no escape from it. There are only varying practical suggestions of approximate utility which emerge out of this tragic interplay of forces" (*ST*, 999; *GS* 1:972). Mysticism and the church type, therefore, stand in a problematic relation to each other. While their dominant features are incompatible, it is precisely a blend of their features that seems to be needed, according to Troeltsch, in the modern period.

[117] Troeltsch, "Schleiermacher und die Kirche," 13.

[118] Ibid., 13.

[119] *ST*, 796; *GS* 1:933–34.

[120] *ST*, 985 n. 504a; *GS* 1:936 n. 504a.

[121] "Schleiermacher und die Kirche," 15. After offering the second option (creating new institutions), Troeltsch states, "The latter however is very difficult" (15).

modern religious sensibilities with a practical concern for communal life. The view of the church presented in the *Glaubenslehre* is neither church nor sect,[122] but a new sociological conception of religious community.[123] It nurtures individual piety but locates it in an "organic life context."[124] Troeltsch offers an interesting account of how Schleiermacher gradually moved from a highly individualistic and mystical conception of religious community in the *Speeches on Religion* to a more overtly historical and sociological "church" in the *Glaubenslehre*. In the *Speeches*, true religious fellowship, or the true church, occurs primarily in small intimate circles composed of the uniquely religious. The *Volkskirche*, or the actual church, exists as a "helping institution" for the common person on the way to religious virtuosity. Troeltsch argues that by the time Schleiermacher writes the *Glaubenslehre*, he must give up the sharp distinction between the true and actual church, and therefore turns from the small, free-flowing ideal religious communities of the *Speeches* in favor of a more bounded communal organization.[125]

Troeltsch describes Schleiermacher's new conception of the church in comparison with the traditional church and sect types. Unlike the traditional church type, Schleiermacher's church is no supernatural institution founded miraculously through Christ and separated absolutely from non-Christian forms of religious community. Instead, it is a religious community (*Gemeinschaft*) springing from the human demand for communication and need for spiritual sustenance, representation, and rejuvenation. This community is distinguished from other social forms only by virtue of its particular relation to and dependence upon Christ as the archetype of Christian piety. Its uniqueness as a community comes from the particular source of its

---

[122] In his essay on Schleiermacher, Troeltsch appears at times to be using the term "sect" generally, to encompass the individualistic and personal dimensions of the sect and mysticism types. Troeltsch wrote this essay during the period in which his concept of mysticism as an ideal type was still in formation. Therefore, he does not use the term "mysticism" in this essay, but is clearly making reference to what he would increasingly call the mysticism type.

[123] Ibid., 30.

[124] Ibid., 31.

[125] Ibid., 23–24, 28. Troeltsch explains this change with the statement, "Schleiermacher ist kirchlicher geworden" (28). For more on the influence of Schleiermacher on Troeltsch's ecclesiology and conception of mysticism, see Kristian Fechtner, *Volkskirche im neuzeitlichen Christentum. Die Bedeutung Ernst Troeltschs für eine künftige praktisch-theologische Theorie der Kirche* (vol. 8 of Troeltsch-Studien; Gütersloh: Gütersloher Verlagshaus, 1995) 114–22, esp. 117 n. 18.

drive to community and not from some miraculous source that separates it from other kinds of religious or secular groups.[126] Although Schleiermacher's new church type shares the sect type's emphasis on the active and energetic participation of the individual in the formation of community and in the practice of piety, it differs from the traditional sect type as well. It does not conceive of the community emerging from the individual, or from the idea of an association of individuals whose activity and abilities somehow create the religious fellowship. On the contrary, it shares the traditional church type's assumption that the individual is deeply dependent upon the prior productive power of religious communication, the activity of grace, and the historical legacy of the community.[127] Describing this hybrid of church and sect, Troeltsch writes:

> In such a community the following will be present: tradition and progress, common spirit and individual independence, comprehensive leadership [*Gesamtleitung*] and freedom of congregations, external dynamic multifarious composition and nevertheless a unity of spirit always showing itself to be in agreement.[128]

If this description is read in conversation with Troeltsch's assessment of each of the three ideal types of social organization offered in the historical narrative of the *Social Teachings*, it becomes clear that Troeltsch is here describing a combination of church, sect, and mysticism. He has found in Schleiermacher's conception of the church the element of social cohesion and communal guidance and authority provided by the church type, the energetic participation of individuals native to the sect type, and the doctrinal tolerance and appreciation for individual religiosity characteristic of mysticism.

Troeltsch identifies in Schleiermacher's conception of the church a proposal uniquely suited to certain features of the general modern situation characterized by an independent secular culture and the interiorization of religion. Nevertheless, his deep sense of the nearly insurmountable difficulties facing the religious situation in his own day remains. Even at the end of the Schleiermacher essay he states, "The situation . . . since Schleiermacher's

---

[126] Ibid., 30.
[127] Ibid., 31.
[128] Ibid., 32.

time has not gotten easier, but more difficult."[129] This is certainly the mood at the end of the *Social Teachings* as well.

Conclusion

Troeltsch's use of the ideal types exhibits the two major features of his evolving conception of Christianity that I identify throughout this study. First, Troeltsch conceives of Christianity as a complex amalgam or continuum of diverse ideas and social forms. The use of the types bolsters Troeltsch's efforts to present Christianity as an internally diverse historical entity with no one clear or unchanging essence. There are three ways in particular that the types emphasize Christian diversity. First, they illustrate that Christianity exists in a multiplicity of forms, which develop in reciprocal relation to other social forces, developments, and institutions. There is no pure Christianity that travels unadjusted throughout history. Second, by alluding to the resources and limits of each type both in its own context and with respect to modern situations and needs, Troeltsch illustrates that no single form of Christianity will obviously serve the present or future. Instead, Christianity will have to generate a new form, thus adding to the diversity and complexity of its historical manifestations.

A third way Troeltsch uses the types to support his particular conception of Christianity can be seen indirectly in his admiration for mysticism. Once Troeltsch discovers the uniqueness of modern mysticism as one of the sole expressions of religious toleration, he holds up this trait as indispensable for a successful Christianity of the future. The mysticism type, therefore, helps Troeltsch defend and promote a Christianity freed from either the universal conception of truth held by the church, which Troeltsch associates with its "dogmatic absolutism," or the limiting and rigid view of religious and moral practice held by the sect, which Troeltsch associates with its religious intolerance. Troeltsch presents the religious toleration of modern mystical movements as intrinsic to the radical individualism native to the gospel.

I also argue in this study that Troeltsch conceptualizes Christianity in certain ways in order to contribute to the value of Christianity in the present and the future. By examining the status, meaning, and function of the types in the *Social Teachings*, it becomes apparent that Troeltsch constructs his conception of historical and normative Christianity in dialogue with the

[129] Ibid., 34.

conditions and challenges of his own day. I have shown that the gendered elements of Troeltsch's types and distinctions help him carry out this dialogue. Troeltsch uses the types not simply to emphasize the internal diversity of historical Christianity, but also to explore and demonstrate the ways in which Christianity might best relate to modern society.

CHAPTER FIVE

From Essence to Synthesis

In the *Social Teachings*, Troeltsch delves into Christianity's past in order to explore the ways in which contemporary Christianity might best be shaped in the context of modern societies. For Troeltsch, the past contains a range of resources that one can and must appropriate, evaluate, and reshape in order to inform and guide the present.[1] Troeltsch's attitude toward the past places him in striking continuity with certain kinds of theorists of tradition today.[2] Far from relying on the "impersonal, universal, and disinterested" conception of reason so often associated with "liberalism,"[3] Troeltsch turns to what one might call "tradition" in order to further the self-understanding and to guide

---

[1] The previous three chapters contain various examples of the ways in which Troeltsch explores and assesses the resources of Christianity's past with an eye to contemporary concerns. Some of the resources he identifies as potential contributors to modern life include: the individualism and universalism of earliest Christianity; the capacity for creating and sustaining social cohesion exhibited by the medieval church and its doctrines; the uniquely Christian form of individualism expressed in many eras and forms of Christianity (including that found in the ideal type of mysticism) as contrasted with the rationalistic form of individualism he sees as increasingly dominant in modern society.

[2] These theorists include, for example, those drawing on the work of Alasdair MacIntyre. In addition, Delwin Brown, who is indebted to Hans Georg Gadamer (and to James Clifford), articulates a Christian theology of tradition that resembles certain features of Troeltsch's thought. Brown's claim (*Boundaries of Our Habitation,* 131) that "our futures are built through the reconstruction of our pasts" is a striking (if unintentional) parallel to the principle that guides Troeltsch's efforts in *Historicism and Its Problems,* the book under consideration in the current chapter. Yet, as I shall note in the conclusion to this study, Troeltsch's theory of Christianity also has strong resonances with more constructive conceptions of tradition that are at odds or in tension with those of MacIntyre or Brown.

[3] MacIntyre uses this language to characterize the view of rationality embodied in the version of moral inquiry he labels the "Encyclopedia." See *Three Rival Versions of Moral Enquiry* (London: Duckworth, 1990) 59.

the development of Christianity in his own time. Examining this feature of Troeltsch's thought, which is developed most clearly in his late philosophy of history, is crucial for understanding him as a theorist of Christianity and for discovering new connections between his work and that of theologians and philosophers today.

In the last three chapters, I have demonstrated the degree to which Troeltsch, by undertaking the massive historical research and analysis required for his composition of the *Social Teachings*, complexified his conception of Christianity in particular and his understanding of historical objects[4] or historical phenomena in general.[5] I have shown also that he does not separate his historical investigation from normative questions about Christianity's possible contribution to modern society. In this chapter, I analyze the way in which Troeltsch incorporates and carries forward these insights and concerns in his major work in philosophy of history, *Historicism and Its Problems*,[6]

---

[4] Troeltsch uses the term "historical object" (*historischer Gegenstand*) to designate the basic phenomenon on which the historian focuses as the main object of his or her historical inquiry. It is that unit that is selected from the mass of historical data and made the focus of attention and organization. Unlike Weber or Rickert, Troeltsch's historical object is not simply the historian's mental concept imposed on historical reality from without to give formless history an organization and shape. By the time he is writing the *Historicism* volume, Troeltsch has come to believe more clearly than before that history (*Geschichte*) presents massive totalities that are properly the main object of investigation. Troeltsch calls these totalities either "individual totalities" or "cultural circles." The historian still must engage in selection and must forever determine the boundaries of the historical object; thus, a strong element of construction remains in Troeltsch's conception of historical work. But, especially in the *Historicism* volume, there is a clear insistence that, in the act of historical analysis, one is dealing with real historical objects and not simply one's mental construct of the object.

[5] Troeltsch testifies to the impact of his writing of the *Social Teachings* on his conception of Christianity in his 1923 essay "The Place of Christianity among the World Religions" (in *Christian Thought: Its History and Application* in *KGA* 17 [ed. Hübinger in collaboration with Terwey] 134–48). He writes, "The further investigations, especially into the history of Christianity, of which I have given the results in my *Social Teachings* . . . have shown me how thoroughly individual is historical Christianity after all, and how invariably its various phases and denominations have been due to varying circumstances and conditions of life. . . . The inference from all that is, however, that a religion, in the several forms assumed by it, always depends upon the intellectual, social, and national conditions among which it exists" (142–43; see also German edition, "Die Stellung des Christentums unter den Weltreligionen," in *KGA* 17:113).

[6] *Der Historismus und seine Probleme. Erstes Buch. Das logische Problem der Geschichtsphilosophie* (vol. 3 of *Gesammelte Schriften*, by Ernst Troeltsch; Tübingen: Mohr, 1922). Hereafter *GS* 3.

published in 1922 as the first of an intended two-volume work. Troeltsch's untimely death in 1923 precluded the writing of volume two.[7]

This last chapter returns to the themes of chapter 1. Indeed, both the *Historicism* volume (the subject of the current chapter) and Troeltsch's essay on the essence of Christianity (the subject of chapter 1) concern historical method, historical understanding, and philosophy of history. Thus, they share a number of common themes: the nature of the historical object, including its composition and development; the nature of the historian's knowledge and construction of the historical object; the inevitable ideal or norm that shapes the historian's perspective on the object; the relation between empirical history and philosophical history; the possibility and meaning of the objectivity of historical and normative claims; the significance and extent of the subjectivity of all such claims; and the interrelation of visions of the past, present, and future, as well as the need for a new, contemporary construction of the meaning and value of the historical object in each age.[8]

---

[7] Troeltsch's work on the *Historicism* volume took place after his 1915 move from the theological faculty in Heidelberg to the philosophical faculty in Berlin. In recent decades many Troeltsch scholars have rejected and corrected the conclusion of Karl Barth (and of those who follow his interpretation, such as Benjamin Reist and Walter Bodenstein) that Troeltsch's move to Berlin (and his interest in working out a conception of European culture) signals the end of his work as a Christian theologian. There is no significant discontinuity between Troeltsch's prior work and the work he takes up in Berlin or in the *Historicism* volume. Troeltsch was always interested in the relation between religion and culture, and he directed much of his historical and theological work toward the resolution of pressing questions about the impact of modernization on both Christian traditions and German culture. F. W. Graf provides important historical contextualization of Troeltsch's attitude toward his move from Heidelberg to Berlin. Troeltsch experienced relief at the idea of leaving Heidelberg's theological faculty and at joining a philosophical faculty. This experience of relief must be placed in the context of the culture wars between orthodox and liberal Protestants. The intervention of the official church in matters related to the teaching of doctrine and the appointment of theological faculty was particularly confining for liberal Protestant professors and pastors, who were often obliged to hold themselves to traditional church doctrine. In this context, orthodox Protestants often sought to push many liberal Protestants out of the theological faculty. See Graf, "Protestantische Theologie," 60–62. See also Chapman, *Ernst Troeltsch and Liberal Theology*, 9–12.

[8] Of course, there are clear differences between the themes of the two works. Perhaps the most striking feature of the *Historicism* volume that separates it from Troeltsch's earlier works is its heightened concern with what he viewed as the crisis of modern society in general and the situation of both German and European culture in particular. F. W. Graf notes that Troeltsch's characteristic preoccupation with the "general political context of his cultural philosophy" increased with his move to Berlin, where Troeltsch directed his philosophical-historical inquiry more intensively toward the task of addressing "the challenges constituted by

This common set of themes provides an opportunity for comparison. How did Troeltsch's conception of Christianity change and develop in the nearly twenty years between the first edition of his essence essay (1903) and the *Historicism* volume (1922)? The *Historicism* volume, of course, does not contain a "theory of Christianity." Instead, it seeks to construct a conception of European culture. Nevertheless, insofar as it attempts to offer a complex and detailed conception of historical phenomena (in terms of both their constitution and their potential resources for the present), the *Historicism* volume provides valuable insight into how Troeltsch would likely have conceptualized Christianity during this period of his intellectual development.

In the first part of this chapter, I show that while there are no utter contradictions between the two works, Troeltsch's conceptions of individuality and development, as well as his outline of categories of historical analysis in the *Historicism* volume, demonstrate the degree to which he has complexified his understanding of the nature of historical phenomena since writing the 1903 essence essay.[9] I argue that a more profound awareness of Christianity as a pluriform phenomenon shaped deeply by its participation in complex causal processes leads Troeltsch to turn away from the concept of an essence and toward that of a cultural synthesis (*Kultursynthese*).[10] The concept of cultural synthesis serves two important functions for Troeltsch that were central to his earlier articulation of Christianity's essence. First, as I have just noted, the concept of cultural synthesis more clearly does justice to the complexity of historical objects than had the concept of an essence. Second, as a creative combination of insights from the past intended to serve the needs

---

the world war" ("Einleitung," in *Ernst Troeltschs "Historismus"* [vol. 11 of Troeltsch-Studien; ed. idem; Gütersloh: Gütersloher Verlagshaus, 2000] 12). Fritz Ringer (*Decline of the German Mandarins*, 345) also argues that in the *Historicism* volume "Troeltsch's methodological convictions flowed together with his social, political, and pedagogical concerns."

[9] This complexification occurred in large part through Troeltsch's immersion in studies of the history of Christianity and Protestantism, such as the *Social Teachings*—a point that the last three chapters demonstrate in detail.

[10] This move does not imply that he no longer had an interest in conceptualizing Christianity, nor does it necessarily suggest that he merged Christianity with the larger "European" culture. Rather, I wish to suggest that Troeltsch becomes less interested in the concept of *essence*, and more in that of *synthesis*, regardless of the historical object in question. What Troeltsch means by synthesis (that is, a synthesis of resources from the past, combined afresh in conversation with the needs of the present) will be discussed in greater detail later in this chapter.

of the present, the cultural synthesis accomplishes one of the major tasks that Troeltsch had earlier assigned to the concept of an essence of Christianity: namely, the task of proposing a vision for Christianity's future out of the historical reconstruction and analysis of its past.[11]

In this chapter, I account for Troeltsch's move from the concept of essence to that of cultural synthesis by first indicating the ways in which he complexified his view of historical entities and dynamics as a result of his work on the *Social Teachings*. Second, I discuss the new conception of historical phenomena that he offers in the *Historicism* volume by means of the category and conceptualization of the "individual totality" (*individuelle Totalität*). These two sections provide the groundwork for understanding how and why Troeltsch replaces the concept "essence" with that of "cultural synthesis." In a third section, I detail the place of the concept "essence" in the *Historicism* volume and demonstrate how the concept of cultural synthesis takes on the two most important functions that had earlier been associated with essence construction. Specifically, Troeltsch comes to use the concept of cultural synthesis (and *not* the concept of essence) to portray the complex and pluralistic composition of historical objects and to engage in the ethical task of formulating a vision for the present and future of his particular culture.

In his work on the idea of a European cultural synthesis, Troeltsch was addressing pressing and immediate concerns related to the cultural situation in Germany and in Europe as a whole in the aftermath of the First World War. During this time, as Harrington has noted, Troeltsch was among those European intellectuals who reflected on questions of European identity and the place of Europe in the world in ways that sought to avoid trends toward nationalism, neoconservatism, cultural pessimism, and imperialism.[12] In the face of cultural fragmentation and political division within Germany and among European nations, Troeltsch used the concept of cultural synthesis to work out a sense of cultural cohesion and unity that nevertheless incorporated and respected the radical diversity of philosophical and cultural traditions

---

[11] While Troeltsch shifts his focus in the *Historicism* volume from the particular question of how to construe historical and normative Christianity to the broader question of conceptualizing the European cultural circle (*Kulturkreis*), the two issues he is concerned with are the same, namely, those which I have placed at the center of this study: how to do justice to the complexity of an historical phenomenon while maintaining a sense of its continuity, meaning, and value for the present and future.

[12] Austin Harrington, "Ernst Troeltsch's Concept of Europe," *European Journal of Social Theory* 7 (2004) 482.

in Europe. Thus, the idea of a European cultural synthesis was also an effort to counter divisive nationalisms, to promote peace in postwar Europe, and to embrace democratic ideals and forms of cooperation among European nations.[13]

The Development of Troeltsch's View of Historical Phenomena

The analyses in the previous chapters show how Troeltsch increasingly sought to conceptualize Christianity in a way that acknowledged its internal diversity and its rootedness in multiple processes of historical development and social change. Already in the 1903 essence essay, as I show in chapter 1, he attempts to formulate the essence of Christianity in a way that adequately reflects the complex structure and constitution of an historical object like Christianity.[14] He ponders, for example, how to define the essence so that it does justice to "the multiplicity of formations developing out of the original form" of Christianity.[15]

Through his work on the *Social Teachings*, Troeltsch increases his appreciation for the diversity of Christianity and heightens his awareness of the interaction and interdependence of social and religious events.[16] Thus he comes to recognize the important role that cultural, political, and

---

[13] See F. W. Graf, "Philosophisch reflektierte Kriegserfahrung. Einige Überlegungen zu Ernst Troeltschs 'Kaisergeburtstagsrede'," in *"Geschichte durch Geschichte überwinden." Ernst Troeltsch in Berlin* (ed. idem; vol. 1 of Troeltsch-Studien: New Series; Gütersloh: Gütersloher Verlagshaus, 2006) 231–52. During this period, Troeltsch often reflected on the possibility of a synthesis of German and "Western European" political values. In these writings, Troeltsch was implicitly challenging his German colleagues to temper claims to the superiority of German political and philosophical ideals and to open themselves to the resources of English and French conceptions of reason, natural law, and democracy. For more on the development and transformation of Troeltsch's conception of "England" and of German-British relations, see "Einleitung" to *KGA* 17. See also Troeltsch's essay, "Naturrecht und Humanität in der Weltpolitik" (1922) in *KGA* 15:493–512.

[14] As I have indicated in ch. 1, in the 1903 essence essay Troeltsch states that "the various formations of the Christian spirit display extraordinarily divergent orientations" ("Essence," 153; "¹WCh," 583).

[15] "Essence," 152; "¹WCh," 582.

[16] Graf notes that thanks to the perspectives Troeltsch gained while writing the *Social Teachings*, Troeltsch's *Historicism* volume "includes in the discussion from the outset the question of the interaction of ideal factors, or spiritual formations, and material factors, or societal institutions" ("Einleitung," in *Ernst Troeltschs "Historismus,"* 11).

economic conditions have played in Christianity's development. As I show in earlier chapters, Troeltsch indicates how movements that were "external" to Christianity, such as Stoicism, nevertheless deeply contributed to its shape and history. He also discusses the degree to which socio-economic conditions, such as feudalism or capitalism, affect Christianity's nature and structure in a given period or context. Finally, at least at the close of the *Social Teachings*, Troeltsch explicitly acknowledges that social forces influence Christianity's development significantly—something he increasingly comes to appreciate throughout his composition of this work. Troeltsch continues to insist that some developments are "an independent expression of the religious life" and not, therefore, *mere* products of social forces. He also becomes convinced, however, that social forces play a significant *role* in all such "religious" developments. Concerning these developments or phenomena, he states:

> It is clear that in the causal connection out of which their peculiar form of religious thought gains concrete stimulus, force, movement, and aim, social and even, finally, economic influences are at work. . . . As in all other spheres of life, so also in that of the history of religion, the conception of the causal connection is considerably widened and altered by giving fresh attention to this co-operating element.[17]

Troeltsch, therefore, has come to see more profoundly the extent to which the various theological and religious developments he has charted in the *Social Teachings* were bound up with social changes and cultural contexts.[18]

---

[17] *ST*, 1002; *GS* 1:975–76.

[18] Interestingly, Troeltsch makes this point much more clearly in the conclusion to the *Social Teachings* than he had done, in certain cases, in the rest of the text. In his chapter on the beginnings of Protestantism, for example, one is hard-pressed to find any significant discussion of the influence of social conditions on the emergence of the reform movement. He devotes only one two-page section to such a topic, and he says only the following: "[O]nly very indirectly can we here discern certain traces of the influence of social, economic, and political causes. That is to say: the theories proclaimed by the Nominalism of the later Scholasticism and the mysticism of the Pre-Reformation opposition parties, were doubtless to some extent connected with the social changes which took place during the later Middle Ages" (*ST*, 466; *GS* 1:432). In the rest of this section, Troeltsch focuses on refuting Marxist accounts of the Reformation, and therefore he reverts again, as he had done in his treatment of Christian origins, to his insistence on the "purely religious" nature and origin of the movement. This contrasts sharply with what he states in the conclusion to the *Social Teachings*. Reflecting on his treatment of the Reformation, he states, "[W]e have seen that the individualism of the Reformation presupposed the collapse of mediaeval society, and that the triumphant realization of the Reformation can only be explained from the standpoint of political and

One can find evidence that Troeltsch became more strongly convinced of the interdependence of religious, social, cultural, political, and economic developments in several essays written around the time of his completion of the *Social Teachings*. In "Religion, Economy, and Society" (1913),[19] Troeltsch emphasizes the interaction (*Wechselwirkung*) of religious and economic developments and characterizes their relation as one of reciprocal influence.[20] Again, in "Stoic-Christian Natural Law and Modern Secular Natural Law" (1911), he refers to a reciprocity between ideas and social factors and argues that "just as the sociological situation determines the formation of ideas, so, conversely, the ideology impinges upon the sociological circumstances."[21] Along with this increased appreciation for the social factors that influence Christianity's development, Troeltsch comes to see Christianity itself as pluriform in structure. In "Logos and Mythos in Theology and Philosophy of Religion" (1913), he writes, " 'Christianity' . . . is an extremely ambiguous concept. Its ambiguity is directly evident in the co-existence of the great confessions, all of which have the historical right to identify themselves with Christianity."[22] Similarly, in the "The Dogmatics of the History-of-Religions

---

social conditions" (*ST*, 1003; *GS* 1:976). This contrast suggests that as he wrote the *Social Teachings*, Troeltsch gradually developed an increasing appreciation for what he comes to call the interaction (*Wechselwirkung*) of religious and social forces and developments.

[19] "Religion, Wirtschaft, und Gesellschaft," in *GS* 4:21–33.

[20] Specifically, Troeltsch states that the interaction of religious and economic forces should be understood in terms of the "reciprocal influences and interpenetrations (both conscious and unconscious) of both tendencies" ("Religion, Wirtschaft, und Gesellschaft," *GS* 4:25).

[21] "Stoic-Christian Natural Law and Modern Secular Natural Law," in *Religion in History*, 322; "Das stoisch-christliche Naturrecht und das moderne profane Naturrecht," in *GS* 4:167. Here Troeltsch is actually defending the efficacy of ideas in shaping social circumstances against reductionist readings of historical development, wherein all ideas are "pure reflections and outgrowths of the sociological laws of nature" (ibid). It is nonetheless significant that Troeltsch at this point is willing to admit a reciprocity between ideas (or ideals) and social forces, since earlier he was less clear on how to speak of this relationship, occasionally refusing the reciprocity and focusing more on the independence of religious ideas. For example, in the introduction to the *Social Teachings*, he makes virtually no mention of the relation between religious ideas and social, economic, or political forces, and he does not suggest that this will be his concern in the book. Instead, his main question articulated in the introduction is how certain kinds of religious ideas are related to certain kinds of religious structures; at the close of the *Social Teachings*, however, he has broadened his topic to the consideration of how religious ideas and social forms are influenced by societal structures and economic, political, and social conditions.

[22] "Logos and Mythos in Theology and Philosophy of Religion," in *Religion in History*, 60; "Logos und Mythos in Theologie und Religionsphilosophie," in *GS* 2:823.

School" (1913), Troeltsch refers to "the whole, living, historical complexity known as Christianity," which he describes as "an extraordinarily extensive world of thought and life with widely divergent periods and epochs."[23]

Finally, many of the changes Troeltsch makes to the 1903 essence essay when revising it for inclusion in the second volume of his collected works in 1913 also demonstrate the degree to which he has problematized his view of Christianity's complex structure and development. The first and most obvious way in which Troeltsch modifies his 1903 essence essay is by adding phrases, sentences, or short sections that detail or make explicit some of the diverse features of Christianity's history of which he became more appreciative while writing the *Social Teachings*. For example, in four places[24] Troeltsch makes additions that allude to the ideal types (church, sect, and mysticism) in order to highlight the internal plurality of Christianity. He writes that the sects and mysticism "have their own meaning and independent relationship to the Gospel and to original Christianity."[25] Pointing to the emergence of sect and church tendencies in earliest Christianity,[26] Troeltsch states that from its beginning Christianity was characterized by "two different trends" that had a "distinctive influence through the whole history of Christianity."[27] It is no surprise, therefore, that Troeltsch also adds comments stressing the importance and advantage of expanding traditional church or intellectual histories to include questions and methods relevant to a "general history of culture."[28] Finally, Troeltsch draws attention to the diversity of Christianity's history by adding sentences that point to the way in which Christianity has assimilated "new and alien elements"[29] that cannot be said to have been determined by "the Gospel."[30] All these additions to the 1903 version help Troeltsch emphasize more strongly the complexities and variations that characterize Christianity.

[23] "The Dogmatics," in *Religion in History,* 96; "Die Dogmatik," in *GS* 2:510.

[24] The four places are "Essence," 140, 141, 149, 155; "²WCh," 405, 406, 416, 422.

[25] "Essence," 140; "²WCh," 405.

[26] Here Troeltsch associates the sect tendency (individualism that is "heroically and ethically oriented, living in the salvation of the future") with Jesus, and he connects the church tendency ("present salvation and the certainty of grace") with Paul. See "Essence," 149; "²WCh," 416.

[27] "Essence," 149; "²WCh," 416.

[28] "Essence," 127; "²WCh," 390. In a different passage, Troeltsch speaks against the "one-sided ecclesiastical consideration of Christianity" ("Essence," 140; "²WCh," 405).

[29] "Essence," 150; "²WCh," 416.

[30] "Essence," 126; "²WCh," 388.

The second way in which Troeltsch modifies the 1903 essay follows directly from the first. In recognition of the important insights he has gained into Christianity's history, Troeltsch makes comments that place greater weight on the empirical-historical dimension of defining Christianity's essence. For example, he speaks of the need for any formulation of the essence to be based on "a history which has been historically and scientifically researched."[31] Such research, if it focuses not only on "the development of ideas of belief" but on "sociological" developments and relations as well, "will no longer be able to formulate the essence as simply as Harnack did."[32]

Troeltsch's Late Conception of the Historical Object: The Category of the Individual Totality

As the foregoing discussion shows, in the years between 1903 and 1913, Troeltsch becomes increasingly convinced of Christianity's internal diversity and of the reciprocal relationship among religious, social, economic, and political forces. In the *Historicism* volume, he conceptualizes the historical object and its development by means of the category of the individual totality (*individuelle Totalität*).[33] "Totality" refers to Troeltsch's view that historical phenomena are not simple elements;[34] rather, they are composite amalgams encompassing diverse and ever-fluctuating contents and events that nevertheless constitute a "unity of life." As I shall demonstrate more clearly below, "individual" signals the value and uniqueness of all such major totalities. For Troeltsch, such individual totalities are best represented not by single human beings (as they typically were by many German historians who conceptualized historical epochs by focusing on extraordinary individuals) but rather as "collective individualities," such as "peoples, states, classes,

---

[31] "Essence," 161; "²WCh," 430.

[32] "Essence," 178; "²WCh," 449.

[33] James Luther Adams offers a clear and succinct definition of the individual totality: it is "a complex of data more or less unified by a pervasive meaning and dynamic." "Ernst Troeltsch as Analyst of Religion," *Journal of the Scientific Study of Religion* 1 (1961) 107.

[34] Troeltsch argues that history presents no analogue to natural science's fundamental unit (the element) nor to its abstract general law; instead, history has before itself only complex or composite objects, or what he calls *zusammengesetzte Größen* (combined or composite entities). Thus, the basic unit of history should be conceived as something complex, not as something simple (*GS* 3:32–33).

social castes, cultural epochs, cultural tendencies, religious communities, and complex events of all kinds such as wars and revolutions."[35]

This category proves useful to Troeltsch's purposes because it enables him to emphasize the pluriform structure and fluid constitution of historical objects. Troeltsch can, therefore, also identify these objects' involvement in and indebtedness to complex causal processes without reducing them to mere products of these causal processes. That is, the category of the individual totality 1) offers a sufficiently complex view of historical phenomena and processes, while 2) preserving the integrity or continuity of meaning and the uniqueness or value of each historical object. This section focuses on how Troeltsch achieves this dual result.

The Individual Totality as Complex and Fluid

The "individual totality" is the first of eleven "logical assumptions and principles of selection, formation and connection" that Troeltsch groups together as constituting the logic of history.[36] The second is the concept of development. Together, these two concepts are the most basic and central categories of historical inquiry and understanding.[37] The remaining nine categories are tools or principles for understanding, analyzing, shaping, and defining an individual totality and the complex processes that constitute it. These are: originality, limited selection, representation, unity of value or meaning, tension between the whole and the parts, the unconscious, the creative, freedom, and chance.[38]

In chapter 3, I pointed to some of the ways in which Troeltsch portrays Christianity's internal constitution as influenced by a variety of predictable and unpredictable causal and developmental processes and events.[39] In the *Social Teachings*, he portrays the complexity of Christianity by means of

[35] *GS* 3:33. Also in contrast to a convention among German historians of treating the state as the basic object of historical analysis, Troeltsch proposes that the cultural circle (*Kulturkreis*), which encompasses states and other unities of peoples and their cultural contents, is perhaps the best candidate for the individual totality that historians should adopt as their historical object in the modern world. See *GS* 3:35.

[36] *GS* 3:29.

[37] Troeltsch states that the historical object and historical becoming, or development, are the main concepts of empirical history and also lead into material philosophy of history (*GS* 3:71).

[38] Rubanowice offers a clear interpretive summary of the eleven elements of Troeltsch's logic of history in *Crisis in Consciousness,* 80–89.

[39] See my discussion of Troeltsch's pluralistic causality in ch. 3.

his historical narrative. He articulates, however, no explicit philosophical categories to conceptualize its dynamic and ever-changing constitution. In the *Historismus*, Troeltsch explicitly accounts for the fluidity and contingency of historical objects—including their shape, structure, and development—by means of five of his categories of historical analysis.

The Tension between the Whole and the Parts

The principle that in any totality there will be a tension between the general and the particular, or between the common spirit and individual tendencies that may go against the whole, is itself a by-product of the composite and vital nature of any totality. This suggests, therefore, that the unity of the object does not preclude opposing tendencies that conflict with, challenge, or differ from the principle or source of that unity. By means of this concept, Troeltsch preserves both the dynamism of the object and the open-endedness of its development without simultaneously compromising its integrity. Troeltsch compares the historical object to the biological organism, which exhibits a lively tension between the "whole body" and the "individual cells."[40] In the historical totality there exists among the contents "a continual mutual conditioning, a continual unity and a continual contradiction—a dialectical relationship."[41] This is also expressed in the tension and interrelation, unique to historical objects,[42] between the universal and the individual: "In [the individual totality], every universal refers to an individual and every individual refers to a universal, where the universal is to be understood as the unity of meaning of the totality under consideration."[43] Troeltsch adds that this relation of universal and particular is in no way a formal one, emerging the same way in all totalities, but rather varies from case to case.

The Unconscious

This notion of a common or universal spirit stretching over the whole of the totality leads to another of Troeltsch's categories, that of the unconscious. He uses this concept to underscore the unpredictability and incomprehensibility

---

[40] *GS* 3:44.

[41] Ibid.

[42] Troeltsch emphasizes that this dynamic is peculiar to history and not to be explained by any other mode of analysis, such as psychology or sociology. Presumably, in Troeltsch's view, these analyses would account for this lively tension by means of some reductive causal schema. See *GS* 3:44–45.

[43] *GS* 3:44.

of the total shape, influence, and direction of the historical object. The unconscious dimension of the larger spirit of the whole refers to its ultimate ungraspability at any given time. The whole inevitably surpasses the purview of the individual. Moreover, the power of the whole is always both greater and different than the individual would presume. Troeltsch clarifies that this is not the notion of the unconscious that is used in psychology, but rather refers to the "fact, confirmed by history a thousand times, that our actions, feelings, instincts, aspirations, and decisions carry in themselves many more assumptions than we can know, and that they have a much greater or completely different significance for the whole and in perpetuity than we were even aware at the time they happened."[44] Given this fact, the ultimate development of the totality is also beyond control and comprehension. It cannot be completely guided or predicted beforehand. Hence, Troeltsch states that there can be no "history of the present, as we are not conscious of the weight and significance, the power and extent of our aspirations."[45]

The Creative

The concept of "the creative" balances that of "the unconscious" by maintaining a place for the novel contributions made by individuals that genuinely influence and add to the larger whole. The creative contributes in its own way, therefore, to the open-endedness and uncontrollability of the composition and development of the totality. What proceeds in the life of the whole comes not simply from the force and influence of what has come before, but also from new additions that cannot be derived from previous elements but, instead, insert into the whole "new structures (*Gebilde*), forces, and beginnings."[46] Troeltsch emphasizes that these new contributions do not simply escape or have no relation to causal processes or origins. On the contrary, creative contributions "take place through the impetus and merging together of all kinds of conditions and causes."[47] Nevertheless, the element of novelty is still prominent and significant. Troeltsch explains this by referring to the unique nature of historical causality, which does not mirror the equality of cause and effect in natural science but, rather, displays a more unequal and complex relationality and interaction of disparate elements and forces.

[44] *GS* 3:47.
[45] Ibid.
[46] *GS* 3:48.
[47] Ibid.

Freedom

The concept of the new also entails that of freedom in the sense of choice. Freedom refers to the fact that amidst the variety of causal relations in which a novel contribution arises, there is indeed the possibility of "aberration,"[48] that is, of a decision against the grain of the causal process that enables one to contribute something not only new, but also of value and meaning. Again, the significance of this category for Troeltsch is not simply its preservation of originality, but actually the extent to which it demonstrates the unpredictability and open-endedness of history. This, then, contributes to the complexity of the individual totality.

Contingency

The unpredictability of any individual totality is preserved not only by novel contributions and freedom of choice, but also by contingencies or accidents that arise from the contact or collision of unrelated causal forces.[49] When such forces intersect, they can either have stimulating and strengthening results or destructive and deteriorating ones. Thus, the shape and development of an individual totality can be significantly determined by events, such as natural disasters, sudden deaths of leading personalities, changes in climates, or the collision of these developments with other historical or social forces. Troeltsch assigns this contingency, or chance, a "tremendous role" in history,[50] and he underscores three implications that chance has for understanding the nature of historical objects. First, insofar as historical objects "always develop at the intersection of such heterogeneous effects," they are by nature always "complex creations" (*komplexe Gebilde*).[51] Second, an historical totality's unity of meaning is not only composed by unpredictable contingencies, whether beneficial or detrimental, but is also continually subject to the transforming effects of future contingencies. Thus, the course and stability of historical objects are always potentially threatened or aided by these accidental occurrences and developments. Finally, unified and lasting totalities of meaning, or stable historical objects, therefore, occur only occasionally, in large part when the unpredictable and accidental forces of

[48] *GS* 3:50.
[49] *GS* 3:51.
[50] Ibid.
[51] *GS* 3:52.

history happen to be propitious for such formations. "Great and significant totalities of meaning are rare."[52]

The Continuity (Development) and Value (Individuality) of the Individual Totality

The five categories I have outlined emphasize the constitution of the single historical object as dynamic, unpredictable, uncontrollable, and made of complex and diverse elements. Troeltsch conceptualizes the coherence of individual totalities by means of his categories of development and individuality.

Development

In the midst of this emphasis on the fluidity and even, in some cases, randomness of individual totalities, Troeltsch's concept of development in the *Historicism* volume points to their continuity. Individual totalities are determined by a "unity of meaning or tendency" (*Sinnheit oder Tendenz*)[53] or a "developing unity" (*Werde-Einheit*).[54] This means that there is a coherence to the development or becoming of the individual totality, so that a continuity of meaning or a "living organic fusion"[55] can be discerned throughout its developmental trajectory. For Troeltsch, this unity is inherent to the actual totality itself and is not just the result of the power of the mind of the historian who organizes the data. He writes, "For the historian . . . development is an inner movement of the object itself, into which one can and must immerse oneself intuitively."[56]

Troeltsch is also concerned to include in his analysis of the historical object an account of its connections with larger, coherent processes of becoming. He employs the concept of development, therefore, to refer not only to the unity of meaning internal to the individual historical object but also to the unity of meaning that exists among several objects making up, for example, a larger cultural circle. In this way, the single object is not an isolated phenomenon but, rather, is joined with other objects in a larger connection, continuity, or "flow of becoming."[57] By means of the concept of development, then, one

[52] Ibid.
[53] *GS* 3:54.
[54] *GS* 3:55.
[55] *GS* 3:58.
[56] *GS* 3:235.
[57] *GS* 3:54.

can see not only discrete and random causal events or processes, but also a greater unity or coherence that governs and unites all of these individual events into a meaningful totality such as Christianity, the Renaissance, or feudalism. Furthermore, historical understanding by means of the concept of development can also link these periods or totalities together into a "whole of the Western cultural circle."[58]

Central to Troeltsch's conception of development in the *Historicism* volume is its clear limitation to the purview, standpoint, or cultural circle of the historian.[59] Despite the natural desire to expand the concept of development to ever-widening circles, and even to all of humanity, no such developmental construction is possible. Troeltsch argues that such a construction is not possible because there is no unity of humanity, at least not at present.[60] Insofar as philosophy of history cannot circumscribe all of humanity or all possible systems of value, it is to be limited to reflection on the development or unity of a single cultural circle.[61]

Troeltsch argues that seeing these greater unities—whether at the level of individual totalities or of larger totalities in the form of cultural circles—is the essence of historical understanding.[62] This claim is consistent with the general portrayal of history that Troeltsch offers in the *Historicism* volume. History itself is the realm of individuality[63] and is therefore full of units of meaning

---

[58] *GS* 3:55.

[59] Benjamin Reist (*Towards a Theology of Involvement,* 78) argues that with this move, Troeltsch subsumes the concept of development under that of individuality, so that the latter "begins to dominate, even overwhelm" the former. Reist is critical of this move insofar as it ends ultimately in a relativistic plurality.

[60] *GS* 3:74–75. Troeltsch exclaims, "The development of humanity! That is a massive undertaking."

[61] As Graf and Ruddies state, for Troeltsch, "God is the only universal philosopher of history." See "Ernst Troeltsch: Geschichtsphilosophie," 145.

[62] *GS* 3:54–55. For Troeltsch, being able to discern a unity of meaning is also essential to the process of constructing a cultural synthesis. In such a process, one turns to the past and identifies a continuity that is then further developed through a new combination or synthesis for the present and future. For hints at this connection, see, for example, *GS* 3:82, 167–71. Chapman asserts that Troeltsch's work was driven by a quest for unity in a fragmented culture, and that Troeltsch insisted on achieving this unity within history (instead of escaping, for example, to an ahistorical notion of the moral conscience) and constructing it out of the material of history (*Ernst Troeltsch and Liberal Theology*, 138–39; 183–84).

[63] This is what distinguishes history from other sciences, especially those which ultimately end, in Troeltsch's view, in some form of naturalism.

and value.[64] For this reason, as much as empirical history rightly limits its task to the more or less objective reconstruction of past events, the concept of development will inevitably push it toward philosophical history in the desire to follow the meaningful trajectories of the past into the present and future.[65] Thus, being able to discern the development of meaningful totalities in history is precisely what it means to genuinely grasp historical objects.

Individuality

Troeltsch's notion of individuality is linked to the first category in his formal logic of history: *originality*. Originality is defined as the nonreducibility and utter unrepeatability (*Einmaligkeit*) of any historical object and the events, impulses, and ideas that constitute it. It refers to the unique and underivable givenness[66] of historical objects or historical realities, which, though dynamic and changing, nevertheless constitute "a qualitative unity or uniqueness" that cannot be reproduced or explained.[67] The individuality of all particular historical entities is precisely this originality.

[64] Here Troeltsch's perspective fits Georg Iggers's description of the general understanding of history among German intellectuals who can be roughly grouped into the historical school: namely, that for these thinkers, history is "value-filled diversity" (*The German Conception of History,"* 30). But as Adams points out, Troeltsch's historical method moves beyond the mere interest in individuality and actually places great weight on generalizing analyses of historical objects, for example, by means of typologies. Adams writes, "In these ways Troeltsch transcends the simple distinction between nomothetic and ideographic method, though he would insist that any individual totality as a symbolic construction does not exhaust reality. In this sense the concept of individuality continues to function as an irreducible category of the dynamic, contingent historical dimension. Nevertheless, the characteristic work of the historian, and of Troeltsch as a historian, is more of a generalizing enterprise than his explicit delineation of method seems to recognize" ("Ernst Troeltsch as Analyst of Religion," 107).

[65] See *GS* 3:61.

[66] To express this givenness or actuality of historical objects, Troeltsch uses words such as *Setzung*, *Gesetztheit* (*GS* 3:38), and *Faktizität* (*GS* 3:200).

[67] *GS* 3:38. Troeltsch adds that psychology, for example, can analyze many features and relations of this historical object, but cannot actually explain the thing itself (*die Sache selbst*). While discussing the historian's unique ability to comprehend and analyze an individual totality as constituted by a tension between the spirit of the whole and the spirit of the individual parts, Troeltsch argues that "the phenomenon itself in its immense individual multifariousness belongs first of all to the historian and his penetrating view. The psychologist and sociologist can only construct the general patterns and laws of the expressions of the phenomenon. . . . It is the historian who shows the primary objects of history to the psychologist and sociologist, and not vice versa" (*GS* 3:45–46). While this statement clearly demonstrates Troeltsch's efforts in the *Historicism* volume to defend history against

Yet, critical for Troeltsch's program and proposal in the *Historicism* volume is his claim that individuality refers not only to the nature of historical objects empirically considered, but also to the ideal that is expressed or striven toward (if not necessarily fully realized) in those entities. In other words, individuality encompasses both idea (*Idee*), or that which should be, and actuality (*Tatsächlichkeit*).[68] With this move, Troeltsch is able to connect empirical and philosophical (or normative) history. The concept of individuality, he says, is the portal from history to a doctrine of values.[69] It can facilitate this transition because "the concept of individuality does not simply mean the purely factual distinctiveness of a given historical-spiritual complex, but simultaneously signifies an individualization of the ideal or of that which ought to be; this ideal is striven after and embodied in different fortuitous ways depending on the circumstances, even though this ideal is not realized exhaustively in each particular form."[70] In the concept of individuality, Troeltsch joins "being and ought, actual and ideal."[71] In doing so, he also links the historical with the valuable.

In *The Absoluteness of Christianity and the History of Religions*, Troeltsch asserts that "the historical and the relative are identical."[72] As an historical phenomenon, Christianity could not be shown to possess absolute validity, for to be historical is to be relative. Yet, this does not suggest that Christianity or any other historical phenomenon has *no* validity. On the contrary, Troeltsch argues that relative historical entities partake of the value that is implicit in all such individualities.[73] The task then, is to discern the value in these entities and to compare them to one another in search of the highest but still relative expression of validity.[74]

In the *Historicism* volume, Troeltsch's position moves beyond his earlier claim that "the historical and the relative are identical" to a new equation:

---

reductionist psychological or sociological declarations, it also illustrates the way in which Troeltsch closely associates history with individuality, so that history becomes the domain with unique access to the individual object in its true and underived reality.

[68] *GS* 3:200.

[69] *GS* 3:201.

[70] Ibid.

[71] *GS* 3:208.

[72] *The Absoluteness*, 85; *Die Absolutheit*, in *KGA* 5:166.

[73] *The Absoluteness*, 89; *Die Absolutheit*, in *KGA* 5:170.

[74] *The Absoluteness*, 98; *Die Absolutheit*, in *KGA* 5:178–79.

the historical, the relative, the valuable, and the individual are all identical.[75] This equation is found implicitly in his doctrine of the relativity of values.[76] Insofar as individuality is both the basic unit of history and the locus of all value in history, and insofar as Troeltsch has defined individuality such that it is opposed to general or timeless validity,[77] "the concept of individuality is that of the fundamental relativity of values."[78]

Troeltsch is eager to clarify that the relativity of values is not relativism. It is the affirmation of continually new, creative, and individual validity in history, as opposed to timeless or universal validity. Furthermore, Troeltsch states that the absolute is present in the relativity of values. This affirmation of an absolute that "becomes alive and creative"[79] in the relative is critical to Troeltsch's effort to avoid unlimited relativism. Without it, his doctrine "would be a relativity only, but not a relativity of values."[80] The thesis of a relativity of values, therefore, implies a metaphysic wherein all individualities are grounded in the divine or absolute, which is the source of all value.[81]

---

[75] Troeltsch's increased emphasis on individuality in the *Historicism* volume (compared to *Absoluteness*) means that he gives up the notion even of comparing different value systems and argues, instead, for limiting the question of norms within the confines of each cultural circle considered separately and individually. Troeltsch is working with a view of culture typical for his time, wherein cultures are seen as discrete and bounded wholes, different and largely separate from other such wholes. For an accessible explanation of the modern conception of culture as typically formulated among early twentieth-century European and North American intellectuals, see Kathryn Tanner, *Theories of Culture: A New Agenda for Theology* (Minneapolis: Fortress, 1997) 25–30.

[76] Troeltsch states that "it is clear that this historical relativity of values has a certain analogy to the doctrine of physical relativity," and he quotes Alan Coates Bouquet's description of Troeltsch as "a kind of Einstein of the religious world" (*GS* 3:219). Discussing this comparison, Mark Chapman makes the interesting comment that "at the end of his life, Troeltsch had begun to regard relativity as having virtues of its own" ("*Der Historismus* in England und England in *Der Historismus*," in *Ernst Troeltschs "Historismus"* [ed. Graf] 197).

[77] See *GS* 3:166, 182–83. Troeltsch explains that, just as the actuality and individuality of historical objects are original and unrepeatable, so is the formation of standards a momentous and spontaneous act, appropriate to the individuality of ideals and values.

[78] *GS* 3:211.

[79] *GS* 3:212.

[80] Ibid.

[81] Christoph Schwöbel offers an illuminating discussion of the strong metaphysical dimension of Troeltsch's understanding of individuality in his late work. He comments, "Whoever wants to engage this central aspect of the understanding of individuality in Troeltsch's late work must not have any fear of metaphysics." Schwöbel notes that Troeltsch supports his conception of individuality by grounding it in a Leibnizian monadology that is linked to the notion of value relativity. Schwöbel explains that such a conception of value relativity "keeps all relativism

This brief discussion of Troeltsch's concepts of individuality and development, together with my account of the ways in which Troeltsch portrays the fluidity of the individual totality, illustrates how Troeltsch (in the *Historicism* volume) makes the historical object more pluriform and more engaged in a complex stream of historical processes on the one hand, while also supporting its uniqueness, continuity, and value by means of newly refined philosophical categories on the other.

Troeltsch's Move from Essence to Cultural Synthesis

Given the degree to which Troeltsch problematized and broadened his understanding of historical entities, it is not surprising that he also became increasingly skeptical of the fruitfulness of defining or conceptualizing an historical phenomenon like Christianity by means of an "essence." In this section, I first reflect on the places where this skepticism appears in his writings after his completion of the *Social Teachings*. I then examine what happens to the concept of an essence in the *Historicism* volume, showing first that it is made to occupy a small and very specific place in Troeltsch's categorical scheme, and second, that the cultural synthesis is crafted in ways that resemble aspects of Troeltsch's earlier conception of an essence.

Troeltsch's Gradual Dissatisfaction with the Concept of an Essence

There are points in the 1903 essence essay that foreshadow Troeltsch's later dissatisfaction with the concept of an essence. Already in that essay, Troeltsch argues that the essence must not be a simple concept representing a single idea that all forms of Christianity share, but, rather, must be able to do justice to the various elements in Christianity that "develop with multiple tensions and oppositions" in its history.[82] Nevertheless, in 1903, Troeltsch focuses on complexifying the concept of an essence and does not yet express the more profound skepticism about the possibility and desirability of speaking of an essence of Christianity at all—a skepticism that is more evident in the essay's second edition (1913), where Troeltsch adds the clause "If we are to

---

in check while seeing individuality in a constitutive relation to the absolute" (" 'Die Idee des Aufbaus heißt Geschichte durch Geschichte überwinden.' Theologischer Wahrheitsanspruch und das Problem des sogenannten Historismus," in *Ernst Troeltschs "Historismus*," ed. Graf, 275).

[82] "Essence," 154; "¹WCh," 583.

speak of the essence at all" to one of his convictions about how the essence should be formulated.[83] There are several additional places in the 1913 edition of the essence essay that betray Troeltsch's efforts either to question or to complexify further the concept of an essence of Christianity. In his opening remarks on Harnack's treatment of the essence of Christianity, Troeltsch inserts some extended comments drawing attention to recent works in church history and Christian origins that make "the 'essence' . . . very difficult to determine at all."[84] Importantly, he then adds a footnote (also not included in the 1903 version) that names some of these works, for example, by Adolf Jülicher, August Dorner, Walther Köhler, William Wrede, and Gerhard Löschke. In this same footnote Troeltsch also makes reference to his own *Social Teachings* as having shown "great caution with regard to achieving a purely historical definition of the concept [of an essence]."[85] With these comments, Troeltsch suggests that Christian history is too complicated to yield clearly a single and unitary essence. Thus any essence would be a normative construction and not simply a reflection of historical reality. In other places, Troeltsch adds phrases that reinforce the need for any concept of an essence of Christianity to be dynamically and flexibly construed, so as to mirror adequately the plurality of Christian history.[86]

The *Social Teachings* is instrumental in moving Troeltsch from his initial 1903 view of the essence to his more complicated perspective in the 1913 version. I have argued for the fruitfulness of reading the *Social Teachings* in conversation with the concerns and perspectives of the essence essay. While there is a striking parallel between these two works, it is certainly noteworthy that the term "essence" rarely appears in the *Social Teachings*. Although Troeltsch's picture of Christianity in the *Social Teachings* resonates profoundly with the complex view of Christianity offered in the 1903 essence essay, the usefulness of the concept of an essence itself gradually appears

---

[83] "Essence," 151; "²WCh," 418.

[84] "Essence," 126; "²WCh," 388.

[85] "Essence," 126 n. 4; "²WCh," 388 n. 25.

[86] Specifically, Troeltsch notes that the essence "must go so far as to bear opposites and tensions within itself" ("Essence," 153; "²WCh," 420–21). He also states that the various "accommodations and appropriations" that Christianity has made (in various epochs) in conversation with its social and historical settings "themselves belong to the essence" ("Essence," 155; "²WCh," 423). Finally, Troeltsch is more explicit than he had been in the 1903 version in defining the essence as "a continuum" ("Essence," 152; "²WCh," 419).

inadequate for the divergent and complicated developments in Christian history that are the subject of Troeltsch's study.

One of the few places where the phrase "essence of Christianity" shows up in the *Social Teachings* is toward the beginning of Troeltsch's chapter on medieval Catholicism. As I indicate in chapter 2, Troeltsch argues against the suggestion presumably held by Protestant theologians that medieval Catholicism is a "perversion" of the essence of Christianity. Following his criticism of such claims, Troeltsch states, "The religious life, even that of Christianity, in each of its great forms is something new and different, and must first of all be understood as an independent phenomenon."[87] Although Troeltsch here does not state outright that there are "many essences" of Christianity, he uses language that is similar to that employed in one section of his essay "The Dogmatics of the History-of-Religions School" (1913). There he suggests more explicitly that there is no one essence of Christianity. Troeltsch writes, "Thus the essence of Christianity can be understood only as the new interpretations and new adaptations, corresponding to each new situation, produced by Christianity's historical power. The essence of Christianity differs in every epoch, resulting from the totality of the influences in each age."[88]

The context in which this statement appears provides a striking illustration of the way in which Troeltsch becomes convinced of the limits of the concept of an essence of Christianity and, therefore, gradually shifts his own view away from this concept and toward that of a cultural synthesis.[89] Troeltsch raises the issue of the essence of Christianity in his discussion of what he identifies as the second task of a history-of-religions approach to dogmatics, that is, the task of formulating a definition of Christianity. After indicating the way Locke, Schleiermacher, Hegel, and Harnack each had attempted to define an essence of Christianity, Troeltsch states that "the essence of Christianity cannot be determined in this fashion."[90] The reason for this is

---

[87] *ST*, 207; *GS* 1:186.

[88] "The Dogmatics," in *Religion in History*, 97; "Die Dogmatik," in *GS* 2:511. See also the original version published in *American Journal of Theology* 17 (1913) 12–13.

[89] I am not suggesting that at this time Troeltsch was making this move from essence to cultural synthesis intentionally, but rather that, in retrospect, we can see foreshadowings of such a change.

[90] "The Dogmatics," in *Religion in History*, 97; "Die Dogmatik," in *GS* 2:511. Similarly, in "Logos and Mythos in Theology and Philosophy of Religion," also written in 1913, Troeltsch states that the previous efforts to construct an essence of Christianity "cannot succeed."

that an historical consideration of Christianity "reveals to us such a variety of interpretations, formulations, and syntheses that no single idea or impulse can dominate the whole."[91] Troeltsch then makes his points, quoted above, about the essence differing in every age. He follows these observations with a description of the nature of all formulations of the essence that resembles many of the features that he will eventually ascribe to a cultural synthesis. He writes, "[T]his essence is actually the subjective, personal interpretation and synthesis which present thinking derives from the entire situation, with reference to the actual living issues and for the purpose of directing future activity."[92]

The Limitation of the Essence in the Historicism *Volume*

Given this gradually developing sense of the limits of the term "essence," it is perhaps not surprising that the category "essence" has a relatively minor place in the *Historicism* volume. What has happened to Troeltsch's concept of an essence of an historical complex (such as Christianity)? Has Troeltsch dispensed with this term altogether?

In the 1903 essence essay, Troeltsch uses the question of an essence of Christianity as an opportunity to reflect on a number of methodological and theoretical questions about the nature of historical inquiry and historical construction in general. He shows how the task of formulating Christianity's essence inevitably bumps up against such questions and offers a definition of essence that can do justice to the complexities raised by his discussion. The essence is not just an abstraction characterizing a past epoch or object, but also a normative vision of the continuity and development of the object and its possibilities for the future. The essence has both an objective and a subjective status. The essence is both the historian's construct and history's

---

Speaking against Hegel, for example, Troeltsch writes, "Those very tendencies which have the best prospects for future growth are by no means a fulfillment of the 'idea,' or a synthesis of all earlier stages; they are rather tumultuous adaptations to a new intellectual situation, radically different from that which gave birth to Christianity" (*Religion in History*, 61–62; "Logos und Mythos in Theologie und Religionsphilosophie," in *GS* 2:824–25).

[91] "The Dogmatics," in *Religion in History*, 97; "Die Dogmatik," in *GS* 2:511.

[92] "The Dogmatics," in *Religion in History*, 97; "Die Dogmatik," in *GS* 2:511. Although Troeltsch seems to be expanding his conception of the essence in the direction of a cultural synthesis, he certainly has not given it up. On the contrary, in the paragraphs that follow these statements I have just quoted, Troeltsch nevertheless notes that dogmatics proceeds with an exposition of the essence of Christianity.

object. Defining the essence is a task located at the boundary between empirical and philosophical history.

I have shown in chapter 1 that the concept of an essence of Christianity encompasses at least four different kinds of claims or statements about the historical object, including not only those that are directed to describing or conceptualizing Christianity's past and present, but also those that help construct its future. In fact, the formulation of the essence of Christianity is described as a—if not *the*—central element and task of empirical and philosophical history. Troeltsch writes, "The definition of the essence is the crown of historical theology, it is the unification of the historical element of theology with the normative element."[93]

In the *Historicism* volume, Troeltsch again raises a number of the issues and tasks that were central to the essence essay, but he does so with a new set of categories and classifications. In the essence essay, the concept "essence" had to be conceived in such a way that it could accommodate and do justice to the numerous complexities Troeltsch raises about history and historical knowledge, in addition to serving as the ideal for the future. In the *Historicism* volume, Troeltsch limits the role of the concept of essence, forcing it to do less work, so to speak, and treating several of the issues and complexities originally connected to the essence under new concepts and categories. Troeltsch now relates the essence to the logical categories of "narrow selection," "representation," and "unity of meaning," but the task of constructing a vision for the future becomes that of the cultural synthesis. In other words, the concept of cultural synthesis replaces the concept of essence in the area of ethical construction for the future. The *Historicism* volume by no means offers a clear and systematic resolution of all the tensions that Troeltsch was treating before his untimely death. With these adjustments, however, it offers additional theoretical support for some of the underdeveloped claims and ideas of the essence essay.

The Place of the Essence in Troeltsch's Logic of History

In the *Historicism* volume, the concept of an essence itself is not included among the categories Troeltsch offers as constituting the formal logic of

---

[93] "Essence," 164; "[1]WCh," 678–79. For the 1913 edition, Troeltsch expands this sentence in the following way: "The definition of the essence is the crown *and at the same time the self-abrogation* of historical theology, it is the unification of the historical element of theology with the normative element *or at least the element which shapes the future*" ([my italics, indicating the additions]; "Essence," 164; "[2]WCh," 433).

history. Instead, as I have suggested, it is implied in three of them: narrow selection, representation, and unity of meaning. Narrow selection plays an important role in formulating and clarifying the originality of an individual totality. Originality refers to the underived, nonreducible, and unrepeatable quality of any individual totality. For Troeltsch, the notion of originality or uniqueness is intrinsic to the notion of an individual totality.[94] Narrow selection enables one to identify that which is original to the totality more clearly by distinguishing the totality from objects around it and emphasizing its "essential or characteristic traits."[95] Troeltsch emphasizes that this formulation of the essential must not be viewed as separating the "spiritual content" from the "surrounding conditions," but must incorporate or synthesize both.[96]

The essential that is formulated by means of narrow selection must also be capable of representation, another concept included among the elements of Troeltsch's logic of history. That which is formulated as the essence of a totality should be able to represent countless details and characteristics that are part of the totality but cannot be portrayed in a single coherent concept. Instead, the essence performs a symbolic role, offering an overarching picture of the object. Here Troeltsch makes reference to such works as Harnack's *Essence of Christianity*, which offers a sweeping historical construction that symbolizes the essential features of the whole, even though, in Troeltsch's view, it does not do justice to the myriad of empirical details in a totality such as Christianity.

Finally, Troeltsch argues that the determination of the essential itself is dependent on the comprehension of a unity of value or meaning implicit in the historical object. This inner structure of meaning is not always a positive value or meaning, and it is not always conscious.[97] Moreover, any conception of such an inner meaning will change over time, insofar as all historical pictures change as history itself changes. Troeltsch argues that this change does not reduce any conception of the object and its meaning to mere subjectivism, but it simply corresponds to the nature of historical knowledge as distinct from knowledge in natural sciences. The former adjusts

[94] *GS* 3:39.
[95] Ibid.
[96] *GS* 3:40. With this statement, Troeltsch appears to be attempting to avoid Harnack's kernel-husk distinction.
[97] *GS* 3:42.

and enlarges to accommodate new perspectives on and changes in the object, while the latter is based on "objective mathematical constructions."[98] While discerning a unity of meaning is related to the task of formulating the essence of an historical object, as a category the unity of meaning is more closely related to Troeltsch's conception of historical development, as will become clear in my discussion of that concept below.

In both editions of the essence essay, the essence was conceived to be central to many aspects of empirical-historical inquiry and philosophical-normative evaluation. In the *Historicism* volume, it is related to only three of Troeltsch's categories of historical analysis and is restricted to the rather narrow function of clarifying the originality of an historical phenomenon.

The Cultural Synthesis

Aside from its inclusion in these three elements of the logic of history, the category "essence" is not central to the act of conceptualizing an individual totality or cultural circle in the *Historicism* volume, and it is no longer said to entail the ethical dimension it had in both versions of the essence essay. Instead, the "cultural synthesis" (*Kultursynthese*) takes over part of the function that Troeltsch had earlier identified as the third aspect of the concept of an essence: the aspect expressing an ideal for the future.[99]

Connecting Past and Present, Actual and Ideal

In his essence essay, Troeltsch wrote that in constructing the essence of Christianity:

> One appeals from past and present understanding to the future understanding which will be produced through correct knowledge and mediation, and one includes the future seen as an ideal as part of the material out of which the inductive definition of the developing essence is constructed.[100]

As one moves from strictly empirical historical examination of Christianity to normative philosophical reflection concerning its future, "the essence changes quite automatically from being an abstracted concept to being an ideal

---

[98] *GS* 3:43.
[99] See "Essence," 156–63; "¹WCh," 650–54; "²WCh," 423–32.
[100] "Essence," 156; "¹WCh," 650; "²WCh," 424.

concept."[101] In the essence essay, therefore, the essence as an ideal concept refers to the ethical act in which one formulates a vision of Christianity that is continuous with past history, but that also looks ahead to the needs of the present and future.[102]

In the *Historicism* volume, this task is reformulated, expanded, and worked out in the concept of the cultural synthesis,[103] a new construction that takes the most important strands of influence and meaning from the past and combines them into a unity that can sustain and rejuvenate the present and future.[104] The act of formulating a cultural synthesis is a central task of material philosophy of history, where one moves from the categories of history (the formal logic of history) to the interpretation and articulation of concrete meanings and standards in history. That is, in material philosophy of history, one takes the understanding of the past yielded by the empirical study of history (which has been guided by the logic of history) and connects the unities of meaning identified in previous history with present and future possibilities; one attempts "a further shaping of historical life out of the historically understood present."[105]

Troeltsch argues that the move to material philosophy of history follows naturally from empirical history. Once one has comprehended the

---

[101] "Essence," 158; "¹WCh," 651–52; "²WCh," 426.

[102] Troeltsch speaks to the ethical urgency of essence construction when he writes that "the essence is not something which is purely historical but is indeed that synthesis of history and the future which has to be created at all the great, crucial junctions" ("Essence," 176; "²WCh," 447).

[103] It is worth noting again that, while Troeltsch's concept of cultural synthesis carries forward a good part of the work that the concept of essence previously had done, the cultural synthesis, of course, is focused on a broader object (the so-called European cultural circle) than the essence of Christianity had been. Nevertheless, I argue that Troeltsch's formulation of the cultural synthesis is indicative of how his views had changed concerning the usefulness of the concept of an essence of Christianity.

[104] Here the connections between Troeltsch's notion of cultural synthesis and MacIntyre's conception of tradition (as a version of moral inquiry) are striking. In the face of cultural fragmentation in Germany after World War I, Troeltsch turns to the resources of the past to inform the possible direction and new syntheses needed for the present culture. Similarly, MacIntyre states that the form of inquiry based on a conception of tradition "treats the past neither as mere prologue nor as something to be struggled against, but as that from which we have to learn if we are to identify and move toward our *telos* more adequately and that which we have to put to question if we are to know which questions we ourselves should next formulate and attempt to answer, both theoretically and practically" (MacIntyre, *Three Rival Versions of Moral Enquiry*, 79).

[105] *GS* 3:79.

continuities of meaning and value in the past, it is impossible not to move from, or attempt to extend, these possibilities into the present and future.[106] Simply stopping with empirical history, or what Troeltsch calls "purely contemplative history,"[107] would lead only to "notorious bad historicism" or "unlimited relativism."[108] One would have only an endless collection of past historical meanings and ideals with no contemporary reflection on, or validation of, these values. Troeltsch argues that, properly understood, empirical history and philosophical history are in a relation of interdependence. Insofar as empirical history without any normative philosophical reflection produces only lifeless past historical objects, philosophical evaluation uninformed by real past formations that are reconstructed by empirical history is "a house without a foundation."[109] There is an antinomy between past and present: "we interpret the past out of the present, and the present out of the past."[110] With these comments, Troeltsch does not collapse the distinction between empirical history and material philosophy of history. Instead, he justifies the continuation of the latter from the former. Empirical history remains focused on discrete, relatively narrowly circumscribed objects from the past, while material philosophy of history works for a continuation of historical life oriented toward the future. Thus, material philosophy of history moves toward ethics.[111]

The cultural synthesis is the means of connecting the past with the present and future. It is, Troeltsch writes elsewhere, "the welding together of . . . cultural values into a homogeneous whole for the present and future within a large given area of culture."[112] In the concept of cultural synthesis, standards for judging or assessing history are produced through "a critical selection out of the cultural stock of a whole great and influential context with a view to the

---

[106] *GS* 3:69.

[107] *GS* 3:70.

[108] *GS* 3:68.

[109] *GS* 3:70.

[110] *GS* 3:76.

[111] *GS* 3:79. Troeltsch places material philosophy of history in a middle position between empirical history and ethics. Ringer explains that Troeltsch "saw the material philosophy of history as an intermediary between empirical history and ethics, an intermediary which would save the historian from thoughtless over-specialization, the moral philosopher from formalism" (Ringer, *Decline of the German Mandarins*, 344–45).

[112] "The Ethics of Cultural Values," in *Christian Thought: Its History and Application*, in *KGA* 17:173; German edition: "Die Ethik der Kulturwerte," in *KGA* 17:89.

forces in it that are living, even though they might currently be repressed."[113] In an act of creative discernment, the historian identifies the unity of meaning or ideal in a particular totality and formulates it anew in conversation with both past and present standards.

The Content and Validity of the Cultural Synthesis

The material for a cultural synthesis is supplied by what Troeltsch calls universal history. It provides the "objective background" for that which is produced anew. Building on what he has already said about historical development, namely, that any conception of a unity of meaning is to be confined to the cultural circle of the historian, Troeltsch argues that here, too, universal history can only be a history of the Western cultural circle. Troeltsch calls this his principle of Europeanism (*Europäertum*). Insofar as "humanity as a uniform historical object does not exist," it is impossible to formulate a history of the development of humankind as a whole.[114] Thus, Troeltsch concludes that "for us there can only be a universal history of Europeanism."[115] Although other cultures can be studied, reflection on the future development of a culture remains within the confines of one's own culture.[116] We are restricted to our own development. The histories of other cultural circles, although valuable in themselves and important tools for

---

[113] *GS* 3:167. Here one finds an important opening in Troeltsch's conception of a cultural synthesis through which one might bring resources that could be employed to criticize the culture in question. If one could draw upon resources that are currently repressed in the contemporary cultural ethos, one presumably could select from history certain resources that stand in tension with the current expressions of the culture and use these as tools of internal critique. This is an interesting way in which Troeltsch's view of the cultural synthesis could be developed in response to critics who (often rightly) state that he links Christianity and European culture so closely that any possibility of a Christian prophetic critique of culture is lost.

[114] *GS* 3:706.

[115] *GS* 3:708, 710.

[116] Wendell Dietrich states that Troeltsch's notion of Europeanism "is not Eurocentric cultural chauvinism" but rather "a modest proposal to reconstruct the particular society and culture of the West." Insofar as Europeanism allows for the bold articulation of an ideal for humanity, but in the confines of a particular culture, Dietrich describes Troeltsch's project in his later works as one that "open[s] out to a universal horizon, modestly and unpretentiously but with robust confidence." Note that "universal horizon" here refers to the horizon of so-called Western culture. See Dietrich, "Troeltsch's Treatment of the Thomist Synthesis in *The Social Teaching* as a Signal of His View of a Cultural Synthesis," *The Thomist* 57 (1993) 398, 401.

comparison and increased self-understanding, are not directly relevant for the current task of synthesis.

The cultural synthesis, therefore, is not a retrieval and creative combination of elements relevant to or normative for all of humanity. Instead, the synthesis draws from the history of what Troeltsch calls the European-Mediterranean-American cultural circle. Troeltsch determines that the four fundamental powers or strands of influence that have informed this European cultural circle up to the present are: Hebrew prophetism and the Hebrew Bible, ancient Greece, the Roman Empire, and the Western Middle Ages.[117] These become the material from which a synthesis is creatively constructed.

By rooting the cultural synthesis in the actual historical life of the cultural circle in the past, Troeltsch argues that the synthesis achieves a significant measure of "objectivity." In other words, it is not merely a product of subjectivism or a construct with no grounding in reality or "facts." Rather, both the historical objects out of which the synthesis is to be constructed and the unity of meaning evident in these objects are historical realities that, in some sense, "ground" the new synthesis. Troeltsch's view of individuality includes the assertion that historical individualities (or individual totalities) are not simply creations of the historian but real historical entities with an actual unity of meaning that is given in history. Although the new synthesis will certainly be a concrete decision and proposal made by the historian, insofar as it seeks to continue developments rooted in the past, it shares to some extent in their objectivity.

The validity of the cultural synthesis is also construed in terms of the concept of individuality. Its validity is not timeless, absolute, or general.[118] Insofar as there is no unified spiritual development of humanity, there is no single or general notion of validity that could apply to all of humanity, or to all cultural circles. Furthermore, the notion of generality is itself incompatible with the notion of individuality. Individuality implies a coherence and value (and validity) inherent in and unique to each individual totality. Validity is tied up with individuality, and individuality is inherently relative. Therefore, absolute validity simply does not correspond to relative individualities, which are ever-changing and unique.[119] Instead, the validity of any synthesis can only come from or be tested within the particular cultural circle. Only

---

[117] *GS* 3:708, 765–68.
[118] *GS* 3:182–83.
[119] *GS* 3:181–83.

God has a supra-individual perspective,[120] and the perspective of a different individuality would have no direct relevance or applicability.

It is important to remember that Troeltsch's methodological and theoretical reflections related to the concept of a cultural synthesis took place in the conflict-ridden context of Europe immediately after World War I. Thus, both the idea of a cultural synthesis and the principle of Europeanism had profound political significance. By means of the idea of a cultural synthesis, Troeltsch sought to sketch a conception of Europe that could unify diverse national cultures, thereby avoiding dangerous nationalisms while also healing divisions particularly between Germany and Western Europe.[121] In addition, by means of a synthesis of identities, traditions, and resources from the various cultures of Europe, Troeltsch sought to craft a nonessentialist conception of Europe. Finally, Troeltsch's conception of a cultural synthesis guided by the principle of Europeanism embraced the relativity of cultures and values while avoiding absolute or "unlimited" relativism. While no universal or absolute validity could be claimed for European cultural values and traditions (or for the values and traditions of any one European nation), these values and traditions could be used to guide ethical reflection within European communities.

The principle of Europeanism is therefore also tied up with Troeltsch's efforts to construct a conception of European culture that could avoid cultural imperialism and Eurocentrism. In the *Historicism* volume, Troeltsch speaks against "naïve or refined European arrogance."[122] By restricting himself to reflection on the history, development, and ethical resources of his own cultural circle, Troeltsch sought to undercut any suggestions that European culture somehow "represents" or is normative for any other culture, and embraced instead the particularity of Europe as one cultural circle among many.[123]

---

[120] *GS* 3:709.

[121] See Harrington, "Ernst Troeltsch's Concept of Europe," 483. Joanne Miyang Cho, "The Crisis of Historicism and Troeltsch's Europeanism," *History of European Ideas* 21 (1995) 202–3.

[122] *GS* 3:707.

[123] On Troeltsch's "de-centering" of Europe, see Harrington, "Ernst Troeltsch's Concept of Europe," 485–86; Cho ("Historicism and Civilizational Discontinuity in Spengler and Troeltsch," *Zeitschrift für Religions- und Geistesgeschichte* 51 [1999] 238–62) states that, with his concept of Europeanism, Troeltsch emphasized "the equality of civilizations" (253) and "articulated perhaps the purest multicultural position in post-war Germany" (254). At the same time, however, Troeltsch's concept of Europeanism results in an isolationist

The Cultural Synthesis and the Essence

This discussion of the main features of the cultural synthesis evokes many of the tasks, themes, and tensions that were earlier part of Troeltsch's analysis and conception of an essence of Christianity. The cultural synthesis clearly takes over the ethical dimension of essence construction. In the essence essay, Troeltsch had described the essence as "no more than the emergence into consciousness of an inner process which really does drive forward the forces of the future out of those of the past."[124] Now, in the *Historicism* volume, it is the cultural synthesis that looks to the development or unity of meaning in past formations and attempts to continue that development into the future. Similarly, in the essence essay, Troeltsch had claimed that the essence was "a living new creation, related afresh to new circumstances."[125] In the *Historicism* volume, the cultural synthesis is described as a new creative construction, even though it is informed by material from the past.

In addition to taking over some of the tasks that earlier had been assigned to the essence, the cultural synthesis also lends clarity to some of the unresolved dimensions of Troeltsch's conception of an essence. There are at least three ways that the cultural synthesis improves upon the essence that are particularly pertinent to the themes of this study. Let us discuss these in turn.

First, "cultural synthesis" entails a clearer conception of the relation between empirical history and philosophy of history than "essence" was able to provide. In the essence essay, Troeltsch claims that the concept of an essence is located at the transition between empirical and philosophical history, but his defense and exposition of this claim is uneven and unclear. On the one hand, Troeltsch resists the temptation to separate absolutely empirical from philosophical (or so-called objective from subjective) historical inquiry. He suggests that a more sophisticated and subtle historical understanding would recognize their interrelation. The essence, in fact, is a concept that demonstrates this interrelation clearly. On the other hand, Troeltsch insists on a strict separation between the empirical and philosophical tasks of history. For example, Troeltsch includes a paragraph in which he praises Harnack's work precisely because it develops a future vision out of empirical

---

view of the relations among cultures. See Cho, "The German Debate over Civilization: Troeltsch's Europeanism and Jasper's Cosmopolitanism," *History of European Ideas* 25 (1999) 310–12.

[124] "Essence," 162; "²WCh," 430 (this appears only in the 1913 edition).

[125] "Essence," 163; "²WCh," 432 (this appears only in the 1913 edition).

history, thereby linking "history to the working out of a normative religious position." He follows this observation, however, with the hesitant admission that, nevertheless, "it is perhaps good to separate more clearly what is the properly historical and what [is] the philosophically historical, normative element."[126] The idea of a cultural synthesis offers a more effective account of the relation between the empirical and the philosophical in several ways. First, it has a clear relation to empirical history insofar as that which is to be synthesized anew is historical material supplied by empirical historical work. At the same time, however, insofar as it is clearly a synthesis and, therefore, a creative recombination of these elements, the cultural synthesis also entails an obvious normative, philosophical dimension. Second, Troeltsch's more developed conception of individuality provides a link between the empirical and the philosophical insofar as it is a category that spans both realms. In other words, individuality refers not only to the given and unrepeatable reality and uniqueness of the empirical historical object, but it also characterizes the ideal contained in the object and formulated by the historian.

It follows from the heightened clarity and unambiguous place of the empirical historical in Troeltsch's conception of the cultural synthesis that it also makes a stronger case for the objectivity of the new construction than the essence had been able to do. By indicating what kind of material from the past will be drawn upon, and by naming four specific historical legacies from which the new synthesis will be elaborated, Troeltsch does a better job of demonstrating the "objective" historical base that will ground the synthesis.

Finally, by positioning the synthesis in a closer relation to ethics, Troeltsch is able to support his claim that the synthesis is a creative construction of the historian. Troeltsch struggles to explain how the essence could be at once a relatively objective representation of an historical phenomenon and a proposal formulated by the historian in order to guide the future. The cultural synthesis clearly has a dual structure consisting of empirical materials that are combined into a new unity for the present cultural circle.

---

[126] "Essence," 177; "²WCh," 449.

Conclusion

The *Historicism* volume presents Troeltsch's late efforts to articulate a method for conceptualizing historical objects in a way that adequately attests to their complex and dynamic constitution while relating them to normative questions about their continued value and meaning for modern life. Although it addresses a broader topic than the essence essay had done—attempting, here, to lay the groundwork for conceptualizing a cultural circle and not simply Christianity—the *Historicism* volume nevertheless stands in clear continuity with the concerns of the 1903 essence essay in which Troeltsch had attempted to conceptualize Christianity as a complex historical phenomenon with abiding value for the future.

I have shown how Troeltsch's proposal in this volume was deeply shaped by his inquiries into the history of Christianity, especially as pursued in the *Social Teachings*.[127] Troeltsch's reflections around the time of his completion of that work suggest that his conception of Christianity as an historical phenomenon had become even more complex. He did not view the concept of an essence as a primary tool in his constructive efforts to conceptualize Christianity and demonstrate its connection and contribution to modern society.

In the *Historicism* volume, the concept of a cultural synthesis comes to serve the understanding of complex historical phenomena that Troeltsch has been reflecting on and moving toward at least since his 1903 essence essay. Of course, Troeltsch is now focused on achieving a conception of the Western cultural circle, and not of Christianity specifically, but his concerns remain the same: he desires to present a sufficiently complex view of historical objects and to demonstrate the possible meaning and value of such objects for the future. The concept of a cultural synthesis is rooted in empirical historical realities and is predicated on the assumption that each cultural circle is internally diverse—informed by a variety of past historical objects, traditions, and tendencies. The cultural synthesis is also clearly oriented toward concerns of the present and future. It seeks to bring together previous historical forces in order to provide a new unity and source of value for the

---

[127] Chapman (*Ernst Troeltsch and Liberal Theology*, 144–45) argues convincingly that the *Social Teachings* "can be understood primarily as preparing the objective 'sociological' or factual basis for the constructive theological task" that Troeltsch was gradually preparing to take up as part of his desire to contribute to a vision of unity for modern society. There are, then, "constructive ethical designs behind the work."

contemporary life of the cultural circle. Troeltsch's untimely death prevented him both from writing the second volume of *Historicism and Its Problems* and from continuing to work out the conceptualization of Christianity he had been formulating in the two versions of the essence essay and in the *Social Teachings* (and in other works as well). I suggest that had he been able to articulate his conception of Christianity in light of what he had formulated concerning cultural circles in the *Historicism* volume, Troeltsch would not have employed the concept of an essence of Christianity. Rather, he would have drawn on the concept of a synthesis to carry out the twofold task that I have claimed was central to his theory of Christianity from the beginning: 1) the conceptualization of Christianity as a complex historical object, and 2) the formulation of a vision of its contemporary meaning and value.

As Troeltsch develops his theory of historical phenomena such as Christianity, he moves from the concept of an essence to that of a synthesis. In his view, the latter improves upon the former not only in offering an adequate conception of the historical object and its complex constitution, but also in providing a new vision of the structure, unity, and character of modern life in the present and future.

Conclusion

The purpose of history is indeed never simply to reflect a past world in the memory. Quite apart from the fact that this is impossible it would also be empty and superfluous. The understanding of the present out of how it came to be, a view of the experience of the human race, or at least of our own people and cultural area, insofar as this is still attainable and can be understood in its total context, the consequent historical disciplining of our thought and the guiding lines for the future which can thereby be achieved: these are the purpose of history.[1]

In his investigations into the history of Christianity, Troeltsch sought to illuminate the present and contribute to the future. In conceptualizing Christianity, he combined historical analysis with normative philosophical reflection, refusing to omit or to privilege one or the other. In asserting that history, or the past, contains potentially vital and sustaining resources for the present, Troeltsch approached a position espoused by many theorists of tradition today.[2] At the same time, Troeltsch also emphasized the creative, constructive, and interested nature of all such attempts to probe one's history. At these moments he resembles those theologians who criticize the appeals to authority and continuity frequently implied in such theories of tradition.

---

[1] "Essence," 157; "¹WCh," 651; "²WCh," 425.

[2] As I suggested in the previous chapter, here Troeltsch stands in obvious continuity with Alasdair MacIntyre. Like MacIntyre, Troeltsch identifies influential and distinctive strands of thought within the history of a tradition and uses these as material for informing and guiding present life. See MacIntyre, *Whose Justice? Which Rationality?* (Notre Dame, Ind.: University of Notre Dame Press, 1988).

For these theologians (and, in many ways, too, for Troeltsch), "tradition" and "identity" are as much constructed as they are inherited.[3]

In the preceding pages, I have shown how Troeltsch gradually brings his conception of Christianity in line with an increasingly complex view of historical phenomena as multiform and dynamic aggregates with abiding meaning and value for the future.[4] In conclusion, I sketch the main contours of Troeltsch's theory of Christianity, discuss the themes that repeatedly surface in Troeltsch's various attempts to conceptualize Christianity, and indicate the ways in which Troeltsch's theory of Christianity could be a resource for Christian theology today.

This study begins with the claim that a theory of Christianity (or, we might say, a theory of tradition) gradually emerges in Troeltsch's works, beginning in 1903 with the first edition of the essence of Christianity essay. There Troeltsch begins to sketch out a view of Christianity that emphasizes the complexity of its historical constitution and seeks new ways to affirm its value for the present and future. I have argued that in articulating this theory, Troeltsch looks beyond the purview of the Harnack-Loisy debate and engages, in particular, the work of Heinrich Rickert to explore methods and strategies for conceptualizing complex historical phenomena like Christianity according to precise principles of historical analysis while simultaneously engaging in normative assessment of their continuing value and meaning. Troeltsch, therefore, introduces new questions and tensions into the discussion about an essence of Christianity. He also begins to envision a sophisticated conception of Christianity as a tradition encompassing multiple and divergent

---

[3] Kathryn Tanner draws on anthropological theories of culture to argue that the "identity of Christianity" is constructed again and again through processes of cultural negotiation and communal debate. She criticizes theorists of tradition for presenting Christian identity as a self-contained and autonomous natural object passed down and appropriated in various times and places. She also criticizes postliberal theologians' appeals to the grammar or rules of a narrative tradition as an authoritarian move that overlooks too much of the complexity of identity formation. See Tanner, *Theories of Culture*, 104–10, 128–38. Gregory P. Grieve and Richard Weiss argue that "religious traditions are social projects, often deliberately constructed to serve particular ideological ends." See "Illuminating the Half-Life of Tradition: Legitimation, Agency, and Counter-Hegemonies," in *Historicizing "Tradition" in the Study of Religion* (ed. Steven Engler and Gregory P. Grieve; Berlin: Walter de Gruyter, 2005) 1.

[4] As I noted in ch. 5, Troeltsch's position overlaps in many ways with that of Delwin Brown, who describes traditions as "dynamic and diverse streams of being and meaning" that offer multiple possibilities for shaping and guiding the future (see *Boundaries of Our Habitation*, 137–38).

truth claims and forms of belief and practice. This developing awareness of Christianity's diversity enables Troeltsch to perceive difficulties and problems that attend all appeals to authority and normativity in Christian tradition: On what grounds can one period of Christian history, one interpretation of revelation, or one set of social doctrines be held up as authoritative for all other forms of Christianity?

I argue that the essence essay presents a set of conceptual commitments, questions, and tensions that Troeltsch will continue to promote, address, and adjust in his subsequent works as he gradually develops his theory of Christianity. In questions such as the following, Troeltsch grapples with tensions inherent in his twofold commitment to do justice to the complexity of Christianity while affirming its continuing value for modern life: How can, and ought, the relation between empirical research and normative evaluation be configured and balanced? How can one simultaneously assert the diversity and the continuity of Christianity's doctrines and social-historical forms? What kind of authority can Christianity have if one embraces a modern historical method, and where is this authority located? Emphasizing the centrality of these questions and the twofold commitment they express enables me to discern four distinct but related ways Troeltsch uses the concept "essence" in the essence essay. In so doing, I lend clarity to what has been considered an interpretive conundrum while showing that, already in 1903, Troeltsch was at pains to stretch the concept of essence in a variety of directions to serve a variety of purposes.

The essence essay sets an agenda that Troeltsch pursues by delving into the history of Christianity. That is, in order to explore how Christian identity might be shaped and articulated in his own day, he explores the variety of its configurations in the past. A major claim of this study is that *The Social Teachings of the Christian Churches and Groups* mirrors and develops the theoretical conceptualization of Christianity spelled out provisionally in the essence essay. In both of these works, Troeltsch portrays Christianity as an internally pluralistic historical tradition whose authority and meaning cannot be reduced to one essence but, rather, must be determined in conversation with the needs and situation of the present on the one hand, and with the diverse insights and resources of the past on the other. The *Social Teachings* is therefore among the most important sources for understanding Troeltsch's evolving views on the essence of Christianity. While it clearly carries forward many of the claims of the essence essay, the *Social Teachings* also further problematizes the concept of an essence of Christianity.

Underscoring the relation between these two works enables me to make explicit the theory of Christianity Troeltsch is working out as he crafts his historical narrative in the *Social Teachings*. In chapters 2, 3, and 4, I show how he portrays Christianity as a complex and multiform historical phenomenon by means of several central categories and organizing concepts in the *Social Teachings*. For example, Troeltsch locates a variety of tendencies in Christianity's origins, and he shows how these help produce diverse forms of Christianity throughout its subsequent history. Troeltsch also resists the temptation to subject the various forms of Christianity to a single criterion found in the origins, allowing, instead, for a much more complicated picture of its possible development. Troeltsch construes historical development in a way that expects a variety of outcomes and expressions to arise in Christianity, especially as it emerges in different historical, social, political, and economic contexts. In Troeltsch's account of Christian history, "external" thought-forms and social practices merge with Christian ideas and create new amalgams that then become internal to Christianity. Similarly, economic and political developments help produce doctrines and approaches to social organization in Christianity. Finally, Troeltsch's threefold typology of church, sect, and mysticism emphasizes Christianity's internal diversity. By crafting a theory of Christianity as a diverse and pluralistic tradition, Troeltsch challenges what he sees as overly authoritarian and dogmatic conceptions of normative and historical Christianity. In addition, Troeltsch criticizes the one-sided portraits of Christianity crafted by various historians and theologians seeking to vindicate certain forms of German Lutheranism in his day. These scholars tended to hold up the Lutheran Reformation as the normative period of Christian history, or to view Christian origins through a Reformation lens, or both. Troeltsch turns to a wider range of movements in the early modern history of Christianity so as to yield what he sees as a more historically defensible theory of Christianity, as well as a broader set of resources and options for guiding modern life.

At the same time, chapters 2, 3, and 4 identify the strategies Troeltsch employs to preserve the continuity of Christianity. While resisting the instinct to locate normative Christianity in the origins of Christianity, Troeltsch finds ways to demonstrate how later developments in Christianity carry forward in a novel yet continuous manner many of the original social tendencies and theological affirmations of the earliest Christians. Similarly, Troeltsch employs terms such as *Keim* ("germ" or "seed") to indicate the connections between earlier and later developments without implying any kind of strong determinism or necessity. Finally, Troeltsch traces each one of his ideal types of social organization back to the beginnings of Christianity, showing how the church, sect, and mysticism possibilities—while not fully explicit in earliest Christianity—were present in or anticipated by certain ideas and tendencies in the original communities. In forging continuities across distant forms of Christianity, Troeltsch seeks material for the creative shaping of Christian identity in his own day.

My study, therefore, uncovers important ways in which Troeltsch crafts the historical narrative of the *Social Teachings* in conversation with the challenges and possibilities facing Christianity in the modern world. Such a move reflects the second part of Troeltsch's quest for a theory of Christianity—the part that seeks to demonstrate the continuing value of Christianity in the present and future. There are several tools Troeltsch employs to carry out his dialogue with modernity. In chapter 3, I showed how he uses the category of Stoicism to express his ambivalence about certain modern conceptions of the individual and radical forms of democracy. While celebrating the fortuitous syncretization of Christian and Stoic thought in late antiquity—a syncretism that makes invaluable contributions to Christianity's stock of resources for social organization and ethics—Troeltsch also worries about the consequences of this merger. For Troeltsch, Stoicism's conception of equality and inequality is based on a model of the person that becomes the basis for rationalistic individualism in the modern period. Troeltsch holds this form of individualism largely responsible for the fragmentation of modern society. In his view, institutions such as capitalism and bureaucracy are allowed to take their harshest and coldest forms when supported by a doctrine of rationalistic individualism. As he maps out the historical relation between Stoic thought and Christianity, Troeltsch therefore nudges his historical narrative in certain directions in order to separate the two at precisely those moments where rationalistic individualism expresses itself. Troeltsch makes it clear that this form of individualism is the legacy of Stoic and not Christian thought. In so doing, he makes a normative claim about the nature of true Christian ideals and suggests that Christianity might be able to contribute positively to modern society by providing an alternative to its model of rationalistic individualism. By drawing out the various subtexts in Troeltsch's account of

Christian history, I show that Troeltsch's assessment of modernity was much more complicated than is often assumed.

In his dialogue with modernity, Troeltsch also uses the ideal types of Christian social formation to explore and test possible models for how Christianity might best relate to and serve modern society. In his account of the church type, he testifies to the importance of Christianity serving as a source of social cohesion in a fragmented society; at the same time, he makes it clear that a fundamentally medieval institution cannot serve a modern society. Troeltsch uses the sect type to demonstrate the continuities between modern and Christian conceptions of freedom and personality, pointing to some ways in which Christianity has had an activating effect on the transformation of society. In his analysis of the mysticism type, Troeltsch engages in a comprehensive ethical inquiry into the strengths and weaknesses of a kind of individualism that can do justice to the sanctity and depth of the individual personality (and that therefore can be a source of doctrinal tolerance in the modern world) but that cannot produce any significant source of unity or guidance for the larger society. Finally, through his portraits of the gender ethic of each type, Troeltsch participates in debates over the proper shape of (German) society in his own time. Once again, he searches for a Christian model of individualism that can avoid both authoritarian and radically individualistic conceptions of community.

By making explicit the developing theory of Christianity that Troeltsch struggles to formulate while writing the *Social Teachings*, I demonstrate that even as it stands in continuity with the theoretical program articulated in the 1903 essence essay, the *Social Teachings* also reflects Troeltsch's heightened awareness of the shortcomings of the concept "essence of Christianity" as a tool for conceptualizing historical and normative Christianity. Troeltsch's obvious omission of the term from his historical narrative, and his expressions of ambivalence toward the term in his writings around the time of his completion of the *Social Teachings*, suggest that he is seeking an alternate concept to serve his twofold theory of Christianity as a complex, internally diverse phenomenon with resources for shaping the present and future.

I argue that Troeltsch arrives at that concept in his late work on the philosophy of history—*Historicism and Its Problems*—where Troeltsch presents the cultural synthesis as a model for conceptualizing large historical complexes and their value for the future. The concept of a cultural synthesis is based on a conception of historical totalities not as unitary but as composite and internally diverse. Such syntheses are formulated through creative and constructive engagement with a plurality of past traditions within a larger tradition or culture. Troeltsch's concept of a cultural synthesis suggests, therefore, that he has come to place increased emphasis on what was once the ethical and normative moment of essence construction. In the context of cultural conflict in German and European society following World War I, Troeltsch seeks to indicate the ways in which the diverse historical traditions and legacies of Europe can be combined afresh in a new synthesis that can guide present and future ethical reflection within and among European nations. The cultural synthesis carries forward the dual elements of Troeltsch's theory of Christianity: its insistence on the pluralistic nature of historical totalities and its desire to indicate the value of such totalities for modern life.

This outline of the way in which the elements of Troeltsch's theory of Christianity emerge in his writings on historical method, history of Christianity, and philosophy of history yields a set of four broad conceptual themes and tensions that have been central to this study and that continue to arise in contemporary theological debates. The first has already been discussed and does not require detailed elaboration: How does one affirm both the internal diversity and the continuity of a single historical complex like Christianity? Troeltsch challenges dogmatic appeals to a singular authoritative form of Christianity and resists efforts to oversimplify its historical complexity by focusing on a few fundamental ideas that best unify the whole. At the same time, in order to demonstrate Christianity's abiding value and meaning for the future, he must preserve some degree of continuity across its diverse expressions.

The second tension is related to the first. I have shown how Troeltsch gradually becomes convinced of the reciprocal relation between religious and social forces. This is demonstrated in his treatment of the mutual development of Calvinism, capitalism, and democracy. As he increasingly emphasizes Christianity's intertwinement with social, economic, and political forces, Troeltsch must also find ways to maintain Christianity's integrity as a religious phenomenon. I argue that this tension is evident in Troeltsch's treatment of Christian origins. Troeltsch attempts to locate the emergence of Christianity in the social situation of late antiquity without reducing it to a mere by-product of social forces, with no integrity of its own. I show that Troeltsch characterizes early Christianity as a "purely religious" movement not simply to make a dubious or essentialist claim for its normativity but precisely to negotiate this tension between religion's interdependence with other social forces and religion's integrity or relative independence as a social force. Similarly, in his model of historical causality, Troeltsch insists on the efficacy of religious ideas and impulses in contributing to larger historical, social, economic, and political developments. This serves to underscore the integrity of Christianity as an historical entity even as it is shaped and influenced by "external" forces. The importance of insisting on the relative autonomy of religion as an element of historical life is intimately related to Troeltsch's desire to indicate the ways in which Christianity might contribute to the shape, quality, and direction of modern European culture. For Troeltsch, if religion is merely a product of other more primary realities, then there is no point in suggesting that it could be a vital and indispensable resource for modern life. Instead, it would be more efficient to turn to those other realities and to forget religion altogether.

The third conceptual theme centers on the relationship between empirical and philosophical history. Throughout this study, I have emphasized that Troeltsch seeks to ground his theory of Christianity in the complex empirical data concerning Christian history. He continually remains abreast of new developments in historical method, therefore, and he gradually articulates his own understanding of how best to conceptualize a complex historical phenomenon like Christianity. At the same time, however, Troeltsch never ceases to insist that there is and should be a connection between this historical work and normative evaluation. Although he certainly argues that empirical history should be done in a more or less "non-partisan" way, he does not give up on the claim that it is not and should not be merely objective. Similarly, he refuses to relegate philosophical history to the merely subjective. In his late work, Troeltsch uses the conception of individuality to link the actual and the ideal, and he directs the concept of a cultural synthesis toward the field of ethics. For Troeltsch, history must serve the needs of the present or it is mere antiquarian curiosity.

The final theme that pervades this study concerns the question of the authority of all claims about the nature of Christianity. From the essence essay in 1903 through his *Historicism* volume in 1922, Troeltsch seeks an authoritative grounding for his theory of Christianity that departs from what he calls a "dogmatic" approach. In the essence of Christianity essay, Troeltsch makes it clear that he rejects any move that appeals to the miraculous authority of scripture or dogma in order to defend a particular construction of normative Christianity. The first part of his theory of Christianity—the part that demands a complex picture of its historical reality—rules out such a move, which could never be defended by the "purely historical" method that Troeltsch employs. Intent on maintaining a rigorously historical perspective on Christianity, Troeltsch resists not only what he sees as dogmatic ploys for defending a particular view of Christianity, but also other kinds of moves that might equate normative Christianity with one particular form of Christianity. Similarly, he denies that Christianity could be summarized in one singular essence for similar reasons—such a claim can be authoritative only if it ignores the patent varieties and divergences in Christianity's history. Nevertheless, because Troeltsch is seeking a theory of Christianity that can speak to his contemporary cultural situation, he needs some kind of authoritative grounding for his claims about Christianity's abiding meaning and value. For this he looks to the resources of the past. Indeed, this is largely what motivates his undertaking of a project such as the *Social Teachings*. In order to work toward a construction of how Christianity could serve the present, Troeltsch investigated the ways it had done so in the past so as to draw on and renew latent resources. Similarly, in the *Historicism* volume the cultural synthesis gets part of its authority from its combination of living historical realities from the past. Yet, Troeltsch does not recommend a simplistic return to past formations or ideas but, rather, a renewal of these in conversation with the future. Troeltsch envisions a dynamic process of continual dialogue between the past, present, and future that results in new proposals and syntheses that guide contemporary life.

By paying attention to these conceptual themes and tensions that preoccupied Troeltsch, we can better understand and assess ambiguous dimensions of his thought that continue to be interesting or problematic for scholars today. Two issues in particular are important for contemporary theories about the nature of tradition (and of Christianity as tradition): first, Troeltsch's conception of Christian origins, and second, Troeltsch's view of the relation between religion and society or culture.

Given his emphasis on the individualism of Jesus, does Troeltsch attempt to legitimate liberal Protestantism by projecting its values back onto the original period?[5] My reading shows that Troeltsch was after something

---

[5] John Milbank (*Theology and Social Theory*, 93) argues that Troeltsch sees Christianity (and particularly liberal Protestantism) as "usher[ing] in the modern world" and therefore projects modern liberal values back onto Christianity's origins, failing to see, for example, modern Christian individualism as a new and contingent development (and change) in

much more complicated than a myth of origins. In fact, Troeltsch sees the problems with many liberal Protestant interpretations of Christian origins and with all appeals to origins for a normative account of Christianity. In ways that anticipate current discourse about Christian origins, Troeltsch refuses to ignore the ambiguity of historical claims about Jesus and earliest Christianity, the subjective and interested character of all reconstructions of both, the diversity within earliest Christianity itself, and the larger problems of reducing the normative or actual "identity" of an historical complex to one form of its expression, namely, the earliest form.

At the same time, Troeltsch recognizes that constructions of Christian origins can serve important goals (and therefore that these constructions do matter), especially when one is seeking, as he is, a vision of Christianity that could serve modern communities. In his own historical narrative, therefore, Troeltsch identifies a set of tendencies and possibilities that are present in or anticipated by early Christian beliefs and practices and that are developed, revised, or carried on in later times and places. He does this in order to forge continuities and trajectories that can make sense of Christianity's present strengths and weaknesses as he understands them, and therefore to serve what he knows is ultimately a constructive project (and not simply an objective rendering of Christianity's historical development). By insisting on this more sympathetic and complex reading of Troeltsch's view of Christian origins, I suggest that contemporary theorists of tradition and historians of earliest Christianity—and particularly those interested in problematizing the category of origins—have more to gain from a fuller engagement with Troeltsch's work in this area than is commonly recognized.

Troeltsch's thought also emerges as an object of critique in contemporary constructions of the relation between religion and society—a topic that is also central in theological theories of tradition. Troeltsch is often said to merge

---

classic Christian doctrine. For Troeltsch, according to Milbank, "the history of the West is turned into the always-coming-to-be of liberal Protestantism and its secular aftermath." As noted in ch. 2 above, Richard Horsley (*Whoever Hears You Hears Me*) traces current individualistic conceptions of Jesus' message (especially among Q scholars) to Harnack and Troeltsch (18). Horsley rightly recognizes that, along with this individualism, scholars such as Harnack and Troeltsch also saw a "social-ethical aspect to Jesus's teaching in general" (20). Their reconstructions of Jesus' message were motivated in part by an "ethical idealism" that (according to Horsley) is absent among the majority of current Q scholars. Horsley seems to recognize something of the "cultural diagnostic" character of Troeltsch's work on the history of Christianity; that is, Troeltsch's aim to provide an historically rigorous account of Christian history while also exploring its resources for contemporary culture.

Christianity with a particular society or culture, that is, European culture.[6] This accusation comes from readings of Troeltsch's late writings in the postwar period, when he devoted much of his work to the task of reconceiving European identity. The theme of Christianity's close relationship to European culture arises especially in his lecture on "The Place of Christianity among the World Religions."[7] Troeltsch's effort to acknowledge the relativity of all religions leads him to link Christianity to a particular (relative) culture instead of arguing for its absoluteness or general validity for all times and places. Troeltsch explains that he has gradually and increasingly come to see that "a religion," in the several forms assumed by it, always depends upon the intellectual, social, and national conditions among which it exists."[8] In the case of Christianity, then, he writes, "It is historical facts that have welded Christianity into the closest connection with the civilizations of Greece, Rome, and Northern Europe. All our thoughts and feelings are impregnated with Christian motives and Christian presuppositions; and, conversely, our whole Christianity is indissolubly bound up with elements of the ancient and modern civilizations of Europe."[9] We see a similar instinct at work in Troeltsch's conception of Europeanism, which he articulates in the *Historicism* volume. There, we will remember from chapter 5, Troeltsch argues that reflection on the history and future of humanity must always be done within the confines of a particular culture, so that any conception of European identity must be self-conscious of its particularity and limited point of view, and not taken to be representative of, or valid for, any other culture. As he works out a conception of Europe in all its particularity (and not universality), Troeltsch points to the centrality of Christian tradition for the development of European cultural values.[10]

---

[6] Tanner makes this claim, as does S. Mark Heim. See Tanner, *Theories of Culture*, 62, 102–3, and Heim, *Salvations: Truth and Difference in Religion* (Maryknoll, N.Y.: Orbis, 1995) 173, 188.

[7] "The Place of Christianity among the World Religions" (1923) in *KGA* 17:134–48; German edition: "Die Stellung des Christentums unter den Weltreligionen" (1924) in *KGA* 17:105–18. This was one of five lectures that Troeltsch was invited to deliver during his planned trip to England and Scotland in March 1923. Troeltsch died on 1 February 1923. For more on the history and development of these lectures, see Hübinger in collaboration with Terwey, "Einleitung," in *KGA* 17:1–32.

[8] "The Place," in *KGA* 17:143: "Die Stellung," in *KGA* 17:113.

[9] "The Place," in *KGA* 17:143–44: "Die Stellung," in *KGA* 17:114

[10] See *GS* 3:718.

In both of these works, Troeltsch is working out a conception of culture (and of religion) that is deeply contextual and that embraces relativity and individuality. The first principle (relativity) promotes a view of religion and culture that resists absolute validity and universality. The second principle (individuality) is in many ways a guard against unlimited relativism, insofar as it draws attention to the particular and unique resources, traditions, and norms of a culture for contemporary ethical reflection. By linking religion and culture Troeltsch seeks to do justice to the historical complexity of Christianity while also avoiding both absolutism and a nihilistic form of relativism.[11] Of couse, Troeltsch's efforts come at a cost, as scholars have noted. His emphasis on the particularity of cultures is so strong that it ignores the interaction of cultures, resulting in isolationism. Troeltsch also ignores the religious diversity of Europe, and overlooks the nature of Christianity as a global religion (and not simply a European and American one).[12]

Yet, there are places in Troeltsch's thought where he does not simply merge religion and society or culture but, instead, seeks grounds on which he can defend the difference between modern European and Christian values so that Christianity can serve as an alternative to some dimensions of modern society. In these cases, Troeltsch appears to separate "the religious" from "the social." Is Troeltsch here falling into an ahistorical or essentialist conception of religion? I have argued that Troeltsch defends the autonomy of religion not to dehistoricize it, but to explore and demonstrate the ways in which Christianity might inform and challenge modern society. In particular, I have shown how Troeltsch repeatedly contrasts the rationalism of modern society with the value system of Christianity. Although Troeltsch did not develop these dimensions of his thought sufficiently, they nevertheless show that he did not intend a simple assimilation of Christianity into a particular culture

[11] As Coakley states (*Christ Without Absolutes*, 35), in rejecting what he calls, "wretched (*schlecht*) historicism," Troeltsch is attempting to avoid "criterial value relativism," which, according to Coakley's definition, "implies the removal of all agreed criteria for arriving at value judgments."

[12] Both of these points have been made in several articles by Cho. See, for example, "The Crisis of Historicism and Troeltsch's Europeanism," *History of European Ideas* 21 (1995) 199–201. Coakley (*Christ Without Absolutes*, 37–40) discusses and challenges Troeltsch's "flirtation" with the thesis of incommensurability. Masuzawa (*Invention of World Religions*, 322) also points to the problematic implications of Troeltsch's close linkage between Christianity and Europe. Yet, in her treatment of Troeltsch's conceptions of both Europe and Christianity, she ignores and misunderstands the historical (post-war, German) context and significance of Troeltsch's writings during this period. I discuss this context in ch. 5 above.

but, rather, wished to underscore the complex interaction of religious and social forces and, occasionally, to distinguish Christian beliefs and practices from modern ones as a mode of cultural critique. Furthermore, Troeltsch's assertion that there is a close link between Christianity and modern (European) society can also be read as part of his conviction that, in the face of the fragmentation of modern society, Christianity should not withdraw into private communities but engage the larger culture, exploring how it might contribute positively to the articulation of broad cultural values.

By constructing what I have called Troeltsch's "theory of Christianity," I have sought to demonstrate that, although Troeltsch surely remains a creature of his time, his thought continues to be instructive and challenging for contemporary theories of tradition and conceptions of the identity of Christianity. Four dimensions of his thought warrant further consideration among theorists of tradition today.

First, Troeltsch avoids an essentialist conception of Christianity and instead emphasizes its complex, contextual, and pluralistic nature as a tradition. Troeltsch exposed the problems of appealing to any one period or expression of Christian practice or belief for an indication of normative Christian identity. Appeals to Jesus, Scripture, or an historical period or institution in Christian history cannot provide a clear or singular indication of what Christianity is or should be. Troeltsch perceived the variety of truth claims within Christianity, and he emphasized the relativity of all formulations of Christian doctrine, showing them to be shaped by and intertwined with particular economic, social, and political situations and practices. Troeltsch nudged histories of Christianity and conceptions of tradition away from their limited focus on institutional churches and considered extra-ecclesial movements a central source for reflecting on the identity of Christianity. In short, Troeltsch knew that "Christianity itself is a theoretical abstraction," and that it "presents no historical uniformity."[13]

Second, Troeltsch was aware of the normative dimension and status of all constructions of "Christianity" and "tradition." That is, Troeltsch saw clearly that all efforts to tell Christian history, to formulate the essence of Christianity, or to identify that which unites the various forms of Christianity are at the same time claims that reflect the theorist's concerns about contemporary cultural and theological issues. Here Troeltsch anticipated what is today called the postmodern insight into the subjective or interested status of all

---

[13] "The Place," in *KGA* 17:138; "Die Stellung," in *KGA* 17:109.

claims about the identity of Christianity.[14] For Troeltsch, proposals about normative Christian identity should be evaluated for their potential to serve the needs of religious and cultural communities, as well as the larger society. Surely such proposals should aim at some measure of "objectivity" and thus be rooted in "the facts"; yet, even his insistence on an empirically grounded theory of Christianity had to do with Troeltsch's concern about the relevance of conceptions of Christianity for the actual life of contemporary communities.

Third, Troeltsch insisted on a complex theory of religion and its relation to society. I have shown that Troeltsch had numerous ways of conceiving the relation between "the religious" and "the social," and that each of these ways was crafted in relation to particular challenges and situations in his own cultural context.[15] Troeltsch consistently argued that religion is a complex phenomenon with multiple and shifting relations to other cultural forces (be they intellectual, political, economic, or social), and he defined "the religious" and "the social" as two overlapping and mutually influential forces that are always in complex relation. Yet, he also emphasized both the independence and the dependence of religion in relation to society. While "religion" cannot be separated from "society," nor can it be equated with the social, especially when one is seeking to explore the possible contribution of religion to the crises and challenges of modern society. Thus, Troeltsch asserted both the (relative) autonomy of religion and the radically contextual nature of religion. Both conceptions of religion were needed to speak to the concerns of his culture, and neither necessarily contradicted the other.

Fourth, especially toward the end of his life, Troeltsch began to outline (but because of his untimely death was not able to complete) an approach to the articulation and adjudication of norms in a culture that has striking affinities with various proposals among theorists of tradition today. It will be recalled that for Troeltsch the cultural synthesis consists primarily of two

[14] Drawing on postmodern theories of culture, Tanner seems to be echoing Troeltsch when she writes, "Materials designated 'traditional' are . . . always a selection from those that could be so designated. The ones selected are those that figure centrally in the organization of Christian materials favored by the party that puts them forward; therefore, what is labeled 'tradition' always has links to a preferred course of Christian behaviors now" (*Theories of Culture*, 163).

[15] John Milbank (*Theology and Social Theory*) misreads Troeltsch's conception of religion when he claims that Troeltsch 1) insists upon a categorical and absolute separation between "the religious" and "the social" (76), and 2) gives "explanatory priority to social causation over religious organization" (89).

moments: an historical one, wherein one looks to the history and resources of a particular tradition in order to identify normative resources in the past; and a constructive one, wherein one seeks to combine these resources anew in conversation with the interests and needs of the present and future. Troeltsch was not able to sketch out in detail the precise manner in which the second moment would be carried out, but it is clear both from what he says in the *Historicism* volume and in the *Christian Thought* lectures that this would be a task for ethics, which for him also included theology.

Troeltsch envisioned a synthesis of inherited tradition and contemporary construction that has not yet been achieved today. Theologians and theorists of tradition drawing on narrative and "tradition-constituted and tradition-constitutive"[16] moral reflection derive norms from the stock of past resources handed down in what is often portrayed as a singular, coherent, and occasionally insular community. Those turning to postmodern anthropological theories of culture locate the articulation of norms in creative and constructive negotiation of identities and in the "invention of traditions." In the *Social Teachings*, Troeltsch took initial steps toward a combination of these two moments, exploring and articulating resources of the past that might be employed and reshaped in new ways to meet present needs and interests. The *Historicism* volume was the beginning of his efforts to theorize this combination, or synthesis. His perception that ethics would be the terrain on which to complete the theory is an indication of the ultimately public orientation of his theology.[17] Troeltsch sought a theory of Christianity and a theory of culture that could engage and serve broad social exigencies of his time. He attempted to achieve it through a process of creative, constructive, and ethically directed engagement with the past in conversation with the present and future.

[16] MacIntyre, "*Whose Justice?*," esp. 349–70.

[17] For an interpretation of Troeltsch as public theologian, see Chapman, *Ernst Troeltsch and Liberal Theology*.

Bibliography

Collected Works by Ernst Troeltsch

Gesammelte Schriften: Until recently, this has been the standard (but not comprehensive) collection of Troeltsch's writings. Troeltsch published the first three volumes between 1912 and 1922. After his death in 1923, Hans Baron edited and published the fourth volume in 1925. The new forthcoming *Ernst Troeltsch Kritische Gesamtausgabe* (see below) will be the first complete edition of Troeltsch's writings.

Gesammelte Schriften. 4 vols. Tübingen: J. C. B. Mohr, 1912–1925:

> *Die Soziallehren der christlichen Kirchen und Gruppen*. Vol. 1, 1912. (*GS* 1)
>
> *Zur religiösen Lage, Religionsphilosophie und Ethik*. Vol. 2, 1913. (*GS* 2)
>
> *Der Historismus und seine Probleme. Erstes Buch. Das logische Problem der Geschichtsphilosophie*. Vol. 3, 1922. (*GS* 3)
>
> *Aufsätze zur Geistesgeschichte und Religionssoziologie*. Edited by Hans Baron. Vol. 4, 1925. (*GS* 4)

Ernst Troeltsch Kritische Gesamtausgabe: This new and complete edition of Troeltsch's writings is currently being published by Walter de Gruyter. To date, seven of twenty volumes have appeared.

Ernst Troeltsch Kritische Gesamtausgabe. 20 vols. Edited by Friedrich Wilhelm Graf, Volker Drehsen, Gangolf Hübinger, and Trutz Rendtorff. Berlin: Walter de Gruyter, 1998–present (13 volumes forthcoming).

> *Rezensionen und Kritiken (1894–1900)*. Edited by Friedrich Wilhelm Graf in collaboration with Dina Brandt. Vol. 2, 2007. (*KGA* 2)
>
> *Rezensionen und Kritiken (1901–1914)*. Edited by Friedrich Wilhelm Graf in collaboration with Gabrielle von Bassermann-Jordon. Vol. 4, 2004. (*KGA* 4)

Die Absolutheit des Christentums und die Religionsgeschichte (1902/1912) mit Thesen von 1901 und den handschriftlichen Zusätzen. Edited by Trutz Rendtorff in collaboration with Stefan Pautler. Vol. 5, 1998. (*KGA* 5)

Protestantisches Christentum und Kirche in der Neuzeit (1906/1909/ 1922). Edited by Volker Drehsen in collaboration with Christian Albrecht. Vol. 7, 2004. (*KGA* 7)

Schriften zur Bedeutung des Protestantismus für die moderne Welt (1906–1913). Edited by Trutz Rendtorff in collaboration with Stefan Pautler. Vol. 8, 2001. (*KGA* 8)

Schriften zur Politik und Kulturphilosophie (1918–1923). Edited by Gangolf Hübinger in collaboration with Johannes Mikuteit. Vol. 15, 2002. (*KGA* 15)

Fünf Vorträge zu Religion und Geschichtsphilosophie für England und Schottland. Der Historismus und seine Überwindung (1924)/Christian Thought: Its History and Application (1923). Edited by Gangolf Hübinger in collaboration with Andreas Terwey. Vol. 17, 2006. (*KGA* 17)

Individual Publications by Ernst Troeltsch

Die Absolutheit des Christentums und die Religionsgeschichte. Tübingen: J. C. B. Mohr, 1902; 2d rev. ed., 1912. All editions in *KGA* 5.

Die Bedeutung der Geschichtlichkeit Jesu für den Glauben. Tübingen: J. C. B. Mohr, 1911.

Die Bedeutung des Protestantismus für die Entstehung der modernen Welt. Munich: Oldenbourg, 1906; 2d rev. ed. Munich: Oldenbourg, 1911. Both editions in *KGA* 8:199–316.

"Calvinismus und Luthertum." *Die Christliche Welt* 23 (8 July 1909) 669–70; (15 July 1909) 678–82. In *GS* 4:254–61. In *KGA* 8:101–7.

Christian Thought: Its History and Application (1923). In *KGA* 17:133–203.

"The Common Spirit" (1923). In idem, *Christian Thought: Its History and Application, KGA* 17:176–87. German edition, "Der Gemeingeist" (1924). In *Der Historismus und seine Überwindung, KGA* 17:92–104.

"Contingency" (1910). In *Encyclopaedia of Religion and Ethics* 4:87–89. Edited by James Hastings. New York: Scribner, 1911.

"Der deutsche Idealismus" (1900). In *GS* 4:532–87.

"The Dogmatics of the 'Religionsgeschichtliche Schule.'" *The American Journal of Theology* 17 (1913) 1–21. 2d rev. German-language edition as "Die Dogmatik der 'religionsgeschichtlichen Schule,'" in *GS* 2:500–24.

"Empiricism and Platonism in the Philosophy of Religion: To the Memory of William James." *Harvard Theological Review* 5 (1912) 401–22. Revised in *GS* 2: 364–85.

"Epochen und Typen der Sozialphilosophie des Christentums" (1911). In *GS* 4:122–56.

"The Ethics of Cultural Values" (1923). In idem, *Christian Thought: Its History and Application*, *KGA* 17:163–75. German edition, "Die Ethik der Kulturwerte" (1924). In *Der Historismus und seine Überwindung*, *KGA* 17:80–92.

"Geschichte und Metaphysik." *Zeitschrift für Theologie und Kirche* 8 (January/February 1898) 1–69.

Glaubenslehre. Nach Heidelberger Vorlesungen aus den Jahren 1911 und 1912. Edited by Gertrud von le Fort. Munich: Duncker & Humblot, 1925. Reprinted with an introduction by Jacob Klapwijk. Aalen: Scientia Verlag, 1981.

"Historiography." In *Encyclopaedia of Religion and Ethics*, vol. 6:716–23. Edited by James Hastings. New York: Scribner, 1913.

"Das Historische in Kants Religionsphilosophie. Zugleich ein Beitrag zu den Untersuchungen über Kants Philosophie der Geschichte." *Kantstudien. Philosophische Zeitschrift* 9 (1904) 21–154.

Der Historismus und seine Probleme. Erstes Buch. Das logische Problem der Geschichtsphilosophie = *GS* 3.

Der Historismus und seine Überwindung. Fünf Vorträge. Edited by Friedrich von Hügel. Berlin: Pan Verlag Rolf Heise, 1924. In *KGA* 17:67–132.

"Idealism." In *Encyclopaedia of Religion and Ethics* 7:89–95. Edited by James Hastings. New York: Scribner, 1914.

"Die Krisis des Historismus." In *Die Neue Rundschau* 33 (1922) 572–90. In *KGA* 15:437–55.

"Die Kulturbedeutung des Calvinismus." In *Internationale Wochenschrift für Wissenschaft Kunst und Technik* 4 (9 April 1910) 449–68; (16 April 1910) 501–8. In *GS* 4:783–801. In *KGA* 8:146–81.

"Logos und Mythos in Theologie und Religionsphilosophie." *Logos. Internationale Zeitschrift für Philosophie der Kultur* 4 (January–April 1913) 8–35. In *GS* 2:805–36.

"Luther und die moderne Welt." In *Das Christentum. Fünf Einzeldarstellungen*, 69–101, 160–64. Edited by Paul Herre. Leipzig: Quelle & Meyer, 1908. In *KGA* 8:59–97.

"Meine Bücher" (1921). In *GS* 4:3–18.

"Moderne Geschichtsphilosophie. I–III." *Theologische Rundschau* 6 (January 1903) 3–28; (February 1903) 57–72; (March 1903) 103–17. Revised in *GS* 2:673–728.

"The Morality of the Personality and of the Conscience" (1923). In idem, *Christian Thought: Its History and Application, KGA* 17, 149–62. German edition, "Die Persönlichkeits- und Gewissensmoral" (1924). In *Der Historismus und seine Überwindung, KGA* 17, 68–80.

"Naturrecht und Humanität in der Weltpolitik" (1922). In *KGA* 15, 493–512.

"The Place of Christianity among the World Religions" (1923). In idem, *Christian Thought: Its History and Application, KGA* 17:134–48. German edition, "Die Stellung des Christentums unter den Weltreligionen" (1924). In *Der Historismus und seine Überwindung, KGA* 17:105–18.

Politische Ethik und Christentum. Göttingen: Vandenhoeck & Ruprecht, 1904.

"Prinzip, religiöses." In *Die Religion in Geschichte und Gegenwart* 4:1842–46. Edited by F. M. Schiele and L. Z. Scharnack. Tübingen: J. C. B. Mohr (Paul Siebeck), 1913.

"Protestantisches Christentum und Kirche in der Neuzeit." In *Die Kultur der Gegenwart. Ihre Entwicklung und ihre Ziele*, part 1, section 4: *Die christliche Religion mit Einschluss der israelitisch-jüdischen Religion*, 1st half: *Geschichte der christlichen Religion*. Edited by Paul Hinneberg. Berlin and Leipzig: Teubner, 1906. 2d rev. ed. in *Die Kultur der Gegenwart*, part 1, section 4, vol. 1. Berlin and Leipzig: Teubner, 1909. Both editions in *KGA* 7.

"Religion." In *Das Jahr 1913. Ein Gesamtbild der Kulturentwicklung*, 533–49. Edited by David Sarason. Leipzig: B. G. Teubner, 1913.

"Religion, Wirtschaft und Gesellschaft" (1913). In *GS* 4:21–33.

Review of *Das Bild des Christentums bei den großen deutschen Idealisten. Ein Beitrag zur Geschichte des Christentums*, by Christian Lülmann. *Historische Zeitschrift* n.s. 53 (1902) 306–8. In *KGA* 4:224–27.

Review of *Die Causalbetrachtung in den Geisteswissenschaften*, by Otto Ritschl. *Theologische Literaturzeitung* 27 (21 June 1902) 387–89. In *KGA* 4:213–16.

Review of *Kulturwissenschaft und Naturwissenschaft*, 2d ed., by Heinrich Rickert. *Theologische Literaturzeitung* 38 (5 July 1913) 440. In *KGA* 4:719–20.

Review of *Lehrbuch der Dogmengeschichte*, 2d half, by Reinhold Seeberg. *Göttingische gelehrte Anzeigen* 163 (1 January 1901) 15–30. In *KGA* 4:87–111.

Review of *Die neue historische Methode*, by Georg von Below; and of *Kulturwissenschaft und Naturwissenschaft*, by Heinrich Rickert. *Theologische Literaturzeitung* 24 (10 June 1899) 375–77.

Review of *Die Philosophie der Geschichte als Soziologie. Erster Teil. Einleitung und kritische Übersicht*, by Paul Barth. *Theologische Literaturzeitung* 23 (1898) 398–401.

Review of *Das Wesen der Religion philosophisch betrachtet*, by Rudolf Eucken. *Theologische Literaturzeitung* 27 (21 June 1902) 386–87. In *KGA* 4:209–212.

"Rückblick auf ein halbes Jahrhundert der theologischen Wissenschaft." *Zeitschrift für wissenschaftliche Theologie* 51, n.s. 16 (April–June 1909) 97–135. Revised in *GS* 2:193–226.

"Schleiermacher und die Kirche." In *Schleiermacher der Philosoph des Glaubens*. Edited by Max Apel, 9–35. Berlin: Buchverlag der "Hilfe," 1910.

Die Soziallehren der christlichen Kirchen und Gruppen = GS 1.

Die Sozialphilosophie des Christentums. Gotha/Stuttgart: Verlag Friedrich Andreas Perthes A.-G., 1922.

"Das stoisch-christliche Naturrecht und das moderne profane Naturrecht." *Historische Zeitschrift* 106 (March/April 1911) 237–67. In *GS* 4:166–91.

Die Trennung von Staat und Kirche, der staatliche Religionsunterricht und die theologische Fakultäten. Tübingen: J. C. B. Mohr (Paul Siebeck), 1907.

"Über historische und dogmatische Methode der Theologie." *Theologische Arbeiten aus dem rheinischen wissenschaftlichen Predigerverein*, n.s. 4 (1900) 87–108. Revised in *GS* 2:729–53.

"Was heißt 'Wesen des Christentums'?," *Die Christliche Welt* 17 (1903) 443–46, 483–88, 532–36, 578–84, 650–54, 678–83. Revised in *GS* 2:386–451.

"Das Wesen des modernen Geist." *Preußische Jahrbücher* 128 (April 1907) 21–40. In *GS* 4:297–338.

"Wesen der Religion und der Religionswissenschaft." In *Die christliche Religion mit Einschluss der israelitisch-jüdischen Religion*, 461–91. Part 1, section 4, 2d half of *Die Kultur der Gegenwart. Ihre Entwicklung and ihre Ziele.* Edited by Paul Hinneberg. Berlin: B. G. Teubner, 1906. 2d revised edition in *Systematische Christliche Religion*, 1–36. Part 1, section 4, 2d half of *Die Kultur der Gegenwart. Ihre Entwicklung and ihre Ziele.* Edited by Paul Hinneberg. Berlin: B. G. Teubner, 1909. Revised in *GS* 2:452–99.

"Die Zukunftsmöglichkeiten des Christentums im Verhältnis zur modernen Philosophie" (1911). In *GS* 2:837–62.

"Zum Begriff und zur Methode der Soziologie." Review of *Die Philosophie der Geschichte als Soziologie*, 2d ed. (1915), by Paul Barth. *Weltwirtschaftliches Archiv* 8 (1916) 259–76. In *GS* 4:705–20.

"Zur Frage des religiösen Apriori. Eine Erwiderung auf die Bemerkungen von Paul Spieß." *Religion und Geisteskultur* 3 (1909) 263–73. Revised in *GS* 2:754–68.

Correspondence by Ernst Troeltsch

Briefe an Friedrich von Hügel: 1901–1923. Edited by Karl-Ernst Apfelbacher and Peter Neuner. Paderborn: Bonifacius-Druckerei, 1974.

"Ernst Troeltschs Briefe an Heinrich Rickert." Edited by F. W. Graf. *Mitteilungen der Ernst-Troeltsch-Gesellschaft* VI (1991): 108–28.

Works by Ernst Troeltsch in English Translation

The Absoluteness of Christianity and the History of Religions. Translated by David Reid. Richmond, Va.: John Knox Press, 1971.

The Christian Faith: Based on Lectures Delivered at the University of Heidelberg in 1912 and 1913. Translated by Garrett E. Paul. Minneapolis: Fortress Press, 1991.

Christian Thought: Its History and Application. Translated into English by various hands and edited with an introduction by Baron F. Von Hügel. London: University of London Press, 1923. In *KGA* 17:133–203.

"The Dogmatics of the 'Religionsgeschichtliche Schule.'" *The American Journal of Theology* 17 (1913) 1–21.

"Empiricism and Platonism in the Philosophy of Religion: To the Memory of William James." *Harvard Theological Review* 5 (1912) 401–22.

Writings on Theology and Religion. Translated and edited by Robert Morgan and Michael Pye. London: Gerald Duckworth & Co., 1977. Repr., Louisville, Ky.: Westminster/John Knox, 1990.

"The Idea of Natural Law and Humanity in World Politics." In Otto Gierke, *Natural Law and the Theory of Society 1500–1800*, 201–22. Cambridge: Cambridge University Press, 1950.

Protestantism and Progress: A Historical Study of the Relation of Protestantism to the Modern World. Translated by W. Montgomery. New York: G. P. Putnam's Sons, 1912. First Fortress Press edition as *Protestantism and Progress: The Significance of Protestantism for the Rise of the Modern World*. Foreword by Brian Gerrish. Philadelphia: Fortress Press, 1986.

Religion in History. Essays translated by James Luther Adams and Walter Bense. Minneapolis: Fortress Press, 1991.

The Social Teaching of the Christian Churches. Translated by Olive Wyon. London: George Allen & Unwin, Ltd., 1931. Repr., Louisville, Ky.: Westminster/John Knox Press, 1992.

Other Primary and Secondary Sources

Adams, James Luther. "Ernst Troeltsch as Analyst of Religion." *Journal of the Scientific Study of Religion* 1 (1961) 99–109.

Anselm, Reiner. "Denker des Christentums—Ernst Troeltsch." *Mitteilungen der Ernst-Troeltsch-Gesellschaft* 17 (2004) 6–25.

Antoni, Carlo. *From History to Sociology: The Transition in German Historical Thinking*. Detroit: Wayne State University Press, 1959.

Bainton, R. H. "Ernst Troeltsch: Thirty Years Later." *Theology Today* 8 (1951) 70–96.

Barth, Karl. *Church Dogmatics* 4/1. Translated by G. W. Bromiley. Edinburgh: T&T Clark, 1956.

———. "Evangelical Theology in the Nineteenth Century." In idem, *The Humanity of God*, 11–33. Louisville, Ky: Westminster/John Knox Press, 1960.

Becker, Gerhold. "Die Funktion der Religionsphilosophie in Troeltsch's Theorie des Christentums." In *Protestantismus und Neuzeit*, 240–56. Edited by Horst Renz and Friedrich Wilhelm Graf. Troeltsch-Studien 3. Gütersloh: Gütersloher Verlagshaus Mohn, 1984.

Bendix, Reinhard. *Max Weber: An Intellectual Portrait*. Berkeley: University of California Press, 1977.

Benson, Constance L. *God & Caesar: Troeltsch's "Social Teaching" as Legitimation*. New Brunswick, N.J.: Transaction Publishers, 1999.

Bodenstein, Walter. *Neige des Historismus*. Gütersloh: Gerd Mohn, 1959.

Brown, David. *Tradition & Imagination: Revelation & Change*. Oxford: Oxford University Press, 1999.

Brown, Delwin. *Boundaries of Our Habitation: Tradition and Theological Construction*. Albany, N.Y.: SUNY Press, 1994.

Brown, Marshall. *The Shape of German Romanticism*. Ithaca, N.Y.: Cornell University Press, 1979.

Burant, Aimee. "'A Metaphysical Attitude towards Life': Ernst Troeltsch on Protestantism and German National Identity." *Zeitschrift für Neuere Theologiegeschichte/Journal for the History of Modern Theology* 14 (2007) 81–100.

Burger, Thomas. *Max Weber's Theory of Concept Formation: History, Laws, and Ideal Types*. Durham, N.C.: Duke University Press, 1987.

Bynum, Caroline Walker. "The Mysticism and Asceticism of Medieval Women: Some Comments on the Typologies of Max Weber and Ernst Troeltsch." In eadem, *Fragmentation and Redemption: Essays on Gender and the Human Body in Medieval Religion*, 53–78. New York: Zone Books, 1991.

Campbell, Bruce. "A Typology of Cults." *Sociological Analysis* 39 (1978) 228–40.

Castelli, Elizabeth, and Hal Taussig, eds. *Reimagining Christian Origins: A Colloquium Honoring Burton L. Mack*. Valley Forge, Pa.: Trinity Press International, 1996.

Chapman, Mark D. *Ernst Troeltsch and Liberal Theology: Religion and Cultural Synthesis in Wilhelmine Germany*. Christian Theology in Context. Oxford: Oxford University Press, 2001.

———. "*Der Historismus* in England und England in *Der Historismus*." In *Ernst Troeltschs "Historismus,"* 181–99. Edited by Friedrich Wilhelm Graf. Troeltsch-Studien 11. Gütersloh: Gütersloher Verlagshaus Mohn, 2000.

Cho, Joanne Miyang. "The Advantage and Disadvantage of Europeanism in Ernst Troeltsch: Its Relationship to Nationalism, Eurocentrism, and Universalism." *The European Legacy* 1 (1996) 720–26.

———. "The Crisis of Historicism and Troeltsch's Europeanism." *History of European Ideas* 21 (1995) 195–207.

Cho, Joanne Miyang. "The German Debate over Civilization: Troeltsch's Europeanism and Jaspers's Cosmopolitanism." *History of European Ideas* 25 (1999) 305–19.

———. "Historicism and Civilizational Discontinuity in Spengler and Troeltsch." *Zeitschrift für Religions- und Geistesgeschichte* 51 (1999) 238–62.

Claussen, Johann Hinrich. *Die Jesus-Deutung von Ernst Troeltsch im Kontext der liberalen Theologie.* Tübingen: J. C. B. Mohr, 1997.

Clayton, John Powell. "Can Theology Be Both Cultural and Christian? Ernst Troeltsch and the Possibility of a Mediating Theology." In *Science, Faith, and Revelation: An Approach to Christian Philosophy*, 82–111. Edited by Bob E. Patterson. Nashville, Tenn.: Broadman Press, 1979.

———. *The Concept of Correlation: Paul Tillich and the Possibility of a Mediating Theology.* Theologische Bibliothek Topelmann 37. Berlin: Walter de Gruyter, 1980.

———, ed. *Ernst Troeltsch and the Future of Theology.* Cambridge: Cambridge University Press, 1976.

———. "Was ist Falsch in der Korrelationstheologie?" *Neue Zeitschrift für Systematische Theologie* 16 (1974) 93–111.

Coakley, Sarah. *Christ Without Absolutes: A Study of the Christology of Ernst Troeltsch.* Oxford: Oxford University Press, 1988.

Collingwood, R. G. *The Idea of History.* Oxford: Oxford University Press, 1956.

D'Amico, Robert. *Historicism and Knowledge.* New York: Routledge, 1989.

De Certeau, Michel. *The Mystic Fable.* Translated by Michael B. Smith. Chicago: University of Chicago Press, 1992.

De Mey, Peter. "Ernst Troeltsch: A Moderate Pluralist? An Evaluation of His Reflections on the Place of Christianity among the Other Religions." In *The Myriad Christ: Plurality and the Quest for Unity in Contemporary Christology*, 349–80. Edited by T. Merrigan and J. Haers. Leuven: Leuven University Press, 2000.

De Schrijver, Georges. "Hermeneutics and Tradition." *Journal of Ecumenical Studies* 19 (1982) 32–47.

Dean, William D. *History Making History: The New Historicism in American Religious Thought.* SUNY Series in Philosophy. Albany, N.Y.: SUNY Press, 1988.

Despland, Michel. "Tradition." In *Historicizing "Tradition" in the Study of Religion*, 19–32. Edited by Steven Engler and Gregory P. Grieve. New York: Walter de Gruyter, 2005.

Dietrich, Wendell S. *Cohen and Troeltsch: Ethical Monotheistic Religion and Theory of Culture.* Brown Judaic Studies 120. Atlanta, Ga.: Scholars Press, 1986.

———. "Loisy and the Liberal Protestants." *Studies in Religion* 14 (1985) 303–11.

———. "Troeltsch's Treatment of the Thomist Synthesis in *The Social Teaching* as a Signal of His View of a New Cultural Synthesis." *The Thomist* 57 (July 1993) 381–401.

Dilthey, Wilhelm. *Pattern and Meaning in History: Thoughts on History and Society.* Edited by H. P. Rickman. New York: Harper & Row, 1962.

———. *The Essence of Philosophy.* Chapel Hill, N.C.: University of North Carolina Press, 1954.

Drescher, Hans-Georg. *Ernst Troeltsch: His Life and Work.* Translated by John Bowden. Minneapolis: Fortress Press, 1993.

———. "Ernst Troeltsch's Intellectual Development." In *Ernst Troeltsch and the Future of Theology*, 3–32. Edited by John Powell Clayton. Cambridge: Cambridge University Press, 1976.

Engler, Steven, and Gregory P. Grieve, eds. *Historicizing "Tradition" in the Study of Religion.* New York: Walter de Gruyter, 2005.

Farley, Ed. *Ecclesial Reflection: An Anatomy of Theological Method.* Philadelphia: Fortress Press, 1982.

Fechtner, Kristian. *Volkskirche im neuzeitlichen Christentum. Die Bedeutung Ernst Troeltschs für eine künftige praktisch-theologische Theorie der Kirche.* Troeltsch-Studien 8. Gütersloh: Gütersloher Verlagshaus, 1995.

Fiorenza, Francis Schüssler. "The Crisis of Hermeneutics and Christian Theology." In *Theology at the End of Modernity*, 117–40. Edited by Sheila Davaney. Philadelphia: Trinity Press International, 1991.

———. *Foundational Theology.* New York: Crossroad, 1986.

Forni, Guglielmo. *The Essence of Christianity: The Hermeneutical Question in the Protestant and Modernist Debate (1897–1904).* Atlanta, Ga.: Scholars Press, 1995.

Fredriksen, Paula. *Jesus of Nazareth, King of the Jews: A Jewish Life and the Emergence of Christianity.* New York: Knopf, 1999.

Friesen, Duane K. "Normative Factors in Troeltsch's Typology of Religious Association." *Journal of Religious Ethics* 3 (1975) 271–83.

Gadamer, Hans Georg. *Truth and Method.* 2d ed. New York: Crossroad, 1989.

Gardiner, Patrick L. *The Philosophy of History.* Oxford Readings in Philosophy. Oxford: Oxford University Press, 1974.

Gerrish, Brian. *Continuing the Reformation: Essays on Modern Religious Thought*. Chicago: University of Chicago Press, 1993.

———. "Theology and the Historical Consciousness." In *Revisioning the Past*, 281–97. Edited by Mary Engel and Walter E. Wyman, Jr. Minneapolis: Fortress Press, 1992.

———. *Tradition and the Modern World: Reformed Theology in the Nineteenth Century*. Andrew C. Zenos Memorial Lectures, 1977. Chicago: University of Chicago Press, 1978.

Gerth, H. H., and C. Wright Mills. Introduction to *From Max Weber: Essays in Sociology*. New York: Oxford University Press, 1946; repr., 1958.

Gilkey, Langdon Brown. *Reaping the Whirlwind: A Christian Interpretation of History*. New York: Seabury Press, 1976.

Gisel, Pierre, ed. *Histoire et theologie chez Ernst Troeltsch*. Lieux theologiques, no. 22. Geneve: Labor et Fides, 1992.

Graf, Friedrich Wilhelm. "'endlich große Bücher schreiben.' Marginalen zur Werkgeschichte der *Soziallehren*." In *Ernst Troeltschs Soziallehren. Studien zu ihrer Interpretation*, 27–48. Edited by Friedrich Wilhelm Graf and Trutz Rendtorff. Troeltsch-Studien 6. Gütersloh: Gerd Mohn, 1993.

———. "Ernst Troeltsch. Kulturgeschichte des Christentums." In *Deutsche Geschichtswissenschaft um 1900*, 131–52. Edited by Notker Hammerstein. Stuttgart: Franz Steiner Verlag, 1988.

———, ed. "Ernst Troeltschs Briefe an Heinrich Rickert." *Mitteilungen der Ernst-Troeltsch-Gesellschaft* VI (1991) 108–28.

———, ed. *Ernst Troeltschs "Historismus."* Troeltsch-Studien 11. Gütersloh: Gütersloher Verlagshaus, 2000.

———. "Friendship between Experts: Notes on Weber and Troeltsch." In *Max Weber and His Contemporaries,* 215–33. Edited by Wolfgang J. Mommsem and Jürgen Osterhammel. German Historical Institute; London: Unwin Hyman, 1987.

———, ed. *"Geschichte durch Geschichte überwinden." Ernst Troeltsch in Berlin.* Troeltsch-Studien, n.s., vol. 1. Gütersloh: Gütersloher Verlagshaus: 2006.

———. "Kulturprotestantismus. Zur Begriffsgeschichte einer theologiepolitischen Chiffre." In *Kulturprotestantismus. Beiträge zu einer Gestalt des modernen Christentums*, 21–77. Edited by Hans Martin Müller. Gütersloh: Gerd Mohn, 1992.

Graf, Friedrich Wilhelm. "Philosophisch reflektierte Kriegserfahrung. Einige Überlegungen zu Ernst Troeltschs 'Kaisergeburtstagsrede'." In *Geschichte durch Geschichte überwinden.*" *Ernst Troeltsch in Berlin*, 231–52. Edited by Friedrich Wilhelm Graf. Troeltsch-Studien, n.s., vol. 1; Gütersloh: Gütersloher Verlagshaus, 2006.

————. "Protestantische Theologie in der Gesellschaft des Kaiserreichs." In *Profile des neuzeitlichen Protestantismus*, vol. 2, pt. 1, pages 12–117. Edited by Friedrich Wilhelm Graf. Gütersloh: Gütersloher Verlagshaus, 1992.

————. "Puritanische Sektenfreiheit versus lutherische Volkskirche. Zum Einfluß Georg Jellineks auf religionsdiagnostische Deutungsmuster Max Webers und Ernst Troeltschs." *Zeitschrift für Neuere Theologiegeschichte/Journal for the History of Modern Theology* 9 (2002) 42–69.

————. "Reinhold Seeberg." In *Profile des Luthertums. Biographen zum 20. Jahrhundert*, 617–76. Edited by Wolf-Dieter Hauschild. Gütersloh: Gütersloher Verlagshaus, 1998.

————. "Religion und Individualität. Bemerkungen zu einem Grundproblem der Religionstheorie Ernst Troeltschs." In *Protestantismus und Neuzeit*, 207–30. Edited by Horst Renz and Friedrich Wilhelm Graf. Troeltsch-Studien 3. Gütersloh: Gütersloher Verlagshaus, 1984.

————. "Weltanschauungshistoriographie. Rezensionen zur Erstausgabe der *Soziallehren*." In *Ernst Troeltschs Soziallehren. Studien zu ihrer Interpretation*, 216–29. Edited by Friedrich Wilhelm Graf and Trutz Rendtorff. Troeltsch-Studien 6. Gütersloh: Gütersloher Verlagshaus, 1993.

Graf, Friedrich Wilhelm, and Horst Renz, eds. *Protestantismus und Neuzeit*. Troeltsch-Studien 3. Gütersloh: Gütersloher Verlagshaus, 1984.

Graf, Friedrich Wilhelm, and Hartmut Ruddies. *Ernst Troeltsch Bibliographie*. Tübingen: J. C. B. Mohr, 1982.

————. "Ernst Troeltsch. Geschichtsphilosophie in praktischer Absicht." In *Philosophie der Neuzeit IV*, 128–64. Edited by Joseph Speck. Grundprobleme der großen Philosophen. Göttingen: Vandenhoeck & Ruprecht, 1986.

Graf, F. W., and Trutz Rendtorff, eds. *Ernst Troeltschs Soziallehren. Studien zu ihrer Interpretation*. Troeltsch-Studien 6. Gütersloh: Gütersloher Verlagshaus, 1993.

Grieve, Gregory P., and Richard Weiss. "Illuminating the Half-Life of Tradition: Legitimation, Agency, and Counter-Hegemonies," In *Historicizing "Tradition" in the Study of Religion*, 1–15. Edited by Steven Engler and Gregory P. Grieve. New York: Walter de Gruyter, 2005.

Harnack, Adolf. *The Mission and Expansion of Christianity.* Edited and translated by James Moffat. Gloucester, Mass.: Peter Smith, 1972.

———. *Das Wesen des Christentums.* Academic edition. Leipzig: J. C. Hinrichs, 1902.

———. *What Is Christianity?* Translated by Thomas Bailey Saunders. Introduction by Rudolf Bultmann. Repr., Gloucester: Peter Smith, 1978.

Harrington, Austin. "Ernst Troeltsch's Concept of Europe." *European Journal of Social Theory* 7 (2004) 479–98.

Harvey, Van A. *The Historian and the Believer.* New York: Macmillan, 1966.

Hegel, Georg W. F. *The Philosophy of History.* New York: Dover, 1956.

Heim, S. Mark. *Salvations: Truth and Difference in Religion.* New York: Maryknoll, 1995.

Heschel, Susannah. *Abraham Geiger and the Jewish Jesus.* Chicago: University of Chicago Press, 1998.

Hobsbawn, Eric, and Terence Ranger, eds. *The Invention of Tradition.* Cambridge: Cambridge University Press, 1983.

Hodgson, Peter C., ed. *Ferdinand Christian Baur on the Writing of Church History.* New York: Oxford, 1968.

Horsley, Richard, with Jonathan Draper. *Whoever Hears You Hears Me: Prophets, Performance, and Tradition in Q.* Harrisburg, Pa.: Trinity Press International, 1999.

Hübinger, Gangolf. "Confessionalism." In *Imperial Germany: A Historiographical Companion*, 156–84. Edited by Roger Chickering. Westport, Conn.: Greenwood Press, 1996.

———. "Ernst Troeltschs Berlin. Im 'Bund der Intellektuellen'." In *Ernst Troeltschs "Historismus,"* 164–80. Edited by F. W. Graf. Troeltsch-Studien 11. Gütersloh: Gütersloher Verlagshaus, 2000.

———. *Kulturprotestantismus und Politik. Zum Verhältnis von Liberalismus und Protestantismus im wilhelminischen Deutschland.* Tübingen: J. C. B. Mohr/Paul Siebeck, 1994.

Hughes, H. Stuart. *Consciousness and Society: The Reorientation of European Social Thought, 1890–1930.* New York: Alfred A. Knopf, 1961.

Iggers, Georg. *The German Conception of History: The National Tradition of Historical Thought from Herder to the Present.* Middletown, Conn.: Wesleyan University Press, 1968; rev. ed., 1983.

———. "Historicism." In *Dictionary of the History of Ideas.* New York: Scribner, 1973.

Johnson, Roger A. "Idealism, Empiricism, and 'Other Religions': Troeltsch's Reading of William James." *Harvard Theological Review* 80 (1987) 449–76.

Kasch, Wilhelm. *Die Sozialphilosophie von Ernst Troeltsch*. Tübingen: J. C. B. Mohr, 1963.

Kaufman, Gordon. *In Face of Mystery*. Cambridge, Mass.: Harvard University Press, 1993.

Kawerau, Gustav. "Sektenwesen in Deutschland." In *Realenzyklopädie für protestantische Theologie und Kirche* 18:157–66. Edited by Albert Hauck. Leipzig: J. C. Hinrichs, 1906.

Kippenberg, Hans. *Discovering Religious History in the Modern Age*. Translated by Barbara Harshav. Princeton, N.J.: Princeton University Press, 2001.

Köpf, Ulrich. "Kirchengeschichte oder Religionsgeschichte des Christentums? Gedanken über Gegenstand und Aufgabe der Kirchengeschichte um 1900." In *Der deutsche Protestantismus um 1900*, 42–66. Edited by F. W. Graf and H. M. Müller. Gütersloh: Gütersloher Verlagshaus, 1996.

Lannert, Berthold. "Die Bedeutung der religionsgeschichtlichen Forschungen zur Geschichte des Urchristentums." In *Ernst Troeltschs Soziallehren. Studien zu ihrer Interpretation*, 80–102. Edited by F. W. Graf and Trutz Rendtorff. Troeltsch-Studien 6. Gütersloh: Gütersloher Verlaghaus, 1993.

Lee, Dwight E., and Robert N. Beck. "The Meaning of 'Historicism'." *American Historical Review* 59 (1953–1954) 568–77.

Lehmann, Hartmut. "The Suitability of the Tools Provided by Ernst Troeltsch for the Understanding of Twentieth-Century Religion." *Religion, State & Society* 27 (1999) 295–300.

Lehmann, Hartmut, and Guenther Roth, eds. *Weber's Protestant Ethic: Origins, Evidence, Contexts*. Cambridge: Cambridge University Press, 1987.

Lessing, Eckhard. *Die Geschichtsphilosophie Ernst Troeltschs*. Theologische Forschung no. 39. Hamburg-Bergstedt: Herbert Reich, 1965.

Liebersohn, Harry. *Fate and Utopia in German Sociology, 1870–1923*. Cambridge, Mass.: MIT Press, 1988.

————. *Religion and Industrial Society*. Transactions of the American Philosophical Society 76. Philadelphia: American Philosophical Society, 1986.

————. "Troeltsch's *Social Teachings* and the Protestant Social Congress." In *Ernst Troeltschs Soziallehren. Studien zu ihrer Interpretation*, 241–57. Edited by F. W. Graf and Trutz Rendtorff. Troeltsch-Studien 6. Gütersloh: Gütersloher Verlaghaus, 1993.

Lindbeck, George. *The Nature of Doctrine*. Philadelphia: Westminster Press, 1984.

Linge, David E. "Dilthey and Gadamer: Two Theories of Historical Understanding." *Journal of the American Academy of Religion* 41 (1973) 536–53.

Little, David. *Religion, Order, and Law*. Chicago: University of Chicago Press, 1984.

Loisy, Alfred. *The Gospel and the Church*. Translated by Christopher Home. Repr., Philadelphia: Fortress Press, 1976.

MacIntyre, Alasdair. *Three Rival Versions of Moral Enquiry: Encyclopedia, Genealogy, and Tradition*. Notre Dame, Ind.: University of Notre Dame Press, 1990.

———. *Whose Justice? Which Rationality?* Notre Dame, Ind.: University of Notre Dame Press, 1988.

Mandelbaum, Maurice. *The Problem of Historical Knowledge: An Answer to Relativism*. 1938. Repr., New York: Harper & Row, 1967.

Masuzawa, Tomoko. *The Invention of World Religions: Or, How European Universalism Was Preserved in the Language of Pluralism*. Chicago: University of Chicago Press, 2005.

Meinecke, Friedrich. *Historism: The Rise of a New Historical Outlook*. London: Routledge and K. Paul, 1972.

Meyerhoff, Hans, ed. *The Philosophy of History in Our Time*. New York: Anchor Books, 1959.

Milbank, John. *Theology and Social Theory: Beyond Secular Reason*. Oxford: Blackwell, 1990.

Molendijk, Arie L. *Zwischen Theologie und Soziologie. Ernst Troeltschs Typen der christlichen Gemeinschaftsbildung. Kirche, Sekte, Mystik*. Troeltsch-Studien 9. Gütersloh: Gütersloher Verlagshaus, 1996.

Mommsen, Wolfgang J., and Jürgen Osterhammel, eds. *Max Weber and His Contemporaries*. The German Historical Institute. London: Allen & Unwin, 1987.

Morgan, Robert. "Ernst Troeltsch and the Dialectical Theology." In *Ernst Troeltsch and the Future of Theology*, 33–77. Edited by John Powell Clayton. Cambridge: Cambridge University Press, 1976.

———. "Ernst Troeltsch on Theology and Religion." Introduction to *Ernst Troeltsch: Writings on Theology and Religion*, 1–51. Edited by Robert Morgan and Michael Pye. London: Gerald Duckworth & Co., 1977. Repr., Louisville, Ky.: Westminster/John Knox, 1990.

Nathusius, Martin von. *Die Mitarbeit der Kirche an der Lösung der sozialen Frage*. 3d rev. ed. Leipzig: Hinrichs, 1904.

Newman, John Henry. *An Essay on the Development of Christian Doctrine*. Edited by Charles F. Harrold. New York: Longmans, Green and Co., 1949.

Niebuhr, H. Richard. "Ernst Troeltsch's Philosophy of Religion." Ph.D. Diss., Yale University, 1924.

Oakes, Guy. *Weber and Rickert: Concept Formation in the Cultural Sciences*. Cambridge, Mass.: MIT Press, 1988.

Oexle, Otto Gerhard. "Troeltschs Dilemma." In *Ernst Troeltschs "Historismus*," 23–64. Edited by F. W. Graf. Troeltsch-Studien 11. Gütersloh: Gütersloher Verlagshaus, 2000.

Ogletree, Thomas. *Christian Faith and History*. New York: Abingdon Press, 1965.

Pauck, Wilhelm. *Harnack and Troeltsch: Two Historical Theologians*. New York: Oxford University Press, 1968.

Paul, Garrett. "Why Troeltsch? Why Today? Theology for the Twenty-First Century." *The Christian Century* 110 (1993) 676–81.

Pearson, Lori K. "Conceptualizing Christianity: Troeltsch on Christian Origins in *Die Soziallehren*." *Mitteilungen der Ernst-Troeltsch-Gesellschaft* 13 (2000) 35–47.

————. "Gendered Dimensions of Troeltsch's Typology of Church-Sect-Mysticism." *Zeitschrift für Neuere Theologiegeschichte/Journal for the History of Modern Theology* 13 (2006) 23–40.

Pelikan, Jaroslav. *Historical Theology: Continuity and Change in Christian Doctrine*. New York: Corpus, 1971.

Penzel, Klaus. "Ernst Troeltsch on Luther." In *Interpreters of Luther: Essays in Honor of Wilhelm Pauck*, 275–303. Edited by Jaroslav Pelikan. Philadelphia: Fortress, 1968.

Plantinga, Theodore. *Historical Understanding in the Thought of Wilhelm Dilthey*. Toronto: University of Toronto Press, 1980.

Pye, Michael. "Ernst Troeltsch and the End of the Problem of 'Other' Religions." In *Ernst Troeltsch and the Future of Theology*, 171–95. Edited by John Powell Clayton. Cambridge: Cambridge University Press, 1976.

————. "Troeltsch and the Science of Religion." In *Ernst Troeltsch: Writings on Theology and Religion*, 234–52. Edited by Robert Morgan and Michael Pye. London: Gerald Duckworth & Co., 1977. Repr., Louisville, Ky.: Westminster/John Knox: 1990.

Pye, Michael. "Reflections on the Treatment of Tradition in Critical Perspective, with Special Reference to Ernst Troeltsch and Gerardus van der Leeuw." In *Religionswissenschaft and Kulturkritik*, 101–11. Edited by Hans G. Kippenberg and Brigitte Luchesi. Marburg: Diagonal Verlag, 1991.

Rand, Calvin G. "Two Meanings of Historicism in the Writings of Dilthey, Troeltsch, and Meinecke." *Journal of the History of Ideas* 25 (1964) 503–18.

Reist, Benjamin A. *Toward a Theology of Involvement: The Thought of Ernst Troeltsch*. Philadelphia: Westminster Press, 1966.

Renz, H., and F. W. Graf, eds. *Untersuchungen zur Biographie und Werkgeschichte*. Troeltsch-Studien 1. Gütersloh: Gütersloher Verlagshaus, 1982.

Rickert, Heinrich. *Die Grenzen der naturwissenschaftlichen Begriffsbildung. Eine logische Einleitung in die historischen Wissenschaften*. Tübingen/Leipzig: J. C. B. Mohr, 1902.

———. *Kulturwissenschaft und Naturwissenschaft*. Freiburg: J. C. B. Mohr, 1899.

———. *The Limits of Concept Formation in Natural Science: A Logical Introduction to the Historical Sciences*. Translated from the revised 1929 edition by Guy Oakes. Cambridge: Cambridge University Press, 1986.

Ringer, Fritz. *The Decline of the German Mandarins: The German Academic Community, 1890–1933*. Cambridge, Mass.: Harvard University Press, 1969. Repr., Hanover, N.H.: Wesleyan University Press/University Press of New England, 1990.

Ritschl, Albrecht. *The Christian Doctrine of Justification and Reconciliation: The Positive Development of the Doctrine*. 2d ed. Edinburgh: T&T Clark, 1902.

Roof, Wade Clark. "Modernity, the Religious, and the Spiritual." In *Americans and Religions in the Twenty-First Century*, 211–24. Edited by idem. Annals of the American Academy of Political and Social Science 558. Thousand Oaks, Calif.: Sage Publications, 1998.

Roth, Guenther. "Marianne Weber and Her Circle." Introduction to the Transaction edition of *Max Weber: A Biography*, by Marianne Weber, translated and edited by Harry Zohn, xv–lx. New Brunswick, N.J.: Transaction, 1988.

Rubanowice, Robert J. *Crisis in Consciousness: The Thought of Ernst Troeltsch*. Tallahassee, Fla.: University Presses of Florida, 1982.

Ruddies, Harmut. "Ernst Troeltsch und Friedrich Naumann. Grundprobleme der christlichen Ethik bei der Legitimation der Moderne." In *Ernst Troeltschs Soziallehren. Studien zu ihrer Interpretation*, 258–75. Edited by F. W. Graf and Trutz Rendtorff. Troeltsch-Studien 6. Gütersloh: Gütersloher Verlagshaus, 1993.

Rupp, George. *Culture Protestantism.* Missoula, Mont.: Scholars Press, 1977.

Sarot, Marcel, and Gijsbert van den Brink, eds. *Identity and Change in the Christian Tradition.* Frankfurt am Main: Peter Lang, 1999.

Schleiermacher, Friedrich. *Brief Outline of the Study of Theology.* Edinburgh: T&T Clark, 1850.

———. *The Christian Faith.* Edinburgh: T&T Clark, 1928.

Schreiter, Robert J. "A Semiotic-Linguistic Theory of Tradition: Identity and Communication amid Cultural Difference." In *Zur Logik religiöser Traditionen*, 87–118. Edited by Barbara Schoppelreich and Siegfried Wiedenhofer. Frankfurt am Main: Verlag für Interkulturelle Kommunikation, 1998.

Schwöbel, Christoph. "'Die Idee des Aufbaus heißt Geschichte durch Geschichte überwinden.' Theologischer Wahrheitsanspruch und das Problem des sogenannten Historismus." In *Ernst Troeltschs "Historismus,"* 261–84. Edited by F. W. Graf. Troeltsch-Studien 11. Gütersloh: Gütersloher Verlagshaus, 2000.

Shils, Edward. *Tradition.* Chicago: University of Chicago Press, 1981.

Smith, Jonathan Z. "Fences and Neighbors: Some Contours of Early Judaism." In idem, *Imagining Religion: From Babylon to Jonestown*, 1–18. Chicago: University of Chicago Press, 1982.

Sockness, Brent. *Against False Apologetics: Wilhelm Herrmann and Ernst Troeltsch in Conflict.* Beiträge zur historischen Theologie 105. Tübingen: Mohr Siebeck, 1998.

Sösemann, Bernd. "Das 'erneute Deutschland.' Ernst Troeltschs politische Engagement im ersten Weltkrieg." In *Protestantismus und Neuzeit*, 120–44. Edited by Horst Renz and Friedrich Wilhelm Graf. Troeltsch-Studien 3. Gütersloh: Gütersloher Verlagshaus, 1984.

Stackhouse, Max. "A Premature Postmodern?" *First Things* 106 (Oct. 2000) 19–22.

Stanford, Michael. *An Introduction to the Philosophy of History.* Cambridge: Blackwell, 1998.

Steeman, Theodore M. "Church, Sect, Mysticism, Denomination: Periodological Aspects of Troeltsch's Types." *Sociological Analysis* 36 (1975) 181–204.

Stegemann, Wolfgang. "Zur Deutung des Urchristentums in den *Soziallehren*." In *Ernst Troeltschs Soziallehren. Studien zu ihrer Interpretation*, 51–79. Edited by F. W. Graf and Trutz Rendtorff. Troeltsch-Studien 6. Gütersloh: Gütersloher Verlagshaus, 1993.

Stewart, Charles, and Rosalind Shaw, eds. *Syncretism/Anti-Syncretism: The Politics of Religious Synthesis*. London and New York: Routledge, 1994.

Sykes, Stephen. *The Identity of Christianity*. Philadelphia: Fortress Press, 1984.

———. "Troeltsch and Christianity's Essence." In *Ernst Troeltsch and the Future of Theology*, 139–71. Edited by John Powell Clayton. Cambridge: Cambridge University Press, 1976.

Tal, Uriel. *Christians and Jews in Germany: Religion, Politics, and Ideology in the Second Reich, 1870–1914*. Translated by Noah Jonathan Jacobs. Ithaca, N.Y.: Cornell University Press, 1975.

Tanner, Kathryn. *Theories of Culture: A New Agenda for Theology*. Guides to Theological Inquiry. Minneapolis: Fortress Press, 1997.

Tanner, Klaus. "Das *Kulturdogma* der Kirche: Ernst Troeltschs Naturrechtsdeutung." In *Ernst Troeltschs Soziallehren. Studien zu ihrer Interpretation*, 122–32. Edited by F. W. Graf and Trutz Rendtorff. Troeltsch-Studien 6. Gütersloh: Gütersloher Verlagshaus, 1993.

Thiel, John E. *Senses of Tradition: Continuity and Development in Catholic Faith*. New York: Oxford University Press, 2000.

Tillich, Paul. "Ernst Troeltsch: Historismus und seine Probleme." *Journal for the Scientific Study of Religion* 1 (1961) 109–14.

Tracy, David. *Plurality and Ambiguity: Hermeneutics, Religion, Hope*. San Francisco: Harper & Row, 1987.

Voigt, Friedemann, *"Die Tragödie des Reiches Gottes"? Ernst Troeltsch als Leser Georg Simmels*. Troeltsch-Studien 10. Gütersloh: Gütersloher Verlagshaus, 1998.

Wagenhammer, Hans. *Das Wesen des Christentums. Eine begriffsgeschichtliche Untersuchung*. Mainz: Matthias-Grünewald Verlag: 1973.

Ward, W. R. "Max Weber and the Lutherans." In *Max Weber and His Contemporaries*, 203–14. Edited by Wolfgang J. Mommsem and Jürgen Osterhammel. German Historical Institute; London: Unwin Hyman, 1987.

———. *Theology, Sociology and Politics: The German Protestant Social Conscience 1890–1933*. Berne: Peter Lang, 1979.

Weber, Marianne. *Ehefrau und Mutter in der Rechtsentwicklung*. Tübingen: J. C. B. Mohr/Paul Siebeck, 1907.

Weber, Marianne. *Max Weber: A Biography*. Translated and edited by Harry Zohn. New York: John Wiley & Sons, 1975.

Weber, Max. *Economy and Society*. Berkeley and Los Angeles: University of California Press, 1978.

―――. *From Max Weber: Essays in Sociology*. Translated, edited, and with an introduction by H. H. Gerth and C. Wright Mills. New York: Oxford University Press, 1946.

―――. "Kirchen und Sekten in Nordamerika. Eine kirchen- und sozialpolitische Skizze." *Die Christliche Welt* 20 (14 June 1906) 558–62; (21 June 1906) 577–83.

―――. *The Methodology of the Social Sciences*. Edited and translated by Edward Shils and Henry Finch. New York: Free Press, 1949.

―――. "'Objectivity' in Social Science and Social Policy," in *The Methodology of the Social Sciences*, 50–112. Translated and edited by Eward Shils and Henry Finch. New York: Free Press, 1949.

―――. *The Protestant Ethic and the Spirit of Capitalism*. Translated by Talcott Parsons. London and New York: Routledge, 1992.

―――. "The Protestant Sects and the Spirit of Capitalism." In *From Max Weber: Essays in Sociology*, 302–22. Edited by H. H. Gerth and C. Wright Mills. London: Routledge, 1991.

―――. *Sociology of Religion*. Boston: Beacon Press, 1993.

White, Hayden. *Metahistory: The Historical Imagination in Nineteenth-Century Europe*. Baltimore: Johns Hopkins University Press, 1973.

Wiedenhofer, Siegfried. "The Logic of Tradition." In *Zur Logik religiöser Traditionen*, 11–84. Edited by Barbara Schoppelreich and Siegfried Wiedenhofer. Frankfurt am Main: Verlag für Interkulturelle Kommunikation, 1998.

Willey, Thomas E. *Back to Kant: The Revival of Kantianism in German Social and Historical Thought, 1860–1914*. Detroit, Mich.: Wayne State University Press, 1978.

Witsch, Norbert. *Glaubensorientierung in "nachdogmatischer" Zeit. Ernst Troeltschs Überlegungen zu einer Wesensbestimmung des Christentums*. Paderborn: Bonifatius, 1997.

Wuthnow, Robert. *Experimentation in American Religion: The New Mysticisms and Their Implications for the Churches*. Berkeley: University of California Press, 1978.

Wyman, Walter E., Jr. *The Concept of Glaubenslehre: Ernst Troeltsch and the Theological Heritage of Schleiermacher*. Chico, Calif.: Scholars Press, 1983.

Yamin, George J. *In the Absence of Fantasia: Troeltsch's Relation to Hegel.* Gainesville, Fla.: University Press of Florida, 1993.

Yasukata, Toshimasa. *Ernst Troeltsch: Systematic Theologian of Radical Historicality.* Atlanta, Ga.: Scholars Press, 1986.

Yinger, J. Milton. *The Scientific Study of Religion.* New York: Macmillan, 1970.

———. "The Sociology of Religion of Ernst Troeltsch." In *An Introduction to the History of Sociology*, 307–13. Edited by H. E. Barnes. Chicago: University of Chicago Press, 1966.

Index

Harvard Theological Studies

61. Schifferdecker, Kathryn. *Out of the Whirlwind: Creation Theology in the Book of Job*, 2008.

58. Pearson, Lori. *Beyond Essence: Ernst Troeltsch as Historian and Theorist of Christianity*, 2008.

57. Hills, Julian V. *Tradition and Composition in the* Epistula Apostolorum, 2008.

56. Nickelsburg, George W. E. *Resurrection, Immortality, and Eternal Life in Intertestamental Judaism and Early Christianity*. Expanded Edition, 2006.

55. Johnson-DeBaufre, Melanie. *Jesus Among Her Children: Q, Eschatology, and the Construction of Christian Origins*, 2005.

54. Hall, David D. *The Faithful Shepherd: A History of the New England Ministry in the Seventeenth Century*, 2006.

53. Schowalter, Daniel N., and Steven J. Friesen, eds. *Urban Religion in Roman Corinth: Interdisciplinary Approaches,* 2004.

52. Nasrallah, Laura. *"An Ecstasy of Folly": Prophecy and Authority in Early Christianity*, 2003.

51. Brock, Ann Graham. *Mary Magdalene, The First Apostle: The Struggle for Authority,* 2003.

50. Trost, Theodore Louis. *Douglas Horton and the Ecumenical Impulse in American Religion*, 2002.

49. Huang, Yong. *Religious Goodness and Political Rightness: Beyond the Liberal-Communitarian Debate*, 2001.

48. Rossing, Barbara R. *The Choice between Two Cities: Whore, Bride, and Empire in the Apocalypse*, 1999.

47. Skedros, James Constantine. *Saint Demetrios of Thessaloniki: Civic Patron and Divine Protector, 4th–7th Centuries c.e.*, 1999.

46. Koester, Helmut, ed. *Pergamon, Citadel of the Gods: Archaeological Record, Literary Description, and Religious Development*, 1998.

45. Kittredge, Cynthia Briggs. *Community and Authority: The Rhetoric of Obedience in the Pauline Tradition*, 1998.

44. Lesses, Rebecca Macy. *Ritual Practices to Gain Power: Angels, Incantations, and Revelation in Early Jewish Mysticism*, 1998.

43. Guenther-Gleason, Patricia E. *On Schleiermacher and Gender Politics*, 1997.

42. White, L. Michael. *The Social Origins of Christian Architecture* (2 vols.), 1997.

41. Koester, Helmut, ed. *Ephesos, Metropolis of Asia: An Interdisciplinary Approach to its Archaeology, Religion, and Culture*, 1995.

40. Guider, Margaret Eletta. *Daughters of Rahab: Prostitution and the Church of Liberation in Brazil*, 1995.

39. Schenkel, Albert F. *The Rich Man and the Kingdom: John D. Rockefeller, Jr., and the Protestant Establishment*, 1995.

38. Hutchison, William R. and Hartmut Lehmann, eds. *Many Are Chosen: Divine Election and Western Nationalism*, 1994.

37. Lubieniecki, Stanislas. *History of the Polish Reformation and Nine Related Documents*. Translated and interpreted by George Huntston Williams, 1995.

– Davidovich, Adina. *Religion as a Province of Meaning: The Kantian Foundations of Modern Theology*, 1993.

36. Thiemann, Ronald F., ed. *The Legacy of H. Richard Niebuhr*, 1991.

35. Hobbs, Edward C., ed. *Bultmann, Retrospect and Prospect: The Centenary Symposium at Wellesley*, 1985.

34. Cameron, Ron. *Sayings Traditions in the Apocryphon of James*, 1984. Reprinted, 2004,

33. Blackwell, Albert L. *Schleiermacher's Early Philosophy of Life: Determinism, Freedom, and Phantasy*, 1982.

32. Gibson, Elsa. *The "Christians for Christians" Inscriptions of Phrygia: Greek Texts, Translation and Commentary*, 1978.

31. Bynum, Caroline Walker. Docere Verbo et Exemplo: *An Aspect of Twelfth-Century Spirituality*, 1979.

30. Williams, George Huntston, ed. *The Polish Brethren: Documentation of the History and Thought of Unitarianism in the Polish-Lithuanian Commonwealth and in the Diaspora 1601–1685*, 1980.

29. Attridge, Harold W. *First-Century Cynicism in the Epistles of Heraclitus*, 1976.

28. Williams, George Huntston, Norman Pettit, Winfried Herget, and Sargent Bush, Jr., eds. *Thomas Hooker: Writings in England and Holland, 1626–1633*, 1975.

27. Preus, James Samuel. *Carlstadt's* Ordinaciones *and Luther's Liberty: A Study of the Wittenberg Movement, 1521–22*, 1974.

26. Nickelsburg, George W. E. *Resurrection, Immortality, and Eternal Life in Inter-testamental Judaism*, 1972.

25. Worthley, Harold Field. *An Inventory of the Records of the Particular (Congregational) Churches of Massachusetts Gathered 1620–1805*, 1970.

24. Yamauchi, Edwin M. *Gnostic Ethics and Mandaean Origins*, 1970.

23. Yizhar, Michael. *Bibliography of Hebrew Publications on the Dead Sea Scrolls 1948–1964*, 1967.

22. Albright, William Foxwell. *The Proto-Sinaitic Inscriptions and Their Decipherment*, 1966.

21. Dow, Sterling, and Robert F. Healey. *A Sacred Calendar of Eleusis*, 1965.

20. Sundberg, Jr., Albert C. *The Old Testament of the Early Church*, 1964.

19. Cranz, Ferdinand Edward. *An Essay on the Development of Luther's Thought on Justice, Law, and Society*, 1959.

18. Williams, George Huntston, ed. *The Norman Anonymous of 1100 A.D.: Towards the Identification and Evaluation of the So-Called Anonymous of York*, 1951.

17. Lake, Kirsopp, and Silva New, eds. *Six Collations of New Testament Manuscripts*, 1932.

16. Wilbur, Earl Morse, trans. *The Two Treatises of Servetus on the Trinity: On the Errors of the Trinity, 7 Books, A.D. 1531. Dialogues on the Trinity, 2 Books. On the Righteousness of Christ's Kingdom, 4 Chapters, A.D. 1532*, 1932.

15. Casey, Robert Pierce, ed. Serapion of Thmuis's *Against the Manichees*, 1931.

14. Ropes, James Hardy. *The Singular Problem of the Epistles to the Galatians*, 1929.

13. Smith, Preserved. *A Key to the Colloquies of Erasmus*, 1927.

12. Spyridon of the Laura and Sophronios Eustratiades. *Catalogue of the Greek Manuscripts in the Library of the Laura on Mount Athos*, 1925.

11. Sophronios Eustratiades and Arcadios of Vatopedi. *Catalogue of the Greek Manuscripts in the Library of the Monastery of Vatopedi on Mt. Athos*, 1924.

10. Conybeare, Frederick C. *Russian Dissenters*, 1921.

9. Burrage, Champlin, ed. *An Answer to John Robinson of Leyden by a Puritan Friend: Now First Published from a Manuscript of A.D. 1609*, 1920.

8. Emerton, Ephraim. *The Defensor pacis of Marsiglio of Padua: A Critical Study*, 1920,

7. Bacon, Benjamin W. *Is Mark a Roman Gospel?* 1919.

6. Cadbury, Henry Joel. 2 vols. *The Style and Literary Method of Luke*, 1920.

5. Marriott, G. L., ed. Macarii Anecdota*: Seven Unpublished Homilies of Macarius*, 1918.

4. Edmunds, Charles Carroll and William Henry Paine Hatch. *The Gospel Manuscripts of the General Theological Seminary*, 1918.

3. Arnold, William Rosenzweig. *Ephod and Ark: A Study in the Records and Religion of the Ancient Hebrews*, 1917.

2. Hatch, William Henry Paine. *The Pauline Idea of Faith in its Relation to Jewish and Hellenistic Religion*, 1917.

1. Torrey, Charles Cutler. *The Composition and Date of Acts*, 1916.

Harvard Dissertations in Religion

In 1993, Harvard Theological Studies absorbed
the Harvard Dissertations in Religion series.

31. Baker-Fletcher, Garth. *Somebodyness: Martin Luther King, Jr. and the Theory of Dignity*, 1993.

30. Soneson, Jerome Paul. *Pragmatism and Pluralism: John Dewey's Significance for Theology*, 1993.

29. Crabtree, Harriet. *The Christian Life: The Traditional Metaphors and Contemporary Theologies*, 1991.

28. Schowalter, Daniel N. *The Emperor and the Gods: Images from the Time of Trajan*, 1993.

27. Valantasis, Richard. *Spiritual Guides of the Third Century: A Semiotic Study of the Guide-Disciple Relationship in Christianity, Neoplatonism, Hermetism, and Gnosticism*, 1991.

26. Wills, Lawrence Mitchell. *The Jews in the Court of the Foreign King: Ancient Jewish Court Legends*, 1990.

25. Massa, Mark Stephen. *Charles Augustus Briggs and the Crisis of Historical Criticism*, 1990.

24. Hills, Julian Victor. *Tradition and Composition in the* Epistula apostolorum, 1990.

23. Bowe, Barbara Ellen. *A Church in Crisis: Ecclesiology and Paraenesis in Clement of Rome*, 1988.

22. Bisbee, Gary A. *Pre-Decian Acts of Martyrs and* Commentarii, 1988.

21. Ray, Stephen Alan. *The Modern Soul: Michel Foucault and the Theological Discourse of Gordon Kaufman and David Tracy*, 1987.

20. MacDonald, Dennis Ronald. *There Is No Male and Female: The Fate of a Dominical Saying in Paul and Gnosticism*, 1987.

19. Davaney, Sheila Greeve. *Divine Power: A Study of Karl Barth and Charles Hartshorne*, 1986.

18. LaFargue, J. Michael. *Language and Gnosis: The Opening Scenes of the Acts of Thomas*, 1985.

12. Layton, Bentley, ed. *The Gnostic Treatise on Resurrection from Nag Hammadi*, 1979.

11. Ryan, Patrick J. *Imale: Yoruba Participation in the Muslim Tradition: A Study of Clerical Piety*, 1977.

10. Neevel, Jr., Walter G. *Yāmuna's* Vedānta *and* Pāñcarātra*: Integrating the Classical and the Popular*, 1977.

9. Yarbro Collins, Adela. *The Combat Myth in the Book of Revelation*, 1976.

8. Veatch, Robert M. *Value-Freedom in Science and Technology: A Study of the Importance of the Religious, Ethical, and Other Socio-Cultural Factors in Selected Medical Decisions Regarding Birth Control*, 1976.

7. Attridge, Harold W. *The Interpretation of Biblical History in the* Antiquitates judaicae *of Flavius Josephus*, 1976.

6. Trakatellis, Demetrios C. *The Pre-Existence of Christ in the Writings of Justin Martyr*, 1976.

5. Green, Ronald Michael. *Population Growth and Justice: An Examination of Moral Issues Raised by Rapid Population Growth*, 1975.

4. Schrader, Robert W. *The Nature of Theological Argument: A Study of Paul Tillich*, 1976.

3. Christensen, Duane L. *Transformations of the War Oracle in Old Testament Prophecy: Studies in the Oracles Against the Nations*, 1975.

2. Williams, Sam K. *Jesus' Death as Saving Event: The Background and Origin of a Concept*, 1972.

1. Smith, Jane I. *An Historical and Semantic Study of the Term "Islām" as Seen in a Sequence of Qur'an Commentaries*, 1970.